VMware vSphere 6.7 Data Center Design Cookbook
Third Edition

Over 100 practical recipes to help you design a powerful virtual infrastructure based on vSphere 6.7

Mike Brown
Hersey Cartwright

BIRMINGHAM - MUMBAI

VMware vSphere 6.7 Data Center Design Cookbook
Third Edition

Commissioning Editor: Vijin Boricha
Acquisition Editor: Prachi Bisht
Content Development Editor: Deepti Thore
Technical Editor: Varsha Shivhare
Copy Editor: Safis Editing
Project Coordinator: Nusaiba Ansari
Proofreader: Safis Editing
Indexer: Tejal Daruwale Soni
Graphics: Jisha Chirayil
Production Coordinator: Aparna Bhagat

First published: January 2014
Second edition: June 2016
Third edition: March 2019

Production reference: 1280319

Published by Packt Publishing Ltd.
Livery Place
35 Livery Street
Birmingham
B3 2PB, UK.

ISBN 978-1-78980-151-4

www.packtpub.com

`mapt.io`

Mapt is an online digital library that gives you full access to over 5,000 books and videos, as well as industry leading tools to help you plan your personal development and advance your career. For more information, please visit our website.

Why subscribe?

- Spend less time learning and more time coding with practical eBooks and Videos from over 4,000 industry professionals

- Improve your learning with Skill Plans built especially for you

- Get a free eBook or video every month

- Mapt is fully searchable

- Copy and paste, print, and bookmark content

Packt.com

Did you know that Packt offers eBook versions of every book published, with PDF and ePub files available? You can upgrade to the eBook version at `www.packt.com` and as a print book customer, you are entitled to a discount on the eBook copy. Get in touch with us at `customercare@packtpub.com` for more details.

At `www.packt.com`, you can also read a collection of free technical articles, sign up for a range of free newsletters, and receive exclusive discounts and offers on Packt books and eBooks.

Contributors

About the authors

Mike Brown is an army veteran and full stack, data center engineer with over 10 years' experience in IT. At work, he's most comfortable on the data center floor with his laptop, a console cable, and a closed container of coffee. At home, he's the biggest cheerleader for his children at their football and basketball games or just while they're hanging out.

Mike has held many positions in IT, from help desk to systems administrator, to engineer and consultant. He can be found on Twitter at `@VirtuallyMikeB`. His technical achievements include VCIX6-DCV and other VMware, Cisco, NetApp, and Microsoft certifications.

> *I am thankful to have worked with a lot of smart people who have shared their knowledge and given me opportunities to grow. I am fortunate to have mentors and friends such as Michael Mills, Luke Morgan, and Dr. Christopher Seedyk, who have shared this journey with me.*

Hersey Cartwright has worked in the technology industry since 1996 in a variety of roles, from help desk support to IT management. He first started working with VMware technologies in 2006. He is currently a solutions engineer for VMware, where he designs, sells, and supports VMware software-defined data center products in enterprise environments within the healthcare industry. He has experience working with a wide variety of server, storage, and network platforms.

About the reviewer

Mario Russo is a senior solution architect at Atos, based in Italy. He has worked as an IT architect, a senior technical VMware trainer, and in the presales department. He has worked on VMware technology since 2004. He is a VCI level 2 certified instructor of VMware and holds the following certifications: VCAP5-DCA, VCP-Cloud, VMware Certified Professional 6 – Network Virtualization (NSX v6.2), VCP7-CMA, VMware Certified Professional 7 – Cloud Management and Automation, Nutanix Platform Professional AOS5 (NPP5), Zerto Certified Professional (5.0) Implementation Engineer, RecoverPoint Version 2.0 – Associate, and Information Storage and Management Version 3.0. He has also acted as a technical reviewer for many books published by Packt Publishing.

Thanks to my wife, Lina, and my daughter, Gaia, for supporting me and helping me to overcome any challenge that life puts my way.

Packt is searching for authors like you

If you're interested in becoming an author for Packt, please visit `authors.packtpub.com` and apply today. We have worked with thousands of developers and tech professionals, just like you, to help them share their insight with the global tech community. You can make a general application, apply for a specific hot topic that we are recruiting an author for, or submit your own idea.

Table of Contents

Preface

VMware is the industry leader for data center virtualization. This third edition of the *Data center Design Cookbook* covers VMware's vSphere 6.7 suite of products, which provides a robust and resilient platform for virtualizing server and application workloads. The features available in vSphere 6.7 simplify management, increase availability, provide security, and guarantee the performance of workloads deployed in the virtualized data center.

The *VMware vSphere 6.7 Data Center Design Cookbook* provides recipes for creating a virtual data center design using the features of vSphere 6.7 by guiding you through the process of identifying the design factors and applying them to the logical and physical design process.

The *VMware vSphere 6.7 Data Center Design Cookbook* steps through the design process from beginning to end. From the discovery process, to creating the conceptual design, to calculating the resource requirements of the logical storage, compute, and network design, to mapping the logical requirements to a physical design, and finally, creating the design documentation.

The recipes in this book provide guidance on making design decisions to ensure the successful creation and, ultimately, the successful implementation of a VMware vSphere 6.7x virtual data center design.

Who this book is for

If you are an administrator or consultant interested in designing virtualized data center environments using VMware vSphere 6.7 and its supporting components, then this book is for you. This book will help both new and experienced architects to deliver professional VMware vSphere virtual data center designs.

What this book covers

Chapter 1, *The Virtual Data Center*, provides an introduction to the benefits of the virtual data center, VMware vSphere products, and the basic virtualization concepts. This chapter identifies the differences between a data center administrator and a data center architect. An overview of the **VMware Certified Advanced Professional Data center Design (VCAP-DCD)** and **VMware Certified Design Architect (VCDX)** certifications is also covered.

Chapter 2, *The Discovery Process*, explains how to identify stakeholders, conduct stakeholder interviews, and perform technical assessments to discover the business and technical goals of a virtualization project. This chapter covers how to use the following tools—VMware Capacity Planner, Windows Performance Monitor, and vRealize Operations Manager—to collect resource information during the discovery process.

Chapter 3, *The Design Factors*, explains how to identify and document the design requirements, constraints, assumptions, and risks. This chapter details how to use the design factors to create a conceptual design.

Chapter 4, *vSphere Management Design*, describes the vCenter Server components and their dependencies. Recipes for determining which vCenter Server deployment options to use, the Windows server or virtual appliance to be used, and for determining the type of database to use based on the deployment size, are included.

Chapter 5, *vSphere Storage Design*, covers logical storage design. Recipes are included for calculating the storage capacity and performance requirements for the logical storage design. This chapter covers the details of selecting the correct RAID level and storage connectivity to support a design. Recipes for VSAN and VVOLs are provided in this chapter.

Chapter 6, *vSphere Network Design*, provides details on the logical network design. This chapter explains how to calculate bandwidth requirements to support a vSphere design. Details on selecting a virtual switch topology, designing for network availability, and the network requirements to support vMotion and IP connected storage, are also covered.

Chapter 7, *vSphere Compute Design*, provides recipes for calculating the CPU and memory requirements to create a logical compute design. The chapter also covers cluster design considerations for **High Availability (HA)** and the **Distributed Resource Scheduler (DRS)**.

Chapter 8, *vSphere Physical Design*, explains how to satisfy design factors by mapping the logical management, storage, network, and compute designs to hardware to create a physical vSphere design. The chapter also provides details on creating a custom installation ISO to install ESXi and the best practices for host BIOS configurations.

Chapter 9, *Virtual Machine Design,* looks at the design of virtual machines and application workloads running in the virtual data center. Recipes are provided for right-sizing virtual machine resources, enabling the ability to add virtual machine resources, and creating virtual machine templates. This chapter details the use of affinity and anti-affinity rules to improve application efficiency and availability. Converting or migrating physical servers to virtual machines is also covered in this chapter.

Chapter 10, *vSphere Security Design,* provides an overview of the vSphere features available to provide security in the virtual data center. Recipes covering authentication, access controls, and security hardening, which must be incorporated into a data center design to secure the vSphere environment, are also included.

Chapter 11, *Disaster Recovery and Business Continuity,* covers options relating to backup, recovery, and continued operations in the event of system failure. This chapter covers how to create backups of vSphere configurations so they can be quickly restored. The protection of virtual machines using popular products for backup and replication is also covered in this chapter.

Chapter 12, *Design Documentation,* covers documenting a vSphere design. Documentation includes the architecture design document, the implementation plan, the installation guide, the validation and test plan, and the operational procedures. This chapter also provides tips for presenting a design to stakeholders and using the design documentation to implement the design.

To get the most out of this book

The following are the software requirements for this book:

- VMware vSphere ESXi 6.7
- VMware vCenter Server 6.7
- VMware PowerCLI 6.5.1
- VMware vCLI 6.7

Download the color images

We also provide a PDF file that has color images of the screenshots/diagrams used in this book. You can download it here: https://www.packtpub.com/sites/default/files/downloads/9781789801514_ColorImages.pdf.

Conventions used

There are a number of text conventions used throughout this book.

`CodeInText`: Indicates code words in text, database table names, folder names, filenames, file extensions, pathnames, dummy URLs, user input, and Twitter handles. Here is an example: "If jumbo frames are not configured correctly, `vmkping` will fail."

Any command-line input or output is written as follows:

```
esxcli storage nmp satp set –default-psp=<psp policy to set>
  --satp=<SATP_name>
```

Bold: Indicates a new term, an important word, or words that you see onscreen. For example, words in menus or dialog boxes appear in the text like this. Here is an example: "Once the collection process has been completed, you can view the report using the **Reports** section of **Performance Monitor**."

Warnings or important notes appear like this.

Tips and tricks appear like this.

Sections

In this book, you will find several headings that appear frequently (*Getting ready*, *How to do it...*, *How it works...*, *There's more...*, and *See also*).

To give clear instructions on how to complete a recipe, use these sections as follows:

Getting ready

This section tells you what to expect in the recipe and describes how to set up any software or any preliminary settings required for the recipe.

How to do it...

This section contains the steps required to follow the recipe.

How it works...

This section usually consists of a detailed explanation of what happened in the previous section.

There's more...

This section consists of additional information about the recipe in order to make you more knowledgeable about the recipe.

See also

This section provides helpful links to other useful information for the recipe.

Get in touch

Feedback from our readers is always welcome.

General feedback: If you have questions about any aspect of this book, mention the book title in the subject of your message and email us at customercare@packtpub.com.

Errata: Although we have taken every care to ensure the accuracy of our content, mistakes do happen. If you have found a mistake in this book, we would be grateful if you would report this to us. Please visit www.packt.com/submit-errata, selecting your book, clicking on the Errata Submission Form link, and entering the details.

Piracy: If you come across any illegal copies of our works in any form on the internet, we would be grateful if you would provide us with the location address or website name. Please contact us at copyright@packt.com with a link to the material.

If you are interested in becoming an author: If there is a topic that you have expertise in, and you are interested in either writing or contributing to a book, please visit authors.packtpub.com.

Reviews

Please leave a review. Once you have read and used this book, why not leave a review on the site that you purchased it from? Potential readers can then see and use your unbiased opinion to make purchase decisions, we at Packt can understand what you think about our products, and our authors can see your feedback on their book. Thank you!

For more information about Packt, please visit `packt.com`.

The Virtual Data Center 1

This chapter focuses on many of the basic concepts and benefits of virtualization. It provides a quick overview of VMware virtualization, introduces the virtual data center architect, and lays some of the groundwork necessary for creating and implementing a successful virtual data center design using VMware vSphere 6.7.

We will also explore the **VMware Certified Advanced Professional 6-Data Center Virtualization Design (VCAP6-DCV Design)** exam and the new **VMware Certified Design Expert (VCDX)** certification, including a few tips that should help you prepare to successfully complete the exam and certification. Then, we will look over some of the new features of vSphere 6.7. This section will include where to find the current release notes and the latest vSphere product documentation. Finally, we will take a high-level look at the process for planning an upgrade to an existing vSphere deployment to vSphere 6.7.

In this chapter, we will cover the following recipes:

- Becoming a virtual data center architect
- Using a holistic approach to data center design
- Passing the VMware VCAP6-DCV Design exam
- Becoming a VMware Certified Design Expert
- Identifying what's new in vSphere 6.7
- Planning a vSphere 6.7 upgrade

Benefits and technologies of virtualization

If you are already familiar with virtualization, this chapter will provide a review of many of the benefits and technologies of virtualization.

Since the focus of this book is on design, we will not go into great detail discussing the specifics of how to configure resources in a virtual data center. Most of you probably already have a good understanding of VMware's virtualization architecture, so this chapter will just provide a basic overview of the key VMware components that are the building blocks to the virtual data center.

Virtualization creates a layer of abstraction between the physical hardware and the virtual machines that run on it. Virtual hardware is presented to the virtual machine granting access to the underlying physical hardware, which is scheduled by the hypervisor's kernel. The hypervisor separates the physical hardware from the virtual machine, as shown in the following diagram:

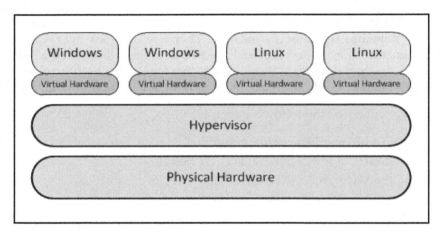

Logical representation of hypervisor layer

The hypervisor separates the physical hardware from the virtual machines. The new release of vSphere 6.7 does not change the design process or the design methodologies. The new functions and features of the release provide an architect with more tools to satisfy design requirements.

The hypervisor

At the core of any virtualization platform is the hypervisor. The VMware hypervisor is named **vSphere ESXi**, simply referred to as **ESXi**. ESXi is a Type 1 or bare-metal hypervisor. This means that it runs directly on the host's hardware to present virtual hardware to the virtual machines. In turn, the hypervisor schedules access to the physical hardware of the hosts.

ESXi allows multiple virtual machines with a variety of operating systems to run simultaneously, sharing the resources of the underlying physical hardware. Access to physical resources, such as memory, CPU, storage, and network, used by the virtual machines is managed by the scheduler, or **Virtual Machine Monitor** (**VMM**), provided by ESXi. The resources presented to the virtual machines can be over committed; this means more resources that are physically available can be allocated to the virtual machines on the physical hardware. Advanced memory sharing and reclamation techniques, such as **Transparent Page Sharing** (**TPS**) and ballooning, along with CPU scheduling, allow for over commitment of these resources to be possible, resulting in greater virtual-to-physical consolidation ratios.

ESXi 6.7 is a 64-bit hypervisor that must be run on a 64-bit hardware. An ESXi 6.7 installation requires at least 1 GB of disk space for installation. It can be installed on a hard disk locally, a USB device, a **Logical Unit Number** (**LUN**) on a **Storage Area Network** (**SAN**), or deployed stateless on hosts with no storage using Auto Deploy. The small footprint of an ESXi installation provides a reduction in the management overhead associated with patching and security hardening.

With the release of vSphere 5.0, VMware retired the ESX hypervisor. ESX had a separate, Linux-based service console for the management interface of the hypervisor. Management functions were provided by agents running in the service console. The service console has since been removed from ESXi, and agents now run directly on ESXi's VMkernel.

To manage a standalone host running ESXi, a **Direct Console User Interface (DCUI)** is provided for basic configuration and troubleshooting. A shell is available that can either be accessed locally from the console or remotely using **Secure Shell (SSH)**.

The esxcli command-line tools and others can be used in the shell to provide advanced configuration options. An ESXi host can also be accessed directly using the vSphere Client. The ESXi DCUI is shown in the following screenshot:

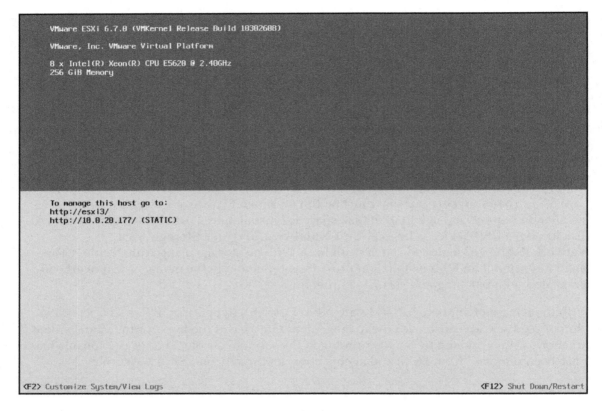

Screenshot of ESXi's DCUI

The DCUI can be accessed remotely using SSH by typing the dcui command in the prompt. Press *Ctrl + C* to exit the remote DCUI session.

Virtual machines

A virtual machine is a software computer that runs a guest operating system. Virtual machines are comprised of a set of configuration files and data files stored on local or remote storage. These configuration files contain information about the virtual hardware presented to the virtual machine. This virtual hardware includes the CPU, RAM, disk controllers, removable devices, and so on, and emulates the same functionality as the physical hardware. The following screenshot depicts the virtual machine files that are stored on a shared **Network File System (NFS)** datastore:

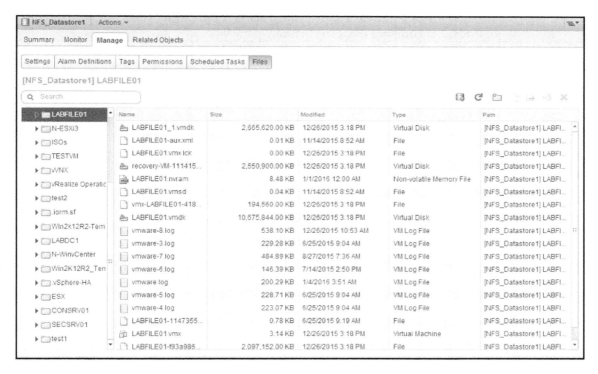

Virtual machine files stored on a shared NFS datastore displayed using the vSphere Web Client

The files that make up a virtual machine are typically stored in a directory set aside for the particular virtual machine they represent. These files include the configuration file, virtual disk files, NVRAM file, and virtual machine log files.

The following table lists the common virtual machine file extensions along with a description of each:

File extension	Description
.vmx	This is a virtual machine configuration file. It contains the configurations of the virtual hardware that is presented to the virtual machine.
.vmdk	This is a virtual disk descriptor file. It contains a header and other information pertaining to the virtual disk.
-flat.vmdk	This is a preallocated virtual disk. It contains the content or data on the disk used by the virtual machine.
.nvram	This is a file that stores the state of a virtual machine's **Basic Input Output System (BIOS)** or **Extensible Firmware Interface (EFI)** configurations.
.vswp	This is a virtual machine swap file. It gets created when a virtual machine is powered on. The size of this file is equal to the amount of memory allocated minus any memory reservations.
.log	This is a virtual machine log file.
.vmsd	This is a virtual machine file used with snapshots to store data about each snapshot active on a virtual machine.
.vmsn	This is a virtual machine snapshot data file.

Virtual machines can be deployed using a variety of methods, as follows:

- Using the New Virtual Machine Wizard in the vSphere Client or vSphere Web Client
- By getting converted from a physical machine using the VMware Converter
- By getting imported from an **Open Virtualization Format (OVF)** or **Open Virtualization Archive (OVA)**
- By getting cloned from an existing virtual machine
- By getting deployed from a virtual machine template

When a new virtual machine is created, a guest operating system can be installed on the virtual machine. VMware vSphere 6.7 supports more than 120 different guest operating systems. These include many versions of the Windows server and desktop operating systems, many distributions and versions of Linux and Unix operating systems, and Apple macOS operating systems.

Virtual appliances are preconfigured virtual machines that can be imported to the virtual environment. A virtual appliance can be comprised of a single virtual machine or a group of virtual machines with all the components required to support an application. The virtual machines in a virtual appliance are preloaded with guest operating systems, and the applications they run are normally preconfigured and optimized to run in a virtual environment.

Since virtual machines are just a collection of files on a disk, they become portable. Virtual machines can be easily moved from one location to another by simply moving or copying the associated files. Using VMware vSphere features, such as vMotion, Enhanced vMotion, or Storage vMotion, virtual machines can be migrated from host to host or datastore to datastore while a virtual machine is running. Virtual machines can also be exported to an OVF or OVA to be imported into another VMware vSphere environment.

Virtual infrastructure management

VMware vCenter Server provides a centralized management interface to manage and configure groups of ESXi hosts in the virtualized data center. The vCenter Server is required to configure and control many advanced features, such as the **Distributed Resource Scheduler (DRS)**, Storage DRS, and VMware **High Availability (HA)**. The vCenter Server management **Graphical User Interface (GUI)** is accessed using the browser-based vSphere Client. Many vendors provide plugins that can be installed to allow third-party storage, network, and compute resources to be managed using the vSphere Client.

 vCenter access using the C#, or Windows vSphere Client, is only available in versions prior to 6.5. Since the release of vSphere 5.5, however, access to, and the configuration of, new features is only available using the vSphere Web Client. The vSphere Web Client can be accessed at `https://FQDN_or_IP_of_vCenter_Server:9443/`.

vCenter Server 6.7 must use a 64-bit architecture if installed on a Windows Server. It can be run on dedicated physical hardware or as a virtual machine. When the vCenter Server is deployed on Windows, it requires either the embedded PostgreSQL database, a Microsoft SQL database, or an Oracle database to store configuration and performance information. IBM DB2 databases are supported with vSphere 5.1, but this support was removed in vSphere 5.5.

With the release of vCenter 6.0, the Microsoft SQL Express database is no longer used as the embedded database. Embedded PostgreSQL is now used as the embedded database for small deployments. The PostgreSQL database on a Windows Server can be used to support environments of less than 20 hosts and 200 virtual machines. When upgrading to vCenter 6.7, if the previous version was using the Microsoft SQL Express database, the database will be converted to the embedded PostgreSQL as part of the upgrade. The embedded PostgreSQL database is suitable for almost all deployments, but using an external database is still supported.

Another option for deploying the vCenter Server is the **vCenter Server Appliance** (**VCSA**). The VCSA is a preconfigured, Linux-based virtual machine preinstalled with the vCenter Server components. The appliance includes an embedded PostgreSQL database that supports the configuration maximums of 2,000 hosts and 25,000 powered-on virtual machines.

Several other management and automation tools are available to aid the day-to-day administration of a vSphere environment: the **vSphere Command-Line Interface** (**vCLI**); vSphere PowerCLI provides a Windows PowerShell interface; vRealize Orchestrator can be used to automate tasks; and the **vSphere Management Assistant** (**vMA**) is a Linux-based virtual appliance that is used to run management and automation scripts against hosts. vMA was deprecated, and its final release only supports vSphere 6.5. These tools allow an administrator to use command-line utilities to manage hosts from remote workstations.

VMware provides a suite of other products that benefit the virtualized data center. These data center products, such as **VMware vRealize Operations** (**vROps**), **VMware Site Recovery Manager** (**SRM**), and **VMware vRealize Automation** (**vRA**), can each be leveraged in the virtual data center to meet specific requirements related to management, disaster recovery, and cloud services. At the core of these products is the vSphere suite, which includes ESXi, the vCenter Server, and the core supporting components.

Understanding the benefits of virtualization

The following table provides a matrix of some of the core VMware technologies and the benefits that can be realized by using them:

VMware technology	Primary benefits	Description
vSphere ESXi	Server consolidation Resource efficiency	ESXi is VMware's bare-metal hypervisor that hosts virtual machines, also known as guests, and schedules virtual hardware access to physical resources.
vSphere HA	Increased availability	HA restarts virtual machines in the event of a host failure. It also monitors and restarts the virtual machines in the event of a guest operating system failure.
vMotion and vSphere DRS	Resource efficiency Increased availability	vMotion allows virtual machines to be live-migrated between hosts in a virtual data center. DRS determines the initial placement of the virtual machine on the host resources within a cluster and makes recommendations, or automatically migrates the virtual machines to balance resources across all hosts in a cluster.

Resource pools	Resource efficiency	These are used to guarantee, reserve, or limit the virtual machine's CPU, memory, and disk resources.
VMware **Fault Tolerance** (**FT**)	Increased availability	FT provides 100 percent uptime for a virtual machine in the event of a host hardware failure. It creates a secondary virtual machine that mirrors all the operations of the primary. In the event of a hardware failure, the secondary virtual machine becomes the primary and a new secondary is created.
Thin provisioning	Resource efficiency	This allows for storage to be over provisioned by presenting the configured space to a virtual machine, but only consuming the space on the disk that the guest actually requires.
Hot add CPU and memory	Resource efficiency scalability	This allows for the addition of CPU and memory resources to a virtual machine while the virtual machine is running.
Storage vMotion	Resource efficiency	This moves virtual machine configuration files and disks between storage locations that have been presented to a host.
vSphere Storage **Application Programming Interface** (**APIs**); data protection	VM backups and disaster recovery	Allows third parties to build agentless backup and disaster recovery solutions that integrate with the vSphere platform
vSphere replication	Disaster recovery	This features provides the ability to replicate virtual machines between sites.
vCenter server	Simplified management	This provides a single management interface to configure and monitor the resources available to virtual data centers.
vCenter server linked mode	Simplified management	This links multiple vCenter Servers together to allow them to be managed from a single client.
Host profiles	Simplified management	This maintains consistent configuration and configuration compliance across all the hosts in the environment.

This is not meant to be an exhaustive list of all VMware technologies and features, but it does provide an insight into many of the technologies commonly deployed in the enterprise virtual data center.

There are many others, and each technology or feature may also have its own set of requirements that must be met in order to be implemented. The purpose here is to show how features or technologies can be mapped to benefits that can then be mapped to requirements and ultimately mapped into a design. This is helpful in ensuring that the benefits and technologies that virtualization provides satisfy design requirements.

Identifying when not to virtualize

Not all applications or server workloads are good candidates for virtualization. It is important that these workloads are identified early on in the design process.

There are a number of reasons why a server or application may not be suitable for virtualization. Some of these include the following:

- Vendor support
- Licensing issues
- Specialized hardware dependencies
- High resource demand
- Lack of knowledge or skillsets

A common reason to not virtualize an application or workload is the reluctance of a vendor to support their application in a virtual environment. As virtualization has become more common in the enterprise data center, this has become uncommon; but, there are still application vendors that will not support their products once virtualized.

Software and operating system licensing in a virtual environment can also be a challenge, especially when it comes to physical server to virtual machine conversions. Many physical servers are purchased with **Original Equipment Manufacturer** (**OEM**) licenses, and these licenses, in most cases, cannot be transferred to a virtual environment. Also, many licenses are tied to hardware-specific information, such as interface MAC addresses or drive signatures. Licensing issues can usually be overcome. Many times, the primary risk becomes the cost to upgrade or acquire new licensing. As with other potential design risks, it is important that any issues and potential impacts licensing may have on the design be identified early on in the design process.

Some applications may require the use of specialized hardware. Fax boards, serial ports, and security dongles are common examples. There are ways to provide solutions for many of these, but often, given the risks associated with the ability to support the application, or the loss of one or more of the potential benefits of virtualizing the application, the better solution may be to leave the application on dedicated physical hardware. Again, it is important that these types of applications be identified very early on in the design process.

Physical servers configured with a large amount of CPU and memory resources where applications are consuming a large amount of these resources may not be good candidates for virtualization. This also holds true for applications with high network utilization and large storage I/O requirements. vSphere 6.7 supports virtual machines configured with up to 128 **virtual CPUs (vCPUs)** and 6 TB of memory, but the high utilization of these configured resources can have a negative impact on other workloads in the virtual environment. These high-utilization workloads will also require more resources to be reserved for failover. The benefits of virtualizing resource-intensive applications must be weighed against the impact placed on the virtual environment. In some cases, it may be better to leave these applications on dedicated physical hardware.

Many administrators may lack knowledge of the benefits or skills to manage a virtualized data center. The administrator of a virtual environment must be well-versed with storage, networking, and virtualization in order to successfully configure, maintain, and monitor a virtual environment. Though this may not necessarily be a reason not to leverage the benefits of a virtualized environment, it can be a substantial risk to the acceptance of a design and the implementation. This is especially true with smaller IT departments, where the roles of the server, application, storage, and network administrators are combined.

Each of these can introduce risks in the design. We will discuss how risk impacts the design process in much more detail in Chapter 2, *The Discovery Process*, and Chapter 3, *The Design Factors*.

Becoming a virtual data center architect

The virtual data center architect, or simply the architect, is someone who identifies requirements, designs a virtualization solution to meet those requirements, and then oversees the implementation of the solution. Sounds easy enough, right?

How it works...

The primary role of the architect is to provide solutions that meet customer requirements. At times, this can be difficult, since the architect may not always be part of the complete sales process. Often, customers may purchase hardware from other vendors and look to us to help them make it all work. In such situations, the purchased hardware becomes a constraint on the design. Identifying and dealing with constraints and other design factors will be discussed in more detail in Chapter 2, *The Discovery Process*, and Chapter 3, *The Design Factors*.

The architect must also be able to identify requirements, both business and technical, by conducting stakeholder interviews and analyzing current configurations. Once the requirements have been identified, the architect must then map the requirements into a solution by creating a design. This design is then presented to the stakeholders, and if, approved, it is implemented. During the implementation phase, the architect ensures that configurations are done to meet the design requirements and that the work done stays within the scope of the design.

The architect must also understand best practice. Not just best practice for configuring the hypervisor, but for management, storage, security, and networking. Understanding best practice is the key. The architect not only knows best practice, but understands why it is considered best practice. It is also important to understand when to deviate from what is considered best practice.

There's more...

The large part of an architect's work is facing customers. This includes conducting interviews with stakeholders to identify requirements and ultimately presenting the design to decision makers. Besides creating a solid solution to match the customer's requirements, it is important that the architect gains and maintains the trust of the project stakeholders. A professional appearance and, more importantly, a professional attitude, are both helpful in building this relationship.

Using a holistic approach to data center design

The virtual data center architect must be able to take a holistic approach to data center design. This means that for every decision made, the architect must understand how the environment as a whole will be impacted.

An architect is required to be, at the very least, familiar with all aspects of the data center. They must understand how the different components of a data center, such as storage, networking, computing, security, and management, are interconnected, as shown in the following diagram:

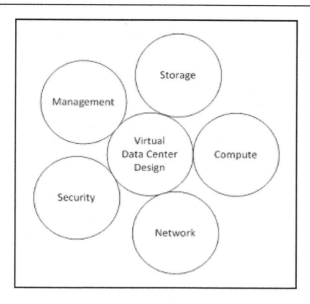

The holistic approach to data center design

It has become very important to understand how any decision or change will impact the rest of the design. Identifying dependencies becomes an important part of the design process. If a change is made to the network, how are computing, management, and storage resources affected? What other dependencies will this introduce in the design? Failing to take a holistic approach to design can result in unnecessary complications during the design process, and potentially costly fixes after the design is implemented.

How to do it...

The following scenario is built as an example which helps illustrate the concept of using a holistic design approach.

You have been engaged to design a virtualization solution for a financial organization. The solution you are proposing is to use 10 GB **Converged Network Adapters (CNA)** to provide connectivity to the organization's network in three 1U rack-mount servers. The organization needs to separate a **Virtual Local Area Network (VLAN)** that is currently configured to be delivered over the CNA onto a physically separate network to satisfy a new compliance requirement. A 1 GB network will provide sufficient bandwidth for this network, and the network should be highly available. Single points of failure should be minimized.

To support this compliance requirement, you, the architect, must take a holistic approach to the design and answer a number of questions about each design decision, for example:

1. Are there network ports available in the current rack-mount servers, or will a network card need to be added? If a card has to be added, are there **Peripheral Component Interconnect (PCI)** slots available?
2. Will a dual-port network card provide sufficient redundancy, or will the network need to be separated across physical cards? Are there onboard network ports available that can be used with a PCI network card to provide in-box redundancy?
3. Has the hardware for the physically separate switch been obtained? If not, how long before the equipment is received and deployed? Will this have an impact on the implementation schedule?
4. How will the virtual switch need to be configured to provide the connectivity and redundancy that is required?

How it works...

The impact can be fairly significant, depending on some of the answers. For example, let's say the 1U rack-mount server will not support the required network adapters needed to satisfy the requirement and a different 2U rack-mount server must be used. This then raises more questions, such as whether there is sufficient space in the rack to support the new server footprint.

What if the requirement had been that the applications connected to this network be virtualized on separate physical server hardware and storage? What parts of the design would have to change? The architect must be able to understand the dependencies of each part of the design and how a change in one place may affect other areas of the design.

As you think through these questions, you should be able to see how a change to a requirement can have a deep impact on many other areas of the design. It becomes very important to identify requirements early on in the design process.

Passing the VMware VCAP6-DCV Design exam

VMware has **VMware Certified Advanced Professional (VCAP)** exams testing the ability of a person to deploy, administer, and design complex virtual environments. The exams for vSphere 6 come in two types: Design and Deployment. Passing both exams earns the designation **VMware Certified Implementation Expert (VCIX)**. The VCIX is not a certification the same way that VCAPs are; rather it is a special designation that proves the earner has deep and wide expertise in designing and deploying complex vSphere 6 infrastructures.

VMware is constantly reviewing and updating their certification system. Recent changes to the vSphere 6.x advanced certifications included adding the VCAP6.5-**Data Center Virtualization (DCV)** Design exam and retiring the VCAP6-DCV Design exam. Overarching changes to the entire VMware certification program include the replacement of product versions in the certification title with the year in which the certification was earned. For example, the only current, advanced DCV Deployment exam is titled VCAP-DCV Deployment 2018. This change was made in an effort to show the timeliness of the certification simply by its name. Reading the certification page for this exam is the only way to understand which product version is tested within the exam.

The current, high-level VMware certification path is mapped out in the following flowchart:

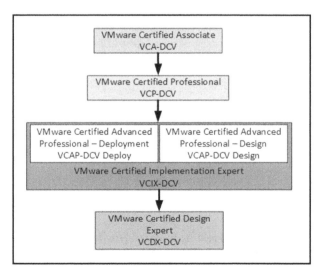

VMware certification path for data center administrators and architects

The VCAP-DCV Design exam tests your ability to design enterprise virtualized environments. To be successful, you must have an in-depth understanding of VMware's core components and the relationship they share with other components of the data center, such as storage, networking, and application services, along with a mastery of VMware's data center design methodologies and principles. All the exam objectives, including study resources, can be found in the exam blueprint. VMware exam roadmaps and the VCAP exam blueprints can be found on the VMware Certification portal page at `https://mylearn.vmware.com/portals/certification/`.

Getting ready

Before you are eligible to take a VCAP6.5-DCV Design exam, you should have obtained the relevant **VMware Certified Professional-Data Center Virtualization (VCP6.5-DCV)** certification. Besides the training required for the VCP6.5-DCV certification, there is no other requisite training that must be completed in order to sit the VCAP6.5-DCV Design exam. When you are ready to schedule your VCAP6.5-DCV Design exam, you must submit an exam authorization request to VMware. When you submit the exam authorization request, VMware will verify that you have met the certification prerequisites and provide you with the access necessary to schedule the exam.

The VCAP6.5-DCV Design exam consists of 60 questions with a time limit of 135 minutes. The passing score is 300 out of 500. The exam questions are comprised of a mixture of multiple choice, matching, and drag and drop. VMware has removed the Visio-style design scenario formatted questions from this exam. Refer to the VMware Certification Portal for details: `https://mylearn.vmware.com/portals/certification/`.

How to do it...

The VCAP-DCV Design exam for vSphere 6 was one of the most challenging exams I have ever taken. Here are a few tips to help you prepare for and successfully sit the VCAP6-DCV Design exam:

1. **Study the material on the exam blueprint**: The exam blueprint lists all the objectives of the exam, along with links to documentation related to each exam objective.
2. **Review the vSphere 6 release notes and product documentation**: The release notes and product documentation will provide an overview of the features available, the requirements that must be met to support implementation of the new features, and the best practices for implementing features to support design requirements.

3. **Schedule your exam**: Scheduling your exam sets a goal date for you to work toward. Setting the date can provide motivation to help you stay on track with your studying efforts.

4. **Watch the APAC vBrownBag DCD5 series**: The APAC vBrownBag did a series of podcasts focusing on the VCAP-DCD exam for vSphere 5 exam objectives. Even though these podcasts focus on version five of the exam, many of the design methodologies and concepts are similar. These podcasts are still relevant and provide a valuable study resource. The podcast can be found at `http://www.professionalvmware.com/brownbags`.

5. **Get familiar with the exam design interface**: On VMware's VCAP Certification page for the Design exam, there is a UI Demo that will help get you familiar with the design interface that is used on the exam.

6. **Practice time management**: It is very important that you are aware of the amount of time you are taking on a question, and how much time remains. If you get hung up on a multiple choice question, take your best guess and move on. Conserve time for the more complex drag and drop and design scenario questions.

7. **Answer every question**: A question left unanswered will be marked incorrect and will not benefit your score in any way. A guess has some chance of being correct.

8. **Study the material on the exam blueprint**: I know this has already been mentioned once, but it is worth mentioning again. The exam blueprint contains all the testable objectives. Study it!

There's more...

For up-to-date information on the VCAP-DCV Design certification, to download the exam blueprint, and to book the exam once it has been released, visit the VMware Certification Portal page at `https://mylearn.vmware.com/portals/certification/`.

The final stop on the VMware Certification path is **VMware Certified Design Expert-Data Center Virtualization (VCDX)**. The VCDX certification requires creating a VMware vSphere design, submitting the design to VMware for review, and then defending the design before a panel of VMware design experts.

Becoming a VMware Certified Design Expert

The VCDX is the pinnacle of VMware's certifications. A VCDX certification validates an architect's ability to design, implement, test, document, present, and defend the design of complex, enterprise solutions based on VMware products. Earning the certification ultimately comes down to two things: creating a design, and defending your design in front of a panel of VCDX veterans.

Before attempting the VCDX certification, an architect usually has experience designing the same level of advanced, vSphere designs that the VCDX defense panel is looking for. Before designing such solutions, a VCDX candidate also usually has experience implementing and administering complex vSphere designs. While these experiences are not hard requirements, it is a natural progression that sets the candidate up for success and gives them the best chance of succeeding in the VCDX process. The only other prerequisites to attempt the VCDX6 is to hold either a **VMware Certified Professional 6-Data Center Virtualization (VCP6-DCV)** or **VCP6.5-DCV**, and earn the VCIX6-DCV or VCIX6.5-DCV badge.

This section discusses the VCDX6-DCV that is based on vSphere 6.x designs, but there are other current tracks that lead to VCDX and include the following:

- **VCDX6: Network Virtualization (VCDX6-NV)**—this certification is focused on both vSphere and NSX 6.x
- **VCDX7: Cloud Management and Automation (VCDX7-CMA)**—this certification is based on vRealize Automation 7.x
- **VCDX6: Desktop and Mobility (VCDX6-DTM)**—this certification is based on the Horizon Suite

No matter which track is chosen, understand the VCDX certification process well. VMware has published two documents for most tracks that cover this information: the blueprint and the handbook. The blueprint describes the rules of the VCDX process, including things such as what format the process uses, time limits, and the language in which the process is held. It also covers the objectives of the specific test format used and explains what the VCDX panelists are looking for in a VCDX candidate.

The handbook offers some details on how to choose a good design on which to base a VCDX defense, VMware's policy on teamwork in the VCDX process, and finally, what to expect during the live defense portion of the defense. Becoming familiar with the contents of each document will help focus a candidate's time and effort while progressing through the VCDX process.

How to do it...

After meeting the prerequisites, there are only two more steps to becoming a VCDX. The fees have changed over time, so be sure to check VMware's website for up-to-date costs. You must do the following:

- Submit a VCDX design application with an application fee of $995
- If successful, defend your design, live, in front of a panel of current VCDXs, and pay a defense fee of $3,000

Getting your VCDX application accepted, however, is a lot of work and a big hurdle to overcome. If your application is accepted, the VCDX program is telling you that the documentation, by itself, is of expert quality, and the only thing left to do is prove to them during the live defense panel that you are, indeed, an expert.

The VCDX application consists of a set of documents. Aside from the application itself, you must create a documentation bundle that could follow this order:

1. **Create the design document**: This will be the main document of your submission, where you'll likely spend the most time. This is where you'll document requirements, constraints, assumptions, and risks, and map them to the vSphere components of compute, storage, network, management, and the virtual machine, and ensure that the design qualities of availability, manageability, performance, recoverability, and security are addressed for each component.
2. **Create an installation and configuration document**: This document includes step-by-step instructions on how to install and configure the infrastructure described in the design document. This document is written in such a way that it could be handed off to someone with VCP-level knowledge and they could execute it.
3. **Create the implementation document**: This document describes the implementation at a high-level, to include who is participating, what tasks will be performed and when, and prerequisites for implementation, such as racks that may need to be installed, and redundant power that needs to exist in those racks. This is a common document used in projects run by a project manager.
4. **Create a test plan**: The VCDX candidate will need to be able to prove that the implemented design meets the requirements by describing the tests that need to be passed, as shown in this document.

5. **Create the operations document**: This document is also called the standard operating procedures. It describes common operational tasks that result from maintaining the implemented design over time. Common examples of tasks to include here are how to put a host in maintenance mode, how to deploy a virtual machine from a template, or how to view logs.
6. **Build the bill of materials**: An architect must also be able to describe all the hardware and software needed to implement their design. This is usually shown in a bill of materials document.

Once the VCDX application is submitted and the fee paid, a current VCDX will review the application for completeness and content. Incompleteness is cause for immediate application denial. If it's complete, however, the reviewer will look to see proof of design expertise through thoughtful application of design principles with an emphasis on justifying design decisions and how those decisions impact the design. If your application is sufficient, you'll be invited to defend your design live and in-person at a VMware office. Locations typically include Palo Alto, California; Broomfield, Colorado; Staines, United Kingdom; and Sydney, Australia.

The VCDX has evolved over the years and no longer includes a troubleshooting section. Instead, the defense has two parts: the oral design defense, and the ad hoc design. During the oral design defense, the candidate has 75 minutes to present the design and answer questions from the panelists. VMware recommends the initial presentation take no more than 15 minutes, leaving roughly 60 minutes for the panelists to ask questions that allow the candidate to demonstrate how their design meets the requirements and why they made certain design decisions. Most VCDX certification holders will agree that the most important aspect of this part of the defense is to be able to communicate the **why** of each design decision. If you can justify each decision and make it tie into a customer requirement, you're going to do well.

In the ad hoc design portion, the candidate has 45 minutes to demonstrate their design skills by going through an initial design process in front of the panel. The panelists will pretend to be customers and you, as the virtualization architect, will need to be able to gather their requirements, constraints, make assumptions, identify risks, and begin to build a design based on those inputs. The panel doesn't expect you to create a whole design in 45 minutes; rather, they're trying to assess your design method. To do this, the panel recommends the candidate think out loud and make use of the whiteboard as much as possible. You should try to give the panelists a window into your mind while engaged in your design process.

After finishing both sections of the defense, you'll make the long trip back home. If all went well, you'll receive an email within 10 days stating that you have passed, and welcoming you to the elite VCDX club.

There's more...

The VCDX certification is well known these days, and because of that, there are many more resources online to help you. Your first stop should be the blueprint that can be found at `https://www.vmware.com/content/dam/digitalmarketing/vmware/en/pdf/certification/vmw-vcdx6-dcv-blueprint.pdf`. You'll also want to review the handbook that can be found at `https://www.vmware.com/content/dam/digitalmarketing/vmware/en/pdf/certification/vmw-vcdx6-dcv-handbook.pdf`.

Beyond the official documents linked previously, the boot *IT Architect: Foundation in the Art of Infrastructure Design: A Practical Guide for IT Architects* by VCDX-001, John Arrasjid, is a good book to read. You can find it on Amazon.com at `https://www.amazon.com/Architect-Foundation-Infrastructure-Practical-Architects/dp/0996647708/ref=sr_1_2?ie=UTF8qid=1543255581sr=8-2keywords=the+it+architect`.

VMware also offers VCDX workshops, held monthly, that educate candidates on the VCDX process and helps to prepare them for the application and defense. The best resources, however, will be VMware community members who are going through the same experiences as the VCDX candidate. You should use Twitter and the VMware Technology Network forums to connect with like-minded technologists who share the same goal of becoming a VCDX and work with them to review your documentation and application and hold mock defenses. Many successful VCDX holders will say that mock defenses helped them to achieve VCDX status.

Identifying what's new in vSphere 6.7

vSphere 6.7 is the latest release of VMware's virtual data center platform. This release includes features that provide increased scalability, enhanced security, increased availability, and simplified management of the virtual data center infrastructure. A few of the new features and enhancements include the following:

- Support for an embedded **Platform Services Controller (PSC)** with **Enhanced Linked-Mode (ELM)**, which simplifies the vCenter architecture
- vSphere Quick Boot, which reduces ESXi upgrade times by rebooting only ESXi and not the server hardware
- 95% feature parity of the HTML5 vSphere Client versus the Flash-based Web Client
- Encrypted vMotion across vCenter Servers and versions, easing cloud or data center migrations
- **Persistent Memory (PMEM)**, increasing storage performance capabilities

- **Hybrid Linked Mode** (**HLM**), enabling ease of management between an on-premises vCenter and VMware Cloud on AWS
- Per-VM **Enhanced vMotion Compatibility** (**EVC**), enabling easier cloud migrations
- Instant Clones, formerly known as Project Fargo and vSphere vmFork
- Storage enhancements to UNMAP **vStorage APIs for Array Integration** (**VAAI**) primitive, **Virtual Volumes** (**VVOLs**), and more
- With 6.7 Update 1, the new vSphere Health feature in the HTML5 client

These are just a few of the new features and enhancements introduced with the release of vSphere 6.7. A new version of vSphere, with the new features and enhancements, does not directly change the design process of methodology. The enhancements and features provide an architect with more tools and options for meeting requirements, but can also introduce complexity into the design.

How to do it...

It is important for the architect to understand all the new features and enhancements available. This is a simple, but important, process that includes the following:

1. Access the vSphere 6.7 release notes here: https://docs.vmware.com/en/VMware-vSphere/6.7/rn/vsphere-esxi-vcenter-server-67-release-notes.html
2. Access the vSphere documentation sets found here: https://docs.vmware.com/en/VMware-vSphere/index.html

How it works...

Reading the vSphere 6.7 release notes gives the architect a summary of the additional features, bug fixes, and known issues. There is also information on the upgrade process and workarounds for known issues.

Reviewing the vSphere documentation, including the Installation and Setup Guide, Upgrade Guide, and Administration Guides, gives the architect a deeper look at new features and how to implement new functionality. The documentation also provides specific requirements that must be satisfied in order to enable a new feature or function. These documentation sets are available online or can be downloaded in PDF, EPUB, or MOBI formats.

There's more...

In the VMware communities, `https://communities.vmware.com/`, there are forums available to discuss vSphere Upgrade and Install at `https://communities.vmware.com/community/vmtn/vsphere/upgradecenter`, and ESXi 6.7 located at `https://communities.vmware.com/community/vmtn/vsphere/esxi`, along with other communities dedicated to each vSphere product. In these forums, an architect or administrator can find real-world issues encountered by other vSphere administrators and architects. Questions and discussions can be posted related to features and issues related to all vSphere products. If you run into issues, or have questions about a specific feature, there are people in the community who are always happy to help.

Planning a vSphere 6.7 upgrade

Upgrading an existing vSphere environment to vSphere 6.7 is a fairly simple process, and can be completed with minimal impact to production with the proper planning.

In this recipe, we will look at the steps required to properly plan an upgrade to vSphere 6.7. We will not cover the specifics of upgrading vCenter Server, ESXi hosts, or any other component of the virtual data center. Specific recipes for upgrading vCenter Server and ESXi host have been included in `Chapter 4`, *vSphere Management Design,* and recipes for upgrading virtual machines to the latest hardware are included in `Chapter 9`, *Virtual Machine Design.*

How to do it...

The following tasks should be completed when planning a vSphere 6.7 upgrade:

1. Verify existing hardware is on the VMware **Hardware Compatibility List** (**HCL**) at `https://www.vmware.com/go/hcl`.
2. Check for interoperability between VMware products using the VMware Product Interoperability Matrix at `http://partnerweb.vmware.com/comp_guide2/sim/interop_matrix.php`.
3. Determine interoperability and support between VMware vSphere 6.7 and third-party hardware and software products.
4. Determine the proper upgrade path and sequence.
5. Note that direct upgrades from vSphere 5.x to 6.7 are not supported. You'll need to upgrade your 5.x environment to 6.0 or 6.5 before upgrading to 6.7.

Completing these steps to properly plan a vSphere 6.7 upgrade will ensure the upgrade can be completed successfully.

How it works...

With each release of vSphere, VMware adds support for new hardware and firmware for devices such as disk controllers, server platforms, and **Network Interface Cards (NICs)**. VMware also removes support for older hardware and firmware. It is important to verify that the hardware is on the supported compatibility list prior to attempting an upgrade. Using the VMware Hardware compatibility list is covered in more detail in Chapter 8, *vSphere Physical Design*. Failure to validate support for hardware on the HCL can cause significant issues after the upgrade; unsupported hardware may not be available for use or may cause instability in the environment. Replacing unsupported hardware or upgrading firmware on current hardware to a supported configuration may be required as part of the upgrade process.

Checking for interoperability between vSphere products will help to ensure there is minimal impact on functionality during and after the upgrade process. Just like the hardware and firmware, the interoperability between vSphere products changes with each version. New support is added for newer products and features, while support may be removed for older, end-of-support products and features. Details on using the VMware Product Interoperability can be found in Chapter 4, *vSphere Management Design*.

The virtual data center may contain many third-party products that integrate with the vSphere environment. These products often include backup and recovery software, replication software, and management and monitoring applications. Before upgrading to vSphere 6.7, check with each third-party product vendor to validate support for vSphere 6.7 or to determine the requirements for vSphere 6.7 support. This is the step I see missed most often, typically due to not fully understanding dependencies with these products. It is critical to understand what products require integration with the vSphere environment and the impact changes to the environment may have on this products. Again, this is where proper planning from the beginning ensures a successful vSphere 6.7 upgrade.

The final step is to determine the proper upgrade path. If validation of support and interoperability has been completed correctly, this step will likely be the easiest aspect of the process. Once hardware, VMware product, and third-party product interoperability have been validated, a plan can be formulated for upgrading.

Details are important when it comes to the support of hardware and software in the virtual data center. Spending time Spending time to properly plan will ensure a successful upgrade to vSphere 6.7.

2
The Discovery Process

This chapter will introduce you to design factors and focus on the discovery phase of the design process. The following diagram displays the phases of the design process:

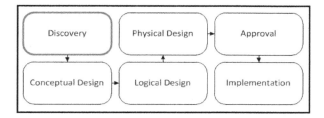

Phases of the design process

Discovery is the most important phase of the design process. It is also the most time-consuming. The discovery process includes a meeting with the stakeholders to determine business requirements that the design must meet. It also includes current state assessments to determine the technical requirements that the design must satisfy in order to meet customer requirements, which in turn become the design requirements.

During the discovery process, an architect must interact with many different individuals in an organization to collect the necessary information that is needed to begin creating the conceptual design. Decision makers, strategic planners, facilities and maintenance providers, network administrators, storage administrators, application administrators, and application end users can, in some way, be impacted by or gain some benefit from a virtual data center design (some directly and others indirectly). Anyone that may be affected by the design should be identified to be included in the discovery process as early as possible.

The current state assessment is the process of collecting information about the physical resources, such as CPU, memory, and storage, currently supporting the environment. Irrespective of whether the environment is physical servers, virtual servers, or a mix of virtual and physical servers, the current state assessment will identify the total resources available and the total resources actually in use. There are a number of different tools available to perform a current state assessment of an environment. The tool used often depends on the size of the environment. VMware offers a **Capacity Planner** tool that provides a good way to automate this assessment.

For a smaller environment of Windows servers, the Windows **Performance Monitor** (**perfmon**) utility can be used to collect the current state information. For Linux systems, tools such as top, Kinfocenter, and Zabbix can be used to collect and analyze performance data. For environments which are already virtualized on vSphere, the **vSphere Optimization Assessment** (**VOA**) provides useful information on the current state of the environment. If you don't work for VMware or a VMware partner, such as InterVision Systems, which grant access to tools, such as Capacity Planner or the VOA software, very limited sizing information can be discovered by using the free utility RVTools.

Once the design factors have been identified and accepted, the design process continues with logical and physical designs. The logical design maps the requirements to the resources required to satisfy the requirements. The physical design then maps the logical design onto the physical hardware that will provide these resources.

In this chapter, we will cover the following recipes:

- Identifying the design factors
- Identifying stakeholders
- Conducting stakeholder interviews
- Using VMware Capacity Planner
- Using Windows Performance Monitor
- Conducting a VMware optimization assessment
- Identifying dependencies

Identifying the design factors

The design factors are the primary considerations that influence the design. These factors define the function that the design must accomplish, how it should accomplish it, and what may prevent the design from accomplishing it.

How to do it...

The design factors encompass much more than just the physical resources, such as the CPU, memory, and storage, necessary to run workloads in a virtual environment.

Identifying the design factors needs the following requirements:

- Functional and nonfunctional requirements
- Constraints
- Assumptions
- Risks

How it works...

Requirements define what a design must do and how it should do it. Requirements can be business or technical. There are two types of requirements: functional and nonfunctional. The requirements should be clearly defined. A good design requirement is verifiable, traceable, feasible, and specific:

- **Functional requirements**: Identify specific functions of the design or simply what a design must do. Functional requirements can be business or technical in nature. The design must provide a capacity for 10 percent growth over the next three years; this is an example of a functional requirement.
- **Nonfunctional requirements**: Specify how the design must perform or operate. While a functional requirement defines something that the design must do, the nonfunctional requirement defines how or how well it must be done. System response time is an example of a nonfunctional requirement. Nonfunctional requirements become constraints on the design.

- **Assumptions**: These are considered valid until they have been proven otherwise. These factors are considered to be true, but further discovery is required to validate them. As part of the design process, assumptions should be documented and then proven or disproven. Sufficient bandwidth being available between different sites to support site-to-site replication is an example of an assumption, if the bandwidth available between the sites or the bandwidth required for replication has not yet been identified.
- **Constraints**: These place limits on the design choices. Constraints can be business policies or technical limitations. Using a specific vendor for a server's hardware is an example of a technical constraint. The project's budget and the deadlines are also common constraints. Nonfunctional requirements, since they specify how the design must perform or behave, will also become constraints on the design.
- **Risks**: These may prevent the design from being successful. Risks should be clearly identified to minimize surprises that may prevent the successful implementation of the design. A good design will address and mitigate risks.

Since the focus of this chapter is on design discovery, I felt it was important to provide this brief introduction to the design factors. We will dive much deeper into determining and defining the requirements, constraints, assumptions, and risks in `Chapter 3`, *The Design Factors*.

Identifying stakeholders

A stakeholder is anyone who has an interest in or benefits from the design. A virtual data center design will have at least some impact on many, if not all, areas of an organization and not just those associated with technology.

How to do it...

Identify the key stakeholders, including the following:

- Project sponsors
- Application owners and providers
- System, network, and storage administrators
- Application users

How it works...

Understanding the role of the stakeholders helps an architect to identify who can provide the information necessary to design a successful virtual data center solution. The details of the stakeholders and their roles are specified in the following table:

Stakeholders	Roles
• C-level executives • **Chief Executive Officer (CEO)** • **Chief Financial Officer (CFO)** • **Chief Technology Officer (CTO)**	• Strategic planning for the organization • Setting up business policies and goals • Budget approval • Project sponsorship
Business unit managers or directors	• Strategic planning for the business unit • Managing day-to-day operations • Influencing business policies and goals • Making and/or influencing decisions
Application owners	• Consumers of IT infrastructure • Documenting the application and dependencies • Managing the application functions • Providing day-to-day support for the application
IT	• Technical **Subject Matter Experts (SMEs)** • Network administrators • System administrators • Storage administrators • Help desk
Application or end users	• Consumers of application services • Relying on the infrastructure and applications to accomplish tasks efficiently

Project sponsors are typically C-level executives, **Vice Presidents (VPs)**, or directors. The project sponsor may also be a committee formed by an organization to evaluate the solutions to business problems or to explore new business opportunities. These stakeholders are often the best resource for obtaining the business requirements that a design must satisfy. If there is a project or a need to explore opportunities, there is a business goal or need driving it. Project sponsors may make the final decision on whether a design has to be approved and accepted for implementation, or they may provide the recommendations for acceptance.

There's more...

Stakeholders or the project team will ultimately be the ones that sign off on or approve the design factors that will be the basis for the logical and physical design. These design factors are identified by analyzing the data collected from the stakeholder interviews and the current state assessments.

The stakeholder's consensus and acceptance of the design factors must be obtained before proceeding with the design process. If you skip this step, you will end up wasting your time and the time of the stakeholders, having to rework areas of the design when requirements are missed, changed, added, or removed.

Define the design factors and obtain acceptance from the project team or stakeholders before taking the next steps in the design process.

Conducting stakeholder interviews

During the discovery process, the primary source of information will be stakeholder interviews. These interviews can be face-to-face meetings or can be done over the phone (or the web). Interviews are not only helpful in collecting information about the business needs and technical requirements, but also keep the stakeholders engaged in the project.

How to do it...

The following are examples of the questions that should be asked in order to determine the business requirements that will influence the design:

- What are the business initiatives, challenges, and goals?
- Are there **Service-Level Agreements (SLAs)** in place? What are they?
- What are the **Recovery Time Objective (RTO)** and **Recovery Point Objective (RPO)** requirements?
- Are there any compliance requirements?
- Who are the SMEs associated with the project?
- Who are the stakeholders?
- Who are the decision makers?
- Are there deadlines that the project must meet?
- Is there a budget for the project? What is the budget for the project?

The following are examples of the questions that should be asked in order to determine the technical requirements that will influence the design:

- Are there any current issues or technical pain points within the environment?
- What are the technology initiatives, challenges, and goals?
- How many servers will be virtualized as part of this project?
- Is there a preferred vendor for the server, network, or storage?
- Have any servers already been virtualized? What hypervisor is being used to host the already-virtualized servers?
- What type of growth is expected over the next three-five years?
- What **Operational Level Agreements** (**OLAs**) are in place?
- Is there a current network, system, storage, and application documentation?

How it works...

Meetings and interviews with stakeholders should maintain some type of structure or formality. Even if it is just a quick call, you should have some type of agenda. I know this may sound like overkill, but it will help you to keep the call or meeting on track and, more importantly, help to ensure that you collect the information you need from the call or meeting.

There are some key items that will help determine the design factors, which are explained as follows:

- **SLAs**: These are a part of a service contract where a service, its availability (uptime and access), and its performance (application response and transaction processing) are defined
- **Service Level Objective** (**SLO**): This defines specific objectives that must be achieved as part of the SLA
- **RTO**: This is the amount of time in which a service must be restored after a disruption or disaster
- **RPO**: This is the maximum amount of data loss acceptable due to a disruption or disaster
- **OLAs**: This is an internal agreement that defines relationships between support groups

Do not expect to complete the discovery in a single meeting or interview, especially for a large enterprise project. There will be follow-up questions that may need to be asked, and there will likely be questions that require more research to be answered.

In situations where more research is required, make sure that someone has been assigned with the responsibility to complete the research. Set an expectation on when the research should be completed and the information should be available. You want to avoid the *I thought so-and-so was getting that* situations and keep the discovery process moving forward.

Using VMware Capacity Planner

VMware's Capacity Planner is an inventory and planning tool available to VMware partner organizations, which collects resource utilization information from systems, analyzes the data against industry-standard reference data, and provides the information needed to successfully consolidate the servers into a virtualized environment.

How to do it...

Follow these steps to complete a Capacity Planner engagement:

1. Determine the amount of time for which the Capacity Planner engagement should run based on the business cycle
2. Choose the type of Capacity Planner assessment to be run: a **Consolidation Estimate (CE)** or a **Capacity Assessment (CA)**
3. Deploy the Capacity Planner collector in the environment to be assessed
4. Verify whether the collector is collecting performance metrics for the systems to be analyzed
5. Collect metrics for the duration of the business cycle
6. Generate Capacity Planner reports

How it works...

A Capacity Planner engagement should typically run for at least 30 days to ensure that it covers a complete monthly business cycle. Thirty days is considered typical since this covers a monthly business cycle where the demand for resources increases during the end-of-month or beginning-of-month processing. It is important that the Capacity Planner capture these increases. The time frame for a Capacity Planner engagement can vary depending on the size and nature of the business.

There are two types of Capacity Planner assessments: CE and CA. The CE assessment provides the sizing estimates of the current environment, while the CA assessment provides a more detailed analysis of the current environment. The CE assessment helps to demonstrate what can be achieved by virtualizing physical workloads, and the CA assessment provides guidance on how systems may be virtualized.

A Capacity Planner collector is installed in the environment that is being assessed. The collector runs as a Windows service and is configured using the VMware Capacity Planner Data Manager. The collector must be installed on a Windows machine, but inventory and performance data can be collected from both Windows and Linux/Unix servers. More than one collector may need to be installed for larger environments. A single collector can collect data from a maximum of 500 systems.

The collector or collectors discover systems in the environment and collect inventory and performance data from the systems. The inventory includes information about the installed physical hardware, operating systems, and installed software.

 If running the VMware Capacity Planner Data Manager on a Windows 7 workstation, use **Run as Administrator**.

Performance data metrics are collected on CPU utilization, RAM utilization, disk capacity, and disk I/O. This data is then sent securely to the VMware Capacity Planner Dashboard to be analyzed.

There can be some challenges to setting up the VMware Capacity Planner. Issues with setting up the correct credentials required for data collection and configuring Windows Firewall and services to allow the data collection are common issues that may be encountered.

The following table includes the services and ports that must be open on target systems to allow the Capacity Planner collector to collect data:

Service	Port
Remote Procedure Call (RPC)	TCP/135
NetBIOS Name Service (NBNS)	TCP/137
NetBIOS Datagram Service (NBDS)	TCP/138
NetBIOS Session Service (NBSS)	TCP/139
Microsoft-DS	TCP/445
Secure Shell (SSH) (Unix/Linux only)	TCP/22

In order to collect data from Windows systems, **Windows Management Instrumentation (WMI)**, remote registry, and perfmon must be enabled on the target system. For data collection on Linux or Unix systems, port 22 must be open and the **Secure Shell Daemon (SSHD)** must be running. Account credentials provided must have at least local administrator rights on the target systems.

There's more...

Once the inventory and performance data has been collected, the results can be analyzed and reports can be generated. Some of this information can be viewed and exported from the VMware Capacity Planner Data Manager, but detailed analysis reports are generated from the VMware Capacity Planner dashboard.

If server hardware constraints have been identified during the discovery process, report settings can be adjusted. These constraints will then be applied to the Capacity Planner reporting to determine and show the consolidation ratios that can be obtained using the different hardware configurations. The following screenshot shows the report settings:

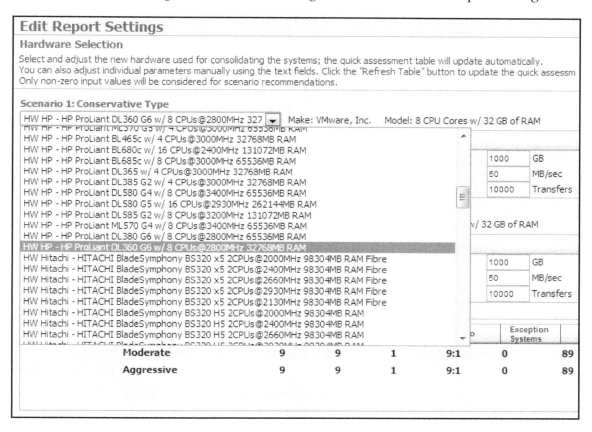

Report Settings in Capacity Planner

The reports that are available include the progress report, which provides an overview of the status of the assessment; the executive summary presentation, which provides a high-level summary of the assessment; and the assessment report, which provides information on consolidation ratios and recommendations. Custom reports can also be generated. The following screenshot shows consolidation recommendations:

System Consolidation Recommendation

Before Virtualization		With VMware Virtualization							
Total Systems	Eligible Systems	Consolidation Scenario and Platform	ESX Hosts	ESX CPU Utilization	ESX Memory Utilization	Average Memory Per VM	Racks Saved	Eligible System Consolidation Ratio	Total System Consolidation Ratio
9	9	Conservative Type	1	23.04%	56.27%	3.25 GB	0	89%	89%
9	9	Aggressive Type	1	23.04%	56.27%	3.25 GB	0	89%	89%

Conservative Type
  Make: VMware, Inc.
  Model: 8 CPU Cores w/ 32 GB of RAM
  CPU: 8
  Memory: 32 GB

Aggressive Type
  Make: VMware, Inc.
  Model: 8 CPU Cores w/ 32 GB of RAM
  CPU: 8
  Memory: 32 GB

Capacity Planner consolidation recommendations

Using Windows Performance Monitor

The Microsoft Windows perfmon can be used to collect performance information, such as CPU utilization, memory utilization, and disk I/O utilization of the Windows servers.

How to do it...

In this example, Microsoft Windows perfmon is used to collect disk I/O metrics, with the following steps:

1. Open **Performance Monitor** and use the **Data Collector Set** wizard to create a user-defined data collector, as displayed in the following screenshot:

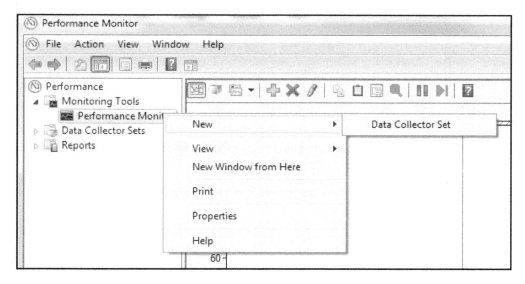

Creating a user-defined data collector in Performance Monitor

2. Once the **Data Collector Set** application has been created, add **New | Data Collector** to the **Data Collector Set**, as shown in the following screenshot:

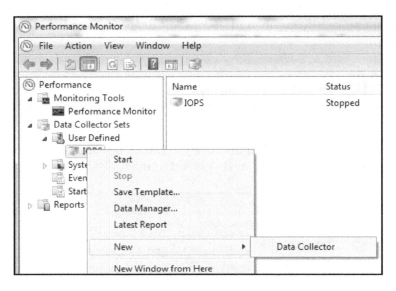

Adding a new Data Collector in Performance Manager

3. Name the new **Data Collector** and select the **Performance counter data collector** radio button, as shown in the following screenshot:

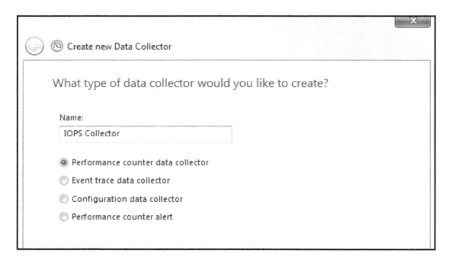

Creating a Data Collector in Performance Manager

4. Add the following counters for the `object _Total` instance to the data collector:

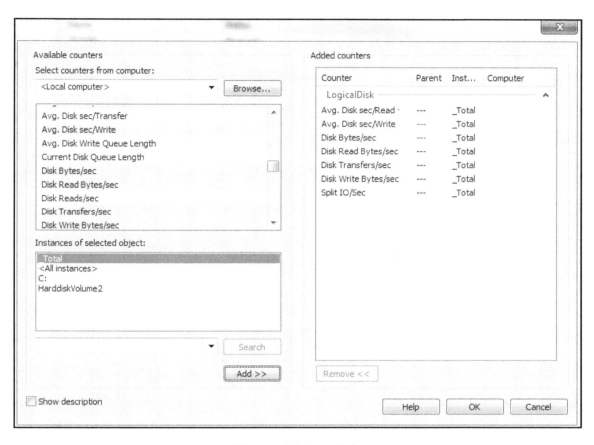

Adding counters in Performance Monitor

5. We will add performance counters as shown in the following screenshot:

Adding performance counters in Performance Monitor

6. Right-click on the new data collector set, select the **Stop Condition** tab, and change the stop condition to the period of time for which you want to monitor the **Input/Output operations Per Second (IOPS)**, as shown in the following screenshot:

Setting stop conditions in Performance Monitor

7. Data collection for the **Data Collector Set** can be configured to start manually or can be scheduled to start at a future date or time. The following screenshot displays setting a **Schedule** for the **Data Collector Set**:

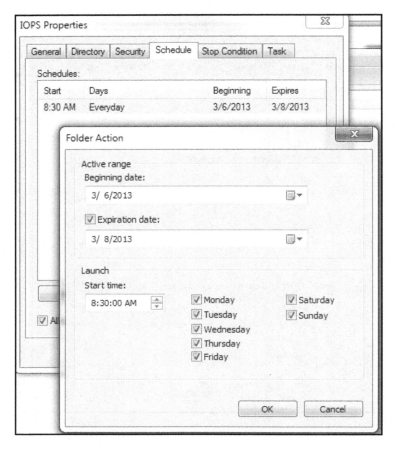

Configuring the monitoring schedule in Performance Monitor

8. Once the collection process has been completed, you can view the report using the **Reports** section of **Performance Monitor**.

9. A template of the **Data Collector Set** application can be created in order to easily import the **Data Collector Set** on other servers/workstations. This is shown in the following screenshot:

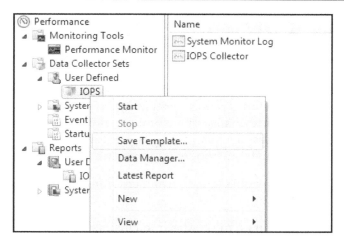

Saving the Data Collector set for use later

How it works...

The total number of IOPS and the I/O profile of a server are necessary to architect the storage required for a virtualized environment correctly. The IOPS and I/O profile are helpful in determining which **Redundant Array of Independent Disks (RAID)** level to use with the number and type of disks to be used in order to support the server storage workload.

Windows perfmon can also be configured to collect metrics associated with CPU and memory usage by simply adding the associated counters to the data collector set.

There's more...

Most organizations will have some form of network-or resource-monitoring system in place, such as Nagios, SolarWinds, Splunk, or vRealize Operations Manager. The information monitored and collected by these systems will be useful for the current state assessments. The SMEs should be asked whether there is monitoring in place and for access to the data collected by these systems.

Many vendors also perform free infrastructure assessments. Often, these free assessments are not thorough enough to provide the details necessary for a complete current state assessment, but they can provide some good information. Again, the project SMEs will be asked whether any type of assessments have been done.

Conducting a VMware optimization assessment

The **VMware Optimization Assessment (VOA)** is an enhanced evaluation of vRealize Operations Manager, which includes reports providing information about the configuration, capacity, and performance of a vSphere environment. This information is useful for an administrator or architect validating an existing vSphere deployment or planning an expansion to an existing vSphere deployment.

The VOA will provide useful insights into a virtual environment by providing detail analytics, including the following:

- Providing information on misconfigured clusters, hosts, and virtual machines
- Identifying potential performance problems with root cause analysis
- Analyzing virtual machine resources to identify undersized and/or oversized virtual machines, providing opportunities to attain a right-size environment

The information gathered during a VOA will allow an administrator or architect the ability to quickly identify health issues, risks to the environment, and areas where efficiency can be improved.

How to do it...

Follow these steps to obtain, deploy, configure, and conduct an optimization assessment using the VOA appliance:

1. Visit `https://www.vmware.com/assessment/voa` and download the VOA appliance.
2. Import the VOA Appliance OVA into the vCenter inventory.

3. Power on the VOA appliance and access the VOA appliance IP address with a web browser to launch the **vRealize Operations Manager Initial Setup** wizard and choose **Express Installation**, as shown in the following screenshot:

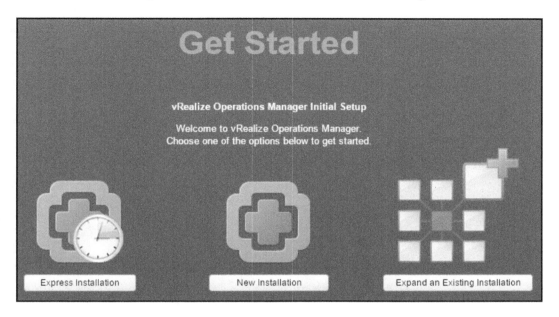

The VOA splash page

4. Set the Administrator Password when prompted by **the vRealize Operations Manager Initial Setup** wizard.

5. Configure the vCenter Adapter by providing a **Display name**, **vCenter Server** IP address, and **Credential**. Use the **Test Connection** button to test connectivity and credentials. Be sure to **Save Settings** once the test is successful. The **vCenter Adapter** configuration window is shown in the following screenshot:

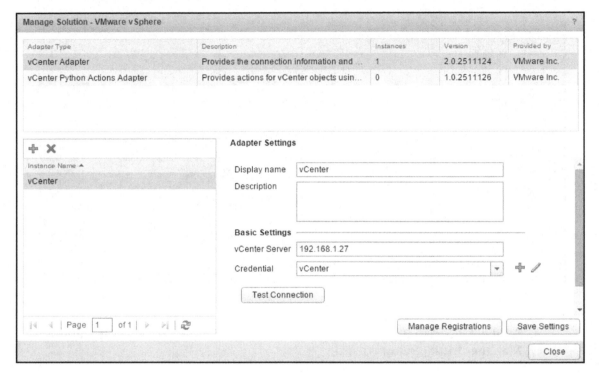

Registering the vCenter adapter in VOA

6. Once the **vCenter Adapter** is configured, it will begin collecting performance and configuration information from the configured vCenter Server.

7. Access the VOA appliance with a web browser to view information on environment health, risks, and efficiency.

How it works...

Once deployed and configured, the VOA appliance begins collecting information about the virtual environment. The information is analyzed and displayed as part of the VOA dashboard. The **Health, Risks**, and **Efficiency** of the environment is displayed in the VOA dashboard, as shown in the following screenshot:

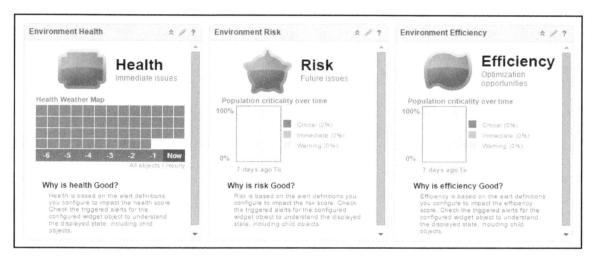

The VOA dashboard

The VOA reporting is split up into three phases. The phases correspond with specific metrics, which will be available over time as the VOA appliance collects and analyzes information from the environment. The following phases make up the optimization assessment:

- **Phase one**: This is the configuration phase. Phase one provides analysis of the configuration of the environment and corresponds with the **Environment Health** dashboard. The information in this phase is available within 24 hours of deploying the VOA appliance.
- **Phase two**: This is the performance phase. Phase two provides analysis of performance information in the environment and identifies risks associated with exceeding available capacity and performance. Phase two requires VOA collection for five to seven days.

- **Phase three**: This is the optimization phase. In this phase, the areas where capacity and performance can be optimized are identified. This includes details such as virtual machines with resources that have been over-allocated. This final phase requires the collection of environment data by the VOA over a period of about 21 days.

Preconfigured reports are included for each phase of the VOA. These reports can be generated for the VOA appliance, as shown in the following screenshot:

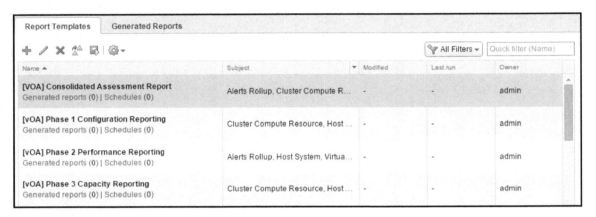

Default reports in VOA

These preconfigured reports provide valuable insight that will assist an architect in determining what will be necessary to meet requirements around growth or expansion of an existing vSphere environment.

Identifying dependencies

A dependency is a relationship among systems or services. During the discovery process, dependencies should be identified and documented. In Chapter 1, *The Virtual Data Center*, we discussed the importance of taking an holistic view when designing a virtualized environment. Identifying dependencies is the key to the holistic approach of designing.

How to do it...

An architect must identify dependencies in order to understand what effect a design decision or change may have on other services. The architect should identify the following dependencies:

- Physical infrastructure dependencies
- Application and service dependencies

How it works...

Dependencies can be service-to-service; for example, a web application depends on a frontend web server and a backend database. Dependencies can be service-to-infrastructure; for example, a web application requires a static IP address and a minimum of 10 MB of network bandwidth.

Physical and infrastructure dependencies are generally easier to discover and are commonly documented. Applications will have dependencies, which include server resources, network resources, and storage resources. Infrastructure dependencies that are not documented are often readily discovered as part of the current state assessment. The following table is an example of how physical application dependencies can be documented:

Application	OS	CPU cores	Speed (GHz)	RAM (GB)	Network (GBps)	Network (VLAN)	Storage
IIS	Win2k8 R2	4	2.7	16	1	22	50 GB
SQL database	Win2k8 R2	8	2.7	32	1	22	1 TB

Service-to-service or application-to-service dependencies can be a bit more difficult to discover. Application owners, application developers, application documentation, and application vendors will be the best sources for determining these dependencies. As with Capacity Planner, if you work for VMware or a VMware partner, you're entitled to use VMware **Application Dependency Planner (ADP)**.

The following diagram is an example of how service dependencies can be mapped and documented:

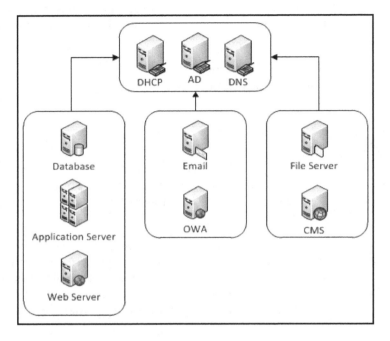

Example application dependency diagram

Understanding the dependencies will help an architect to understand how a change made to one area of the design may have an effect on another area of the design. Mapping and documenting application dependencies will provide the necessary information to properly design a solution for business continuity and disaster recovery. Understanding the dependencies will also aid in troubleshooting issues with the design implementation.

Beware, there may be undocumented dependencies that are not easily discovered. This can often be a risk to the design, especially in an organization with a legacy of unsupported applications or applications developed in-house that have not been properly documented.

I have seen issues where a specific configuration, such as an IP address or a file location, has been hardcoded into an application and not documented. A change is made to the environment and hence the application becomes unavailable. Dependencies of this type can be extremely difficult to plan for and discover.

There are tools available that can help you to discover application dependencies automatically. If you work for VMware or a VMware partner, you have free access to the VMware **Application Dependency Planner** (**ADP**) software. ADP ships as a pre-built OVF virtual appliance and comes with several components. There's a database to store all the dependency information, collector VMs to receive Ethernet traffic, and an Aggregator VM which acts as a manager and central configuration point of the application. The idea of ADP is to sniff Ethernet traffic to understand the communication paths between servers in an environment. ADP then builds a visual map that helps consultants to easily understand application dependencies. The map includes IP addresses, hostnames, port numbers, and protocols which helps to quickly identify which servers are talking with one another.

3
The Design Factors

During the vSphere design discovery process, information is collected on the business and technical goals of the virtualization project. This information must be analyzed in order to determine the vSphere design factors.

The vSphere design factors that must be determined are as follows:

- Requirements
- Constraints
- Assumptions
- Risks

Determining the requirements, making and proving assumptions, determining constraints, and identifying risks forms the conceptual design and provides the foundation to build on for the logical design. Business and technical design factors that are identified as part of the conceptual design will be mapped to the resources that are necessary to satisfy them during the logical design process. The conceptual design phase is highlighted within the overall design and implementation flow diagram:

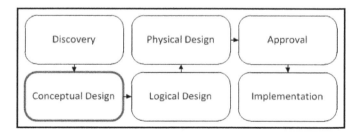

Conceptual design phase of the overall design and implementation workflow

In our example design, after conducting interviews with stakeholders and performing technical assessments of the environment, the following information has been collected about the project's goals, current environment, and business factors that will influence the design:

- Currently, there are 100 physical servers, each hosting a single application. Each application services 10 customers.
- The business expects to add 50 new customers over the next year.
- The solution must support growth over the next 5 years.
- Application uptime and accessibility is very important.
- Consolidate physical servers to reduce hardware costs associated with the maintenance and deployment of new application servers.
- No more than 20 application servers, or 200 customers, should be affected by a hardware failure.
- There should be a 1-hour maintenance window each month for application and hardware maintenance. Hardware maintenance is currently a challenge. Since hardware and application maintenance cannot be performed at the same time, the maintenance window does not typically provide the time that's required to perform both application and hardware maintenance.
- Application servers run Microsoft Windows 2016 as the operating system.
- Each application server is configured with 8 GB of memory. The peak usage of a single application server is approximately 65 percent or approximately 5.2 GB.
- Each application server is configured with two dual-core 2.7 GHz processors. The peak usage of a single application server is approximately 10 percent of the total processing power, or approximately 1 GHz.
- Each application server is configured with 100 GB of disk space. Peak disk capacity usage of a single application server is approximately 65 percent of the total disk space, or 65 GB. Peak disk performance of a single application server is 50 IOPS with an IO profile of 90 percent read and 10 percent write.
- Currently, the stakeholders are using HP DL380 servers. The infrastructure team is very familiar with the management and maintenance of these servers and wants to continue using them.
- Currently, there is no shared storage. The current system and infrastructure administrators are unfamiliar with the shared storage concepts and protocols.
- Cisco switches are used for network connectivity. Separate VLANs exist for management connectivity and production application connectivity.
- Currently, each physical server contains a single gigabit network interface card. Peak network usage is 10 Mbps.

- Server logs are auditable and must be retained for 6 months. All logs should also be sent to a central syslog server that is already in place.
- If an application server fails, the current recovery time is around 8 hours. The solution should reduce this time to less than 4 hours.
- The management team expects the implementation to be completed before the third quarter of the year.
- There is an approved project budget of $200,000.

In this chapter, we will use this information to determine the design factors so that we can create the conceptual design. Throughout the design process, each design decision is mapped back to these design factors.

In this chapter, we will cover the following topics:

- Identifying design requirements
- Identifying design constraints
- Making design assumptions
- Identifying design risks
- Considering infrastructure design qualities
- Creating the conceptual design

Identifying design requirements

The design requirements specify the functions that the design must perform and the objectives that the design must meet.

There are two types of requirements: functional requirements and nonfunctional requirements. Functional requirements specify the objectives or functions that a design must meet. Nonfunctional requirements define how the design accomplishes the functional requirements.

Typical functional requirements include the following:

- Business goals
- Business rules
- Legal, regulatory, and compliance requirements
- Application system requirements
- Technical requirements
- Administrative functions

Typical nonfunctional requirements include the following:

- Performance
- Security
- Capacity
- Availability
- Manageability
- Recoverability

While identifying and defining the requirements, separate the functional requirements from the nonfunctional requirements; nonfunctional requirements are design constraints and will be documented separately.

Since functional requirements define what the design must accomplish, once identified and approved, these requirements typically cannot be easily changed during the design process.

How to do it...

The following high-level steps can be used to fully identify design requirements:

1. Analyze the business and technical information that's collected during the discovery process
2. Determine the functional and nonfunctional requirements of the design
3. Document the design requirements

How it works...

While defining the requirements, each requirement should be clearly stated and specified. Define requirements individually; multiple requirements should not be combined into a single requirement.

During the discovery process, the following information about the current size of the existing environment is identified:

- Currently, there are 100 physical servers, each hosting a single application. Each application services 10 customers.
- Not more than 20 application servers or 200 customers should be affected by a hardware failure.

- Consolidate physical servers to reduce the hardware costs associated with maintaining and refreshing the hardware of the existing application servers.

One of the goals of the project is to consolidate the physical servers to reduce hardware costs. An example design requirement to support this might be as follows: consolidate existing physical servers.

This requirement is vague and with the information that's available from the discovery, the requirement should be more specific. Based on the number of existing physical servers and the maximum number of customers that should be impacted during a hardware failure, a better requirement example may be as follows: consolidate the existing 100 physical application servers down to five servers.

Information about the expected growth of the environment was also discovered:

- The business expects to add 50 new customers each year
- The solution must support growth over the next 5 years

Based on this information, there is a requirement that the environment must be designed to provide the capacity that's necessary to support future growth. An example requirement to support this might be as follows: provide sufficient capacity to support growth.

Again, this requirement is very vague and does not provide any information about how much the growth will be or over what period of time is growth expected. From the discovery, it is known that the business expects to add 50 new customers over the next year. Each server hosts a single application, which will provide service for 10 customers. The solution should support growth over the next 5 years.

Using this information, a requirement that specifies the growth that should be supported and the time period over which this growth is expected is as follows: provide capacity to support growth for 25 additional application servers over the next 5 years.

The architect can also determine the availability of requirements for hardware maintenance and application resiliency:

- The solution must allow a 1-hour maintenance window each month for application and hardware maintenance. Hardware maintenance is currently a challenge. Since hardware and application maintenance cannot be performed at the same time, the maintenance window does not typically provide the time required to perform both application and hardware maintenance.

- Application uptime and accessibility is very important.
- Not more than 20 application servers or 200 customers should be affected by a hardware failure.

From this information, the requirement that might be identified is that the server hardware maintenance should not affect application uptime, and redundancy should be maintained during hardware maintenance operations.

The problem with this requirement is that it includes two separate requirements; one requirement is for application uptime, and another requirement is for redundancy. These requirements should be split into two individual requirements.

 Server hardware maintenance should not affect application uptime. Provide $N+2$ redundancy to support a hardware failure during normal and maintenance operations.

There's more...

Once the functional requirements have been identified and defined, the requirements should be recorded in the design documentation as part of the conceptual design. There are a number of formats that can be used, such as bulleted lists and numbered lists, but a simple table works well. Assigning an ID to each requirement makes it easier to reference the requirement later in the design document:

ID	Requirement
R001	Consolidate the existing 100 physical application servers down to five servers
R002	Provide capacity to support growth for 25 additional application servers over the next 5 years
R003	Server hardware maintenance should not affect application uptime
R004	Provide N+2 redundancy to support a hardware failure during normal and maintenance operations

Identifying design constraints

Design constraints are factors that restrict the options the architect can use to satisfy the design requirements. Once the functional and nonfunctional requirements have been identified, they are separated. The nonfunctional requirements that define how requirements must be satisfied become the constraints on the design.

Design constraints include the following:

- Technology constraints, such as hardware vendors, software solutions, and protocols
- Operational constraints, such as performance and accessibility
- Financial constraints, such as budgets

Unlike functional requirements, the constraints and nonfunctional requirements may change during the design process. This holds true, especially if the constraint introduces risks into the design. For example, if an identified constraint that requires a specific model of hardware to be used prevents the design from satisfying a functional requirement, the constraint may need to be changed or adjusted.

How to do it...

The high-level steps to identify the constraints of a design are as follows:

1. Analyze the business and technical information that's collected during the discovery process
2. Determine the nonfunctional requirements of the design
3. Nonfunctional requirements are constraints on the design
4. Identify any other constraints on the design
5. Document the design constraints

How it works...

As with functional requirements, when defining the nonfunctional requirements or constraints, they should be clearly stated and specified. Define each constraint individually; do not combine multiple nonfunctional requirements into a single constraint.

Currently, HP DL380 servers are used. The infrastructure team is familiar with the management and maintenance of these servers and wants to continue using them.

This statement does not identify something the design must do. It is placing a constraint on the design by providing a specific type of hardware that should be used. The following is an example of the constraint that can be formed from this statement:

- HP DL380 servers should be used for compute resources

Budgetary constraints affect nearly all the projects. There will likely be a limit on the amount of money a company will want to spend to accomplish a goal.

 If a budget has not been established for a project, it is likely that the business has not committed to the project. Beware the infinite budget.

During the design discovery, the following budget was identified for this project: there is an approved project budget of $200,000.

This budget constraint can simply be stated as follows: a project budget of $200,000.

Operational constraints are also common. Often, there will be existing processes or policies in place that will need to be factored into the design. Often, you will need to accommodate the existing monitoring and management applications in the design. An example of an operational requirement is as follows: server logs are auditable and must be retained for 6 months. All logs should also be sent to a central syslog server that is already in place.

Here, a functional and nonfunctional requirement can be identified. The functional requirement is that the server logs are auditable and must be retained for 6 months. This functional requirement defines something the design must do, but there is also a constraint on how the design must accomplish this, and that is by using syslog to send logs to a central server. Based on this information, the constraint is as follows: syslog should be used to send server logs to an existing central syslog server.

There's more...

Constraints should be documented as part of the conceptual design. Just as you used a table to document the design requirements, using a simple table works well when documenting the design constraints. Each constraint is assigned an ID so that it can be easily referenced later in the design document:

ID	Constraint
C001	HP DL380 servers should be used for compute resources
C002	A project budget of $200,000
C003	Syslog should be used to send server logs to an existing central syslog server

Making design assumptions

Assumptions are made by the architect and have not yet been validated. Assumptions are accepted as a fact until they have been validated or invalidated. As part of the design process, each assumption needs to be validated as a fact. If an assumption cannot be validated, a risk will be introduced into the design.

How to do it...

Any assumptions that are made will need to be defined and documented as follows:

1. Identify any assumptions that have been made about the design
2. Document the design assumptions

How it works...

Common assumptions relate to power, space, and cooling. A common example of an assumption that an architect may make is as follows:

- There is sufficient power, cooling, and floor/rack space available in the data center to support both the existing and consolidated environment during the migration

While working through the physical design, the power, cooling, and space requirements will need to be identified and the assumptions validated. A goal of this project is to consolidate the existing physical servers. The overall need for power, cooling, and space will be reduced once the project is complete, but enough of these resources need to be available to support both the existing physical environment and the new consolidated environment during the consolidation process.

Referring to our mock design, a requirement was identified based on the discovery information to provide *N+2* redundancy:

R004	Provide *N+2* redundancy to support a hardware failure during normal and maintenance operations

This requirement was defined based on the following discovery information:

- A 1-hour maintenance window each month for application and hardware maintenance. Hardware maintenance is currently a challenge. Since hardware and application maintenance cannot be performed at the same time, the maintenance window does not typically provide the time that's necessary to perform both application and hardware maintenance.
- Application uptime and accessibility is very important.

What assumption may have been made when defining this requirement?

An assumption was made based on the importance of application uptime and accessibility that there should be sufficient resources to provide redundancy not only during normal operations, but also in the event of a host failure. When a host is unavailable due to maintenance being performed, the following approach should be adopted:

- Resources should be provided to support a host failure during both normal and host maintenance operations

The following requirements relating to growth were also defined:

- The business expects to add 50 new customers over the next year
- Support growth over the next 5 years

ID	Requirement
R002	Provide capacity to support growth for 25 additional application servers over the next 5 years

An expected, the growth of 50 customers over the next year was identified, but the design is expected to support growth over the next 5 years. To create this requirement, an assumption was made that growth would be the same over years two through five, resulting in the documentation of the following assumption: growth is calculated based on the addition of 50 new customers each year over the next 5 years.

The company may have a forecast for growth that exceeds this. If this assumption is incorrect, the design may not meet the defined requirement.

There's more...

Assumptions should be documented in the design document. As with documenting design requirements and constraints, use a table for this. Each assumption is assigned an ID so that it can be easily referenced later in the design document:

ID	Assumption
A001	Sufficient power, cooling, and floor/rack space is available in the data center to support the existing and consolidated environment during the migration
A002	Resources should be provided to support a host failure during both normal and maintenance operations
A003	Growth is calculated based on the addition of 50 new customers each year over the next 5 years

Identifying design risks

Risks include anything that may prevent the design from satisfying the requirements. Design risks include the following:

- Technical risks
- Operational risks
- Financial risks

Risks are often introduced through constraints or assumptions that have not been proven. Risks resulting from assumptions are mitigated by validating them. When risks are not mitigated, the project may not be successful.

How to do it...

Throughout the design process, design decisions should mitigate or minimize risks. The following steps will help you do that:

1. Identify any risks associated with the design requirements or assumptions
2. Validate assumptions to reduce the risks associated with them
3. Determine how design decisions will help mitigate or minimize risks

How it works...

There are a few risks in the design based on the discovery information, assumption, and constraints.

As a part of the discovery process, the following risk was noted:

- Currently, there is no shared storage. The current system and infrastructure administrators are unfamiliar with the shared storage concepts and protocols.

These operational risks were identified during discovery. Operational risks can be minimized by providing implementation and operational documentation.

There is a technical constraint that may also introduce risks, and is as follows:

ID	Constraint
C001	HP DL380 servers should be used for compute resources

This constraint may introduce some risks to the environment if the capabilities of the HP DL380 servers are not able to fulfill the requirements. Can the servers be configured with the processing and memory required by the requirements? Are there enough expansion slots to support the number of network ports or HBAs required? It may be necessary to remove or change this constraint if the HP DL380 server is not able to fulfill the technical requirements of the design.

An assumption was also made with regards to the growth of the environment over the next 5 years: growth is calculated based on the addition of 50 new customers each year over the next 5 years.

If this assumption is not validated and growth is forecasted by the company to be higher in 2 to 5 years, the design will be at risk to not meet the growth requirements. Validating this assumption will mitigate this risk.

Considering infrastructure design qualities

What makes a good infrastructure design? The answer could be summarized by saying that it includes the following qualities:

- Availability
- Manageability

- Performance
- Recoverability
- Security

The infrastructure design qualities, also called design characteristics, should be incorporated into every enterprise design. We saw these when we described them earlier in this chapter as nonfunctional requirements. That is to say, they describe how a design should work. In addition to meeting the customer's requirements and constraints, it may not be a good design overall if the design qualities were not considered.

Throughout the design process, it's a good idea to understand how each design decision impacts the infrastructure design qualities. Continually ask yourself: if the design qualities are my end goal, how does this design decision affect them?

How to do it...

The following steps describe the process you can take to ensure your designs take the infrastructure design qualities into consideration for each requirement, constraint, or assumption:

1. Understand the requirement, constraint, or assumption
2. Make a design decision to meet the requirement, constraint, or assumption
3. Document the impact of the design decision on each infrastructure quality

How it works...

Let's take requirement R003 from earlier in this chapter as an example. This requirement states that server hardware maintenance should not affect application uptime. To meet this requirement, each vSphere cluster will be designed with $N+2$ redundancy to support a host failure during the maintenance of another host. The following table describes how you might document this design decision against the infrastructure qualities:

Infrastructure quality	Impact
Availability	Increases availability by providing additional hosts on which vSphere HA can restart VMs
Manageability	Introduces additional hosts in each cluster that need be managed, patched, and backed up
Performance	Provides additional resources from which VMs can be run

Recoverability	Negligible impact to recoverability
Security	Increased attack surface by introducing an additional host in each cluster

There's more...

So far, we have requirements, constraints, and assumptions mapping to design decisions, which map to infrastructure design qualities. In addition, you should ensure that each component in your design addresses each design quality. Typically, the vSphere design components are identified as follows:

- Compute
- Storage
- Network
- Virtual machine
- Management

So, a simple way to ensure a complete design is to build the following table, which maps each vSphere component to each infrastructure design quality. While building your design, you can check off the mapping of component to quality as you address it in your design. Don't expect to be able to fill in the table with a short description of how you approached each mapping. The topics should be far too large to do so. Rather, use the table as a reference to ensure that each area is addressed in your design:

vSphere component	Availability	Manageability	Performance	Recoverability	Security
Compute	Yes	Yes	Yes	Yes	No
Storage	No	No	No	No	No
Network	Yes	Yes	No	Yes	Yes
Virtual machine	No	yes	Yes	yes	No
Management	Yes	Yes	Yes	Yes	Yes

Creating the conceptual design

The conceptual design is created with the documentation of the requirements, constraints, and assumptions. The design documentation should include a list of each of the design factors. The conceptual design guides the design. All logical and physical design elements can be mapped back to the conceptual design to provide justifications for design decisions.

How to do it...

To create the conceptual design, follow these steps:

1. Use the design factors to form the conceptual design
2. Organize the design factors to be easily referenced during the design process
3. Create high-level diagrams that document the functional blocks of the design

How it works...

The conceptual design should include a brief overview that describes the key goals of the project and any factors that may drive the business decisions related to the project. The conceptual design includes all the identified requirements, constraints, and assumptions.

The following pointers explain an example of conceptual design:

- The primary goal of this project is to lower hardware cost through the consolidation of physical application servers. The design will increase application uptime and resiliency and reduce application recovery time.
- The design will attempt to adhere to the standards and best practices when these align with the requirements and constraints of the design.

Design requirements

Requirements are the key demands on the design. The design requirements are as follows:

ID	Requirement
R001	Consolidate the existing 100 physical application servers down to five servers
R002	Provide capacity to support growth for 25 additional application servers over the next 5 years
R003	Server hardware maintenance should not affect application uptime
R004	Provide $N+2$ redundancy to support hardware failure during normal and maintenance operations

Design constraints

Constraints limit the logical decisions and physical specifications. Constraints may or may not align with the design objectives. The design constraints are as follows:

ID	Constraint
C001	Covered in the *Identifying design constraints* recipe and its *There's more...* section of this chapter
C002	A project budget of $200,000
C003	Syslog should be used to send server logs to an existing central syslog server

Assumptions

Assumptions are the expectations of a system that have not yet been confirmed. If the assumptions are not validated, risks may be introduced. Assumptions are listed as A001, A002, and A003.

There's more...

The conceptual design can also include diagrams that provide high-level overviews of the proposed design. Conceptual diagrams of the functional blocks of the design include the virtualization infrastructure, storage, servers, and networking. A conceptual diagram does not include specifics about the resources that are required, or hardware vendors.

The conceptual diagram should show, at a very high level, how servers will be placed in a vSphere **High Availability (HA)/Distributed Resource Scheduler (DRS)** cluster. The existing physical network infrastructure will be leveraged to provide connectivity for IP storage and the virtual machine networks. The diagram does not include any specifics about the type of servers, type of array, or the resources required, but it does provide an overview of how the different parts of the design will work together.

4
vSphere Management Design

This chapter will cover the design considerations that should be taken into account when designing the management layer of the virtual infrastructure. We will look at the different components that make up vCenter, how to size them correctly, and how to ensure compatibility between the VMware products that are deployed in the environment. This chapter will also cover the different deployment options for vCenter and its components, as well as the importance of the availability, recoverability, and security of these components.

The following diagram displays how management design is integrated into the design process:

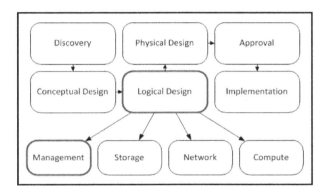

Management design within the vSphere design workflow

Questions that the architect should ask and answer during the management design process include the following:

- What components are necessary to manage the virtual environment?
- How will management components be deployed?
- What resources are required to support the management components?
- What impact will the loss of a management component have on the environment?
- How can we recover from the loss of a management component?
- How can we upgrade and patch management components?

In this chapter, we will cover the following recipes:

- Identifying vCenter components and dependencies
- Selecting a vCenter deployment option
- Determining vCenter resource requirements
- Selecting a database for the vCenter deployment
- Determining database interoperability
- Choosing a vCenter deployment topology
- Designing for management availability
- Designing a separate management cluster
- Configuring vCenter mail, SNMP, and alarms
- Using Enhanced Linked Mode
- Using the VMware Product Interoperability Matrix
- Backing up vCenter Server components
- Planning vCenter HA to increase vCenter availability
- Upgrading vCenter Server
- Designing a vSphere Update Manager Deployment

Identifying vCenter components and dependencies

The vCenter Server provides the central configuration and management of the ESXi servers and the services provided by the virtual infrastructure. vCenter 6.7 is composed of several components and services, such as the **Platform Services Controller** (**PSC**), the vCenter Server database, and the vCenter Server.

How to do it...

Following are the procedure to identify vCenter components and dependencies:

1. Identify the following core components and services of vCenter 6.7:
    - The VMware PSC was introduced in version 6.0. The PSC handles security functions in the vSphere infrastructure. The PSC provides the vCenter **Single Sign-On** (**SSO**) service, licensing management, registration services, and the **VMware Certificate Authority** (**VMCA**). The PSC can be deployed as a standalone server or embedded on the same server with other required vCenter components.
    - vCenter SSO is deployed as a part of the PSC in vSphere 6.x. SSO provides identity management for administrators, users, and applications that interact with the VMware vSphere environment. **Active Directory** (**AD**) domains and **Open Lightweight Directory Access Protocol** (**OpenLDAP**) authentication sources can be added to provide authentication to the vCenter management components.
    - VMware Certificate Authority issues certificates for users accessing vCenter services, machines providing vCenter services, and ESXi hosts. The VMCA service is new to vSphere 6.x and is deployed with the PSC. The VMCA not only issues and manages certificates to vSphere services and components, but also acts as the **Certificate Authority** (**CA**) for these certificates. The VMCA can be used as a subordinate CA in an enterprise CA environment.

- **VMware vCenter Server**: This provides the configuration, access control, and performance monitoring of ESXi/ESX hosts and virtual machines that have been added to the inventory of the vCenter Server. In vSphere 6.x, the VMware vCenter Inventory Service, the VMware vSphere Web Client, the VMware Content Library Service, and other services not provided by the PSC, are all installed with the vCenter Server.
- **VMware vCenter Inventory Service**: This maintains application and inventory data so that inventory objects, including data centers, clusters, folders, and virtual machines, can be searched and accessed. In a vCenter 6.x deployment, the vCenter Inventory Service is installed on the vCenter Server.
- **VMware vSphere Web Client**: This allows the connections made to vCenter to manage objects in its inventory by using a web browser. Many of the new features and capabilities since vSphere Version 5.1 can only be configured and managed using the VMware vSphere Web Client. To access and configure new features in vSphere 6.x, the vSphere Web Client is required. The vSphere Web Client Server is installed with the vCenter Server.
- **vCenter Database**: vCenter Server requires a database to store configurations, logs, and performance data. The database can be an external Microsoft SQL or Oracle database server or the embedded vPostgreSQL database. An external Microsoft SQL database is only supported with a Windows vCenter deployment.

2. Identify the common dependencies required to install vCenter and the PSC:
    - **DNS**: Forward and reverse name resolution should be working properly for all systems. Ensure that systems can be resolved by the **Fully Qualified Domain Name** (**FQDN**), the short name or hostname, and the IP address.
    - **Time**: Time should be synchronized across the environment.

How it works...

Each vCenter Server component or service has a set of dependencies. The following diagram illustrates the core vCenter Server dependencies:

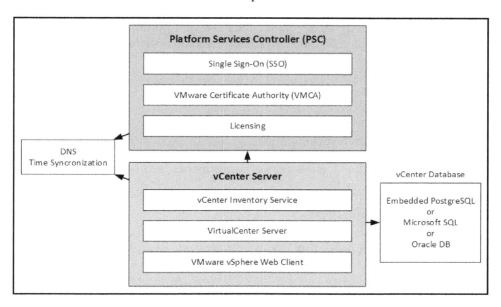

Core vCenter Server dependencies

As with earlier vCenter versions, the vCenter 6.7 Windows installation media includes several other tools that provide support and automation to deploy, manage, patch, and monitor the vSphere virtual environment. These tools can be installed on the same server as other vCenter Server components, or on a separate server. The tools that are included are as follows:

- **VMware vSphere Update Manager (VUM)**: This provides a central automated patch and version management for ESXi hosts and virtual appliances. VUM can be installed on the vCenter Server when running on Windows, but it must be installed on a separate Windows server when using the VCSA.
- **ESXi Dump Collector**: This collects memory dumps over the network in the event of an ESXi host encountering a critical error.
- **VMware vSphere Syslog Collector**: This enables network logging and combines the logs from multiple hosts.
- **VMware vSphere Auto Deploy**: This provides the automated deployment and configuration of ESXi hosts.

Selecting a vCenter deployment option

There are a number of deployment options available for deploying vCenter. The vCenter Server can be deployed on a dedicated physical server running a 64-bit Windows server operating system, on a virtual machine running a 64-bit Windows server guest operating system, or as a Linux-based virtual appliance. vCenter components can be installed on a single server, or the components can be installed on separate virtual or physical machines.

How to do it...

Regardless of the deployment option that's selected, the vCenter Server components must be installed and configured in a specific order, so that the service dependencies are met.

The order of installation of the vCenter Server components is as follows:

1. Deploy the VMware **Platform Services Controller (PSC)**
2. Deploy the vCenter Server
3. Deploy the other supporting components: VMware Update Manager, the VMware Syslog Service, ESXi Dump Collector, and so on

How it works...

Deploying the vCenter Server components on a virtual machine is a VMware recommended practice. When vCenter is deployed on a virtual machine, it is possible to take advantage of the portability and availability provided by the virtual infrastructure. One of the primary advantages of deploying vCenter components on virtual machines is that VMware **High Availability (HA)** can be leveraged to protect the management environment from a hardware failure or a virtual machine crash.

The **vCenter Server Appliance (VCSA)** is a preconfigured, Linux-based virtual machine that has been optimized to run the vCenter Server and the associated services. It includes a PostgreSQL-embedded database. A remote database connection can be configured to support larger deployments.

A limitation of the VCSA is that Microsoft SQL is not supported as a remote database. In previous versions of vCenter, VUM had to be installed on a separate Windows server. Since 6.7, VUM is installed within the VCSA, so a separate Windows server just for VUM is no longer needed.

vCenter Linked Mode creates groups of vCenter Servers that can be managed centrally. Logging in to one member of the vCenter Linked Mode group allows an administrator to view and manage the inventories of all the vCenter Servers in the group. vCenter 6.7 provides an Enhanced Linked Mode that allows for linking both VCSA and Windows vCenter Server deployments.

The PSC, vCenter Server services, and other supporting components can all be installed on a single Windows server, or each component can be installed on a separate server. Installing all of the components on a single server simplifies deployment to support a small environment. Installing each component on a separate server adds some complexity, but allows the resources for each service to be adjusted as necessary and provides flexibility for larger deployments.

Determining vCenter resource requirements

The minimum system requirements for the vCenter Server are dependent on the size of the environment that's managed by the vCenter Server. Sizing vCenter Server correctly will ensure proper operation. The size of the vCenter inventory, the number of hosts, and the number of virtual machines all have an impact on the amount of resources required. Running multiple vCenter Server components on a single server (like an embedded PSC, for example) also determines the amount of resources that will need to be allocated to the vCenter Server.

How to do it...

The following steps will help you to determine the vCenter system requirements:

1. Estimate the number of hosts and virtual machines that will be managed by the vCenter Server
2. Determine whether all of the vCenter Server components will be installed on a single server, or on separate servers
3. Size the vCenter Server to support the managed inventory

How it works...

vCenter Server 6.7 with embedded PSC resource requirements are shown in the following table and ordered by inventory size.

Inventory Size	Number of vCPUs	Memory
Tiny 10 hosts/100 virtual machines	2	10 GB
Small 100 hosts/1,000 virtual machines	4	16 GB
Medium 400 hosts/4,000 virtual machines	8	24 GB
Large 1,000 hosts/10,000 virtual machines	16	32 GB
X-Large 2,000 hosts/35,000 virtual machines	24	48 GB

The PSC can be installed on separate physical or virtual machines. The following table lists the minimum requirements for the PCS, if it is installed on separate physical or virtual machines:

Component	2 GHz CPU cores	Memory
PSC	2	2 GB

If the databases are installed on the same machine, additional CPU, memory, and disk resources will be necessary.

In vSphere 6.7, the VCSA sizing requirements mirror those of the vCenter on Windows Server, based on the size of the managed environment. When you are deploying the VCSA, the inventory size is selected (**Tiny**, **Small**, **Medium**, **Large**, or **X-Large**), and the VCSA appliance is configured with the required resources, as shown in the following screenshot:

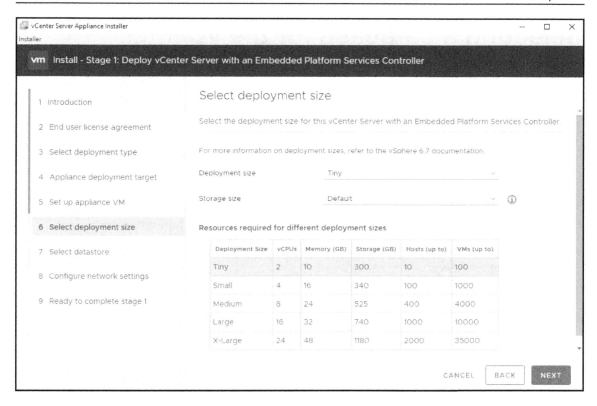

Choosing the VCSA deployment size

There's more...

VMware and third-party plugins and applications may require their own resources. For example, if VUM is installed on the same machine as other vCenter components, the CPU, memory, and disk capacity requirements will need to be adjusted to support the additional resources required.

Selecting a database for the vCenter deployment

The vCenter Server requires a supported database to be deployed to store virtual infrastructure configuration information, logging, and performance statistics. The VCSA and the vCenter Server on Windows both support an embedded or external database.

How to do it...

Perform the following steps to select a database for the vCenter deployment:

1. Estimate the number of hosts and virtual machines that will be managed by the vCenter Server
2. Choose a supported database platform that is suitable to support the vCenter inventory

How it works...

The database stores configuration and performance information. The three database deployment options are as follows:

- Use the embedded vPostgreSQL database on the VCSA or the bundled vPostgreSQL database if installing vCenter Server on Windows
- Install a full database server locally on the same server as the vCenter Server components
- Connect to a database hosted on a remote server

The embedded database included with the VCSA can support an inventory of up to 2,000 hosts and 35,000 virtual machines, which makes it a suitable option, even for very large deployments. The embedded vPostgreSQL on Windows, which can be deployed as a part of the vCenter Server Windows installation, is intended for smaller deployments of up to 20 hosts and 20 virtual machines. If a Windows vCenter Server is deployed using the embedded databases where the inventory is expecting growth beyond 20 hosts and 200 virtual machines, a different supported database option should be selected.

The Microsoft SQL Express Database is no longer supported in vCenter 6.x. When upgrading a vCenter 5.x server that was deployed using the embedded Microsoft SQL Express Database, the vCenter database will be migrated to the vPostgreSQL database as a part of the upgrade process.

Some reasons to use the embedded vPostgreSQL database when deploying a Windows vCenter Server are as follows:

- A small environment of fewer than 20 hosts and 200 virtual machines
- Easy installation and configuration
- Free! no need to license a separate database server software

 Databases are created as a part of the installation process when you are using the bundled vPostgreSQL and vCenter Server. If a full installation of a database server is used, these databases (and the ODBC connections required for them) must be manually created prior to the installation.

Installing a full Microsoft SQL or Oracle database locally (on the same Windows server as the vCenter components) is supported, but this increases the amount of resources that are necessary for the vCenter Server. Additional resources may be required, depending on the size of the vCenter inventory. Hosting the database locally (on the same server) is fully supported, and this can provide faster access, since the access to the database does not rely on network resources.

A full installation of Microsoft SQL or Oracle can also be performed on a separate physical or virtual machine. The vCenter components access the databases hosted on the remote database server. The creation of the databases and the configuration of the vCenter components is the same as with a full database installation on the same server as vCenter. Accessing the databases requires network resources; because of this, network congestion or a network outage can affect the accessibility to the databases.

Some reasons to choose a remotely installed database are as follows:

- Leverage an existing database server that's already available in the environment
- For a separation of roles; database administrators are responsible for administering the database servers, while virtual administrators are responsible for administering the virtual environment
- High availability can be provided to the databases by using Microsoft or Oracle clustering
- It reduces the amount of resources that need to be allocated to the vCenter Server

Determining database interoperability

VMware provides an online Interoperability Matrix to make it easy to determine which database versions are compatible and supported with which versions of VMware products.

How to do it...

To determine database interoperability with VMware products, perform the following steps:

1. Visit: `https://www.vmware.com/resources/compatibility/sim/interop_matrix.php`
2. Select the **Solution/Database Interoperability** tab
3. In the **Select a Solution** option, select **VMware vCenter Server** and a **Version** from the respective dropdown boxes
4. **Add Database** versions by using the **Database** dropdown box. You can add multiple database versions
5. The database's compatibility with the selected product will be displayed in the table, as shown in the following screenshot:

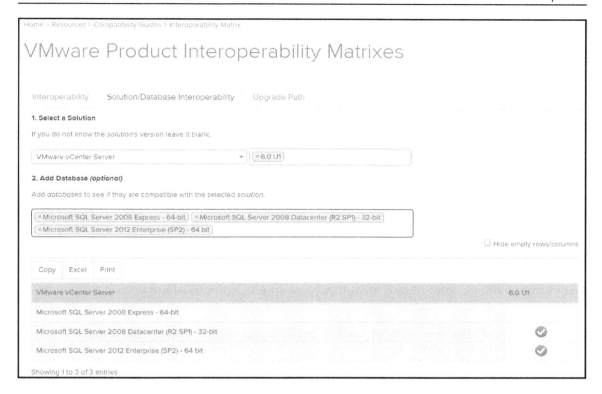

Example of using the VMware Product Interoperability Matrix

How it works...

Verifying database product interoperability ensures the supportability of the database and the version that has been selected for use with a specific VMware product. The VMware Product Interoperability matrices are regularly updated by VMware when new databases or VMware product versions are released.

Database and product interoperability should be checked for new installations, and this should be done prior to upgrading VMware products or applying service packs to database servers.

There's more...

The Interoperability Matrix can be used to determine database operability for all supported VMware products and solutions. It can also be used to determine supported upgrade paths and interoperability between different VMware solutions.

Choosing a vCenter deployment topology

The deployment topology for a vCenter 6.7 deployment is dependent on the size of the environment, the number of vCenters that will be deployed, the number of sites, and the availability required.

How to do it...

To determine the vCenter deployment topology for a vCenter 6.7 deployment, follow these steps:

1. Identify the use cases for each vCenter deployment topology. Factors to consider include the following:
   - The size of the environment
   - The number of vCenters
   - The number of sites

2. Select the vCenter deployment topology based on the environment requirements.

How it works...

vSphere 6 supports up to 10 vCenters linked together in Enhanced Linked Mode, and up to eight PSCs to support the environment. vCenters and PSCs can be deployed on the same site, or across multiple sites. In a small environment with a single vCenter Server, the PSC and vCenter Server can be combined on a single appliance.

The embedded deployment is the topology with the least complexity. The embedded deployment topology is suitable for a small, single-site, single-vCenter environment. In this topology, the PSC and vCenter Server are installed on the same virtual or physical machine. This is represented in the following diagram:

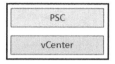

Representation of vCenter with embedded PSC

Multiple vCenter Servers can be deployed with a single external PSC. This deployment topology is used for a small single site with multiple vCenter Servers. These vCenter Servers can be VCSA or Windows, or a mix of both. This enables single-screen management of the environment with Enhanced Linked Mode. This topology is represented in the following diagram:

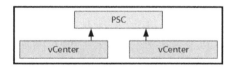

Logical view of multiple vCenters pointing to a single PSC

Multiple PSCs can be deployed to provide high availability to the PSC services. A single vCenter or multiple vCenters can access the PSCs within the same site through a load balancer. There can be up to four PSCs per site, behind a load balancer. The following diagram is a representation of a topology where multiple PSCs are deployed for high availability:

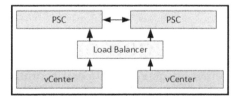

Logical view of a load-balanced PSC

In a multi-site topology, the PSC is deployed at each site. This provides replication of the PSC between sites, and it also enables Enhanced Linked Mode between the vCenters at both sites. The following diagram represents a multi-site deployment topology:

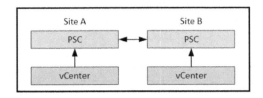

Logical representation of a multi-site PSC topology and Enhanced Linked Mode

Choose a deployment topology that supports the size and requirements of the environment. If Windows-based vCenters are used, the PSC should not be deployed embedded with a vCenter. VMware does not support replication between embedded PSCs for Windows vCenter Servers or using an embedded PSC to provide services to external vCenter Servers.

The latest supported and recommended topology is the VCSA with embedded PSC, as shown in the following diagram, which supports Enhanced Linked Mode for up to 15 VCSAs:

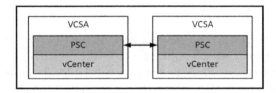

Latest recommended topology with VCSA and embedded PSCs

Designing for management availability

The availability of the management functions of an environment becomes more critical in environments like those that support virtual desktops or self-service provisioning. In these environments, if the vCenter Server is unavailable, so is the ability to provide the provisioning of services.

If the environment does not provide these types of services, the ability to manage the environment, especially during a failure or disaster, is also critical. How can you troubleshoot an issue with a virtual machine (or a group of virtual machines) if the primary tool that is used to manage the environment is unavailable?

How to do it...

To properly design for management availability, follow these steps:

1. Identify the management environment dependencies, as follows:
    - Infrastructure dependencies, including storage, networking, and host hardware
    - Service dependencies, including DNS, DHCP, and Active Directory
    - VMware product dependencies, including the PSC, the vCenter Server, and other supporting components

2. Identify the potential single points of failure in the management environment.
3. Create a management design that ensures the high availability of the management components.

How it works...

When designing the management network, single points of failure should be minimized. Redundant network connections and multiple network interfaces connected to separate physical switches should be configured to provide connectivity.

The storage that hosts the management components should be configured to support the capacity and performance of the management components. The storage should also be configured to be highly available so that a disk or path failure does not interrupt management operations.

In environments where the vCenter Server provides provisioning, such as a virtual desktop or self-service cloud environments, vCenter uptime is critical.

If the vCenter Server is running on a virtual machine, it can be protected with HA. If the host that vCenter is running on or the operating system crashes, the vCenter Server is restarted on a surviving host. There will be some downtime associated with the failure, but when they are designed correctly, the vCenter Server services will be quickly restored.

Sufficient resources should be dedicated to the vCenter Server and its components. We discussed the correct sizing of the vCenter Server earlier in this chapter. Sizing vCenter correctly and reserving resources ensures not only the performance, but also the availability. If a virtual machine is running on the same host as the vCenter Server or one of its components and it consumes too many of the host resources, it may impact the performance and availability of the vCenter Server services. Applying resource reservations to the vCenter Server will prevent resource contention.

Another means of preventing resource contention is to design a separate cluster to host the management components. Management cluster design will be discussed in the *Designing a separate management cluster* recipe.

Designing a separate management cluster

The management components of a virtual environment can be resource intensive. If you are running vCenter and its dependencies as virtual machines in the same cluster as the cluster managed by the vCenter server, the resources required by the management infrastructure must be factored into the capacity calculations of the logical design. Creating a separate management cluster separates the resources required by the vCenter and other management components from the resources required by the applications hosted in the virtual infrastructure.

While a separate management cluster can be beneficial for capacity planning, it can increases the costs associated with building a vSphere environment. A separate management cluster is not required, but it may be a good idea if you need to separate management components from other workloads.

How to do it...

Refer the following steps to design a management cluster:

1. Identify management cluster best practices as follows:
    1. Having the CPU and memory resources to support management applications
    2. Having multiple network interfaces and multiple physical network switches to minimize the single points of failure in the management network
    3. Having multiple paths to the storage to minimize the single points of failure in the storage network
    4. Having storage that's designed to support both the capacity and the performance required for management applications
2. Correctly size the management cluster and identify the services that will be hosted in the cluster. The following questions also need to be answered to size the management cluster.
    1. What is the deployment topology of the vCenter Server environment?
    2. How many PSCs and vCenter Servers will be deployed to support the environment?
    3. Will the cluster also provide the resources needed for the vCenter databases?
    4. What about other management tools, such as vCenter Operations Manager, vCenter Log Insight, or other third-party management tools?

How it works...

The design of a management cluster follows the same process as designing a cluster hosting the production applications. Requirements need to be identified, and a logical design process for storage, networking, and computing resources must be followed. The functional requirements for the management network will likely include high availability, minimizing single points of failure, and quickly recovering failed components.

There's more...

Affinity rules can be used to keep virtual machines together. For example, having the virtual machine running the vCenter Server and the virtual machine running the vCenter Server database on the same host reduces the load on the physical network, since all communication between the two servers never leaves the internal host network.

Anti-affinity rules can also be used to separate virtual machines across hosts or groups of hosts. In an environment where multiple PSCs are deployed to provide high availability, separating the PSCs by using anti-affinity rules will ensure that a single host failure does not impact the services provided by the PSCs.

If you are hosting vCenter in the same cluster as other virtual machine workloads, affinity and anti-affinity rules can be used to keep the vCenter Server running on specific hosts, creating a pseudo-management cluster, so that it can easily be located in the event of the vCenter Server becoming unavailable. If such rules are used for vCenter, consider using should rules and not must rules to allow HA to violate the rules, if required, during an HA event to ensure vCenter gets restarted.

Configuring vCenter mail, SNMP, and alarms

Alarms can be used to notify an administrator of issues (or potential issues) in a vSphere environment. This notification allows an administrator to take corrective actions. Alarms can be configured to send email notifications and/or SMNP traps when conditions are triggered. Alarm definitions contain a trigger and an action. Triggers include issues like hardware failures, or states like increased CPU or memory utilization.

Properly designing alarm notifications can ensure successful ongoing operations in a vSphere environment.

How to do it...

The following steps will configure the **Mail** and **SNMP** settings for a vCenter Server, and will configure a defined alarm to send an email or SNMP notification:

1. Using the vSphere Web Client, access **Manage** | **Settings** | **General** for the vCenter Server, as shown in the following screenshot:

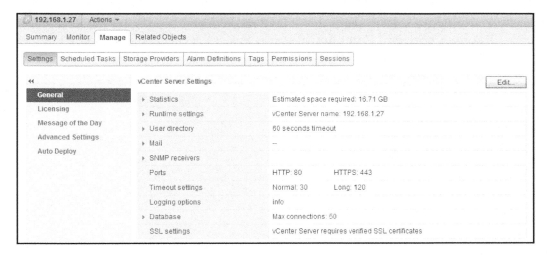

View General Settings in vCenter using the vSphere Web Client

2. Select **Edit** and **Mail**. Provide the **Mail server** FQDN or IP address and the **Mail sender** address. The vCenter **Mail** configuration is shown in the following screenshot:

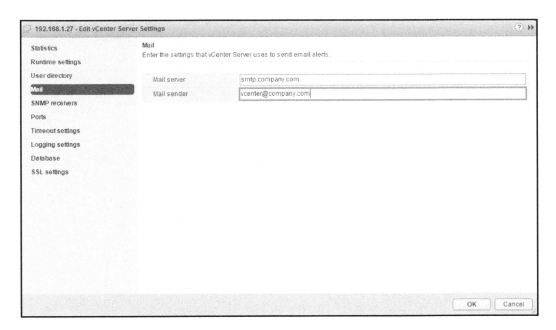

Configure mail in vCenter using the vSphere Web Client

3. To configure SNMP, select the **SNMP receivers** and configure the **Receiver URL**, **Receiver port**, and **Community string**. Select the checkbox to **Enable** the receiver, as shown in the following screenshot:

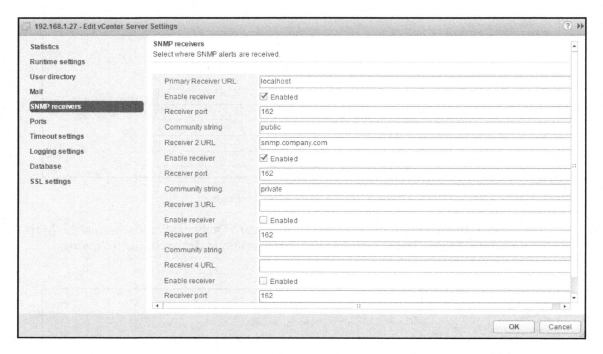

Configure SNMP in vCenter using the vSphere Web Client

4. To configure an alarm, select **Manage** | **Alarm Definitions**. Select the alarm and click on the **Edit** button:

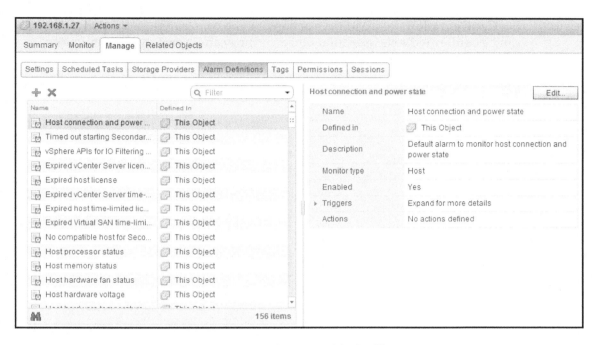

Configure alarms in vCenter using the vSphere Web Client

5. The **Send a notification email** and **Send a notification trap** actions can be configured in the alarm **Actions** section. When configuring the **Send a notification email** action, the email address to send the alert to is configured in the **Configuration** field. Multiple actions can be configured for an alarm. **Actions** can be configured to be executed **Once**, or they can **Repeat** over a configured period of time, as shown in the following screenshot:

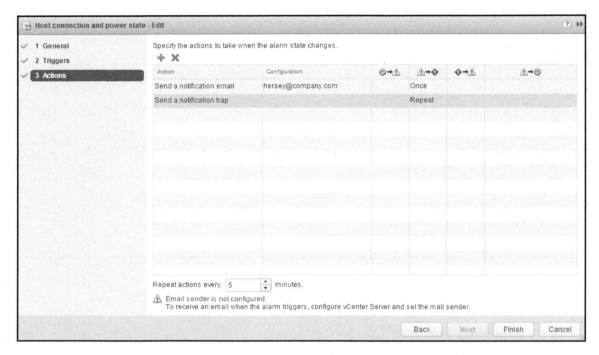

Configure alarm actions in vCenter using the vSphere Web Client

How it works...

For the **Send notification email** alarm action to work, the vCenter **Mail** settings must be configured with both the **Mail server** and the **Mail sender** address. The **Mail sender** address is the mail from address included on the vCenter alarm notification. The **Mail server** is the server that the SMTP mail will be relayed through. The **Mail server** that's specified must be configured to accept and relay mail from the vCenter Server.

Configured SNMP receivers will receive notifications from alarms that have been configured with the **Send a notification trap** action. The SNMP configuration includes the receiver URL, the receiver port, and the receiver community string. Multiple SNMP receivers can be configured and enabled.

There is an extensive list of preconfigured **Alarm Definitions**. Custom alarm definitions can also be created. By default, the **Send a notification email** action is not configured for any of the preconfigured definitions. When an alarm is triggered and the **Send a notification email** action is configured, an email will be sent to the email address (or addresses) in the configuration for the action.

Alarms actions can be configured to send a single notification, or to send a repeated notification. Repeated notifications can be configured to repeat over different intervals while the alarm state is triggered.

Using Enhanced Linked Mode

Enhanced Linked Mode allows for multiple vCenter Servers to be connected together to provide a single point of management. Enhanced Linked Mode enables the ability to view, search, and manage multiple vCenter Servers, and provides the replication of roles, permissions, licenses, and policies between vCenter Servers. This simplifies the management of large environments, with multiple vCenter Servers deployed in the same site or across multiple sites. vCenter 6.x supports linking vCenter Servers that have been deployed as VCSAs and as Windows Servers with external PSCs. Recall from earlier in this chapter that Enhanced Linked Mode is only supported between VCSAs when you are using embedded PSCs.

How to do it...

To enable Enhanced Linked Mode, follow these steps:

1. Ensure that the Enhanced Linked Mode requirements are met:
    *   Ensure that all PSCs are in the same vSphere single sign-on domain
2. Deploy PSCs and vCenter Servers in a supported deployment topology

How it works...

Enhanced Linked Mode enables a single point of management across all vCenter Servers in the same vSphere single sign-on domain. This allows an administrator to easily manage the different environments (for example, a virtual server environment and a virtual desktop environment) across multiple sites:

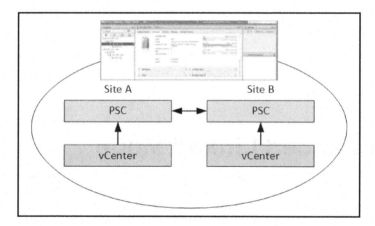

Enhanced Linked Mode in the vSphere Web Client

Once enabled, the inventories of all vCenters in the same single sign-on domain will be linked in Enhanced Linked Mode. The management of these vCenters will then be accessible from a single Web Client interface, as follows:

Hosts and Clusters view of Enhanced Linked Mode in the vSphere Web Client

Using the VMware Product Interoperability Matrix

The VMware Product Interoperability Matrix allows you to ensure compatibility between VMware products. It is important to check for compatibility before deploying or upgrading the components of a vSphere environment to ensure support and interoperability between product versions.

How to do it...

Perform the following steps to validate the interoperability of VMware products in a vSphere deployment:

1. Visit `https://www.vmware.com/resources/compatibility/sim/interop_matrix.php`
2. Select the **Interoperability** tab
3. Under the **Select a Solution** option, select the VMware product and version from the respective dropdown boxes

4. Select Add **Platform/Solution** by using the dropdown box. You can add multiple solutions and versions

5. The interoperability with the selected products and solutions will be displayed in the table, as shown in the following screenshot:

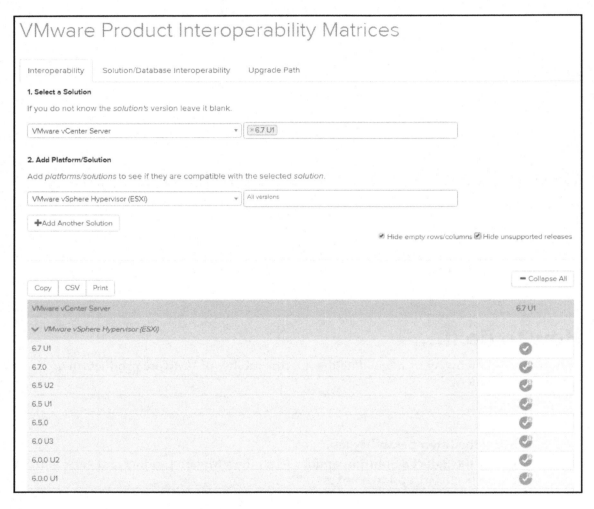

Example use of the VMware Product Interoperability Matrix

How it works...

Verifying product interoperability ensures supportability and interoperability between different VMware products and versions. The VMware Product Interoperability matrices are regularly updated by VMware when new products and versions are released.

Product interoperability should be checked for new installations, and this should be done prior to upgrading VMware products.

There's more...

In many environments, third-party products for monitoring, automation, and protection are used. In a new vSphere design, there will likely be requirements or constraints for integration with these third-party components. It is important to verify interoperability with these products before deploying or upgrading a vSphere environment. The VMware Product Interoperability matrices only include VMware products. Third-party product interoperability will need to be verified with the product vendors.

Backing up the vCenter Server components

vCenter and its components have become a critical piece of the virtual infrastructure. The vCenter Server is no longer just a management interface. Provisioning, protection, and the overall availability of the environment rely on vCenter Server availabilty.

To recover the vCenter Server components in the event of an outage that results in data loss or data corruption, it is necessary to make backups of the databases and the vCenter Server configurations. The PSC and vCenter Server each have specific configuration information that should be backed up.

The frequency of backups depends on the **Recovery Point Objective (RPO)** that has been defined for the management environment. The time to recover the vCenter Server, or the **Recovery Time Objective (RTO)**, is also a critical piece of designing a vCenter backup strategy. The RPO defines the maximum period of data loss that can be tolerated as a result of an outage. If the RPO has been determined to be four hours, this means that backups should occur at least every four hours. The RTO determines how quickly the vCenter must be available after an outage.

How to do it...

Follow this process to design a backup and recovery strategy for the vCenter Server environment:

1. Determine the RPO and RTO requirements for the vCenter Server and the supporting components
2. Develop a backup and recovery strategy that ensures the RPO and RTO requirements are met

How it works...

VMware recommends creating full virtual machine backups of the PSC and vCenter Server when these components are running in virtual machines. There are many third-party backup software products that can also be used to make full virtual machine backups. This allows the virtual machines to be restored quickly in the event of a failure.

If the PSC or vCenter Server is running as a physical machine, a third-party backup application can be used to take a full bare-metal backup. It is important to realize that this type of backup will take longer to restore, impacting the RTO.

File-based backups are also supported for the VCSA. File-based backups are configured through the **Virtual Appliance Management Interface (VAMI)** and sent to remote servers via FTP, FTPS, HTTP, or SCP.

Configuration and performance data is stored in the vCenter Server database. How backups are done depends on the database software that is used to host the database. For example, if the database is a Microsoft SQL database, a backup can be performed on demand in the SQL Management Studio, or as a scheduled SQL job. Third-party backup tools can also be used to back up the vCenter databases.

If the vCenter is using the embedded vPostgreSQL database on either a Windows vCenter Server or the VCSA, it can be backed up using a script from the VMware KB Article 2091961, located at `http://kb.vmware.com/kb/2091961`. There are separate scripts to support a Windows or VCSA vCenter deployment.

The vCenter Server database should be backed up regularly, based on the RPO that has been defined for the management components.

Planning vCenter HA to increase vCenter availability

VCHA is a feature that uses a three-node cluster to protect the vCenter Server from hardware, operating system, or application failures. The three nodes are referred to as active, passive, and witness. VCHA only supports VCSA deployments, not vCenter on Windows, and both embedded and external PSCs are supported. It's important to note that if used with external PSCs, VCHA is not protecting the PSCs—only the vCenter Server itself. Load balanced PSCs would be needed to provide high availability to external PSCs. Keep in mind that it likely doesn't make sense to use vCenter HA if you're not also using load-balanced PSCs, since the idea is to create a highly available management plane.

VCHA is useful when you want to increase vCenter's uptime and you don't necessarily want to only rely on vSphere HA to protect against a host failure. VCHA also protects against service failures. When using an embedded PSC, VCHA will not only monitor vCenter services for failures, but for PSC service failures as well. If a service fails, the passive node becomes the active node.

There are a few simple system requirements for VCHA. Only one vCenter Server license is required, and the vCenter deployment type must not be tiny due to the additional resources that are required.

There are two options to configure VCHA: **Automatic** and **Manual**. If you choose an **Automatic** configuration, the configuration wizard will clone the existing vCenter Server and configure the cluster networking. If you choose the **Manual** method, you must clone the vCenter Server and configure the cluster networking yourself. As of vCenter 6.7 Update 1, however, only the **Automatic** method is available.

After several years of not having a high availability option for vCenter (after VMware deprecated the vCenter Heartbeat product), VCHA provides an internally developed option for those environments that require maximum uptime for their vCenter Server.

How to do it...

To plan and implement vCenter HA, use the following process:

1. Ensure that the VCHA system requirements are met
2. Determine the deployment topology for vCenter and the PSC
3. Choose the **Automatic** or **Manual** configuration method

How it works...

VCHA relies on a heartbeat network and quorum between the three nodes to avoid a split-brain scenario. The active node is the only node with a frontend or production IP address. The passive and witness nodes only have active IP addresses on the heartbeat network. This architecture is shown in the following diagram, with the embedded PSC deployment topology:

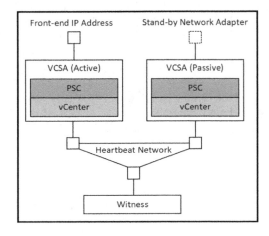

vCenter HA networking overview

There are several failure scenarios that will result in a failover from the active node to the passive node:

- vCenter service failure (or PSC service failure, if an embedded PSC is used)
- VCSA operating system failure
- Entire VM crashes
- Underlying ESXi host crashes due to hardware failure or hypervisor crashes
- Active node isolation on the heartbeat network

There are also several failure scenarios that won't cause a vCenter HA failover from the active node to the passive node:

- Passive node VM failure
- Witness node VM failure
- Frontend network interface failure on the active node

- External PSC failure
- vSphere Client service failure:
    - Services that rely on APIs stay available during this type of failure

Upgrading vCenter Server

Today, most environments will already contain at least some virtualization. A vSphere design will likely involve upgrading an existing environment to enable new features to meet new requirements for availability, security, performance, and manageability.

The management environment for vSphere has become more complex. The vCenter Server and its components have become a critical part of the environment. In the virtualized data center, the vCenter Server is no longer just a management interface; it also provides provision, availability, security, and other services. Other vSphere and third-party components require vCenter Server to operate correctly. Because of this, upgrading a vCenter Server must be planned correctly.

How to do it...

Follow this high-level process to upgrade a vCenter Server:

1. Identify the products and services that depend on vCenter Server, and those that vCenter Server depends on.
2. Verify product interoperability for all of the components and the upgraded vCenter version by using the VMware Product Interoperability matrices. Remember to also validate the compatibility with the third-party products integrated with vCenter.
3. Verify database support for the upgrade version by using the VMware Product Interoperability matrices.
4. Determine the proper upgrade path for upgrading VMware products dependent on vCenter by using the VMware Product Interoperability matrices.
5. Determine the upgrade order to ensure the interoperability of all components.
6. Upgrade vCenter and its supporting components.

How it works...

It is important to validate the support and compatibility of all vCenter Server dependencies before upgrading the vCenter Server. This is the most important process. Secondly, determining the correct upgrade order will ensure that compatibility and interoperability are maintained throughout the upgrade process.

Once the dependencies and interoperability are validated, the upgrade order for components has been determined, and the supporting components have been upgraded to ensure interoperability, the process of upgrading the vCenter Server itself will be a simple process. The Windows installer for vCenter Server on Windows and the VCSA installer both include upgrade installers to upgrade previous versions of vCenter. The following screenshot shows the VCSA installer with the **Upgrade** option:

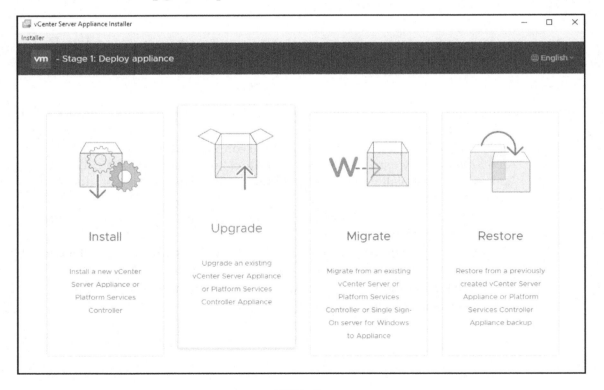

VCSA Installer

To upgrade a Windows vCenter Server, simply run the installer from the installation media. The installer will detect the previous version of vCenter Server and perform an in-place upgrade. This means the existing application will be updated on the existing server. This is different than the Blue-Green upgrade model used for the VCSA.

When you are upgrading an existing vCenter Server environment, consider the following:

- Upgrading a Windows vCenter Server that was deployed using the **Simple Install** will upgrade the vCenter Server with an embedded PSC
- Upgrading a VCSA deployed with embedded SSO will upgrade the VCSA with the embedded PSC
- If Microsoft SQL Express was used for the vCenter deployment, the vCenter database will be migrated to the embedded vPostgreSQL database
- A vCenter Server cannot be downgraded after the upgrade. Back up the vCenter Server databases and other supporting components, in the event that you need to revert back to the previous version after the upgrade

Designing a vSphere Update Manager Deployment

VMware regularly releases patches and updates to provide bug fixes so that it can address security vulnerabilities or add new features. Regularly patching an environment is important to the security and stability of the environment.

VMware **vSphere Update Manager** (**VUM**) is an optional vCenter component when it is installed on Windows, and it provides the patching and upgrading of ESXi hosts, VMware Tools, and VMware Guest Hardware. VUM ensures that compliance is maintained through patch and upgrade baselines. VUM also allows for the remediation of hosts or virtual machines that are not in compliance with the configured baselines.

VUM must be deployed on a Windows server, and it requires a supported database, either embedded or external. The VUM architecture is shown in the following diagram:

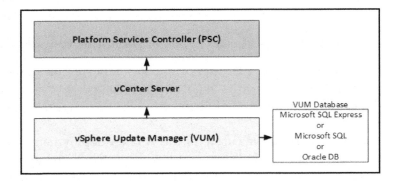

vSphere Update Manager architecture

There is a one-to-one relationship between VUM and vCenter Servers. VUM 6.x is fully integrated into the vSphere Web Client.

VUM is always installed in an embedded fashion with the VCSA.

How to do it...

To deploy VUM in a vSphere environment, perform the following steps:

1. Verify product and database interoperability by using the VMware Product Interoperability matrices.
2. Determine the location and type of database to host the VUM database.
3. Allocate the required compute and storage resources to support the VUM server.
4. Run the vSphere Update Manager Server installation on the Windows server selected for VUM.
5. Once it's deployed, use the vSphere Web Client to create baselines and attach hosts and virtual machines to these baselines. The following screenshot provides an example of critical and non-critical host patch baselines associated with a group of hosts:

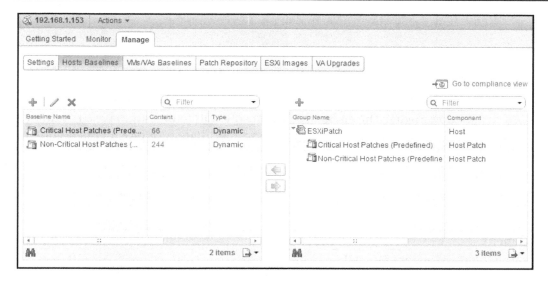

Critical and non-critical host patch baselines

6. Scan for updates and verify compliance with the attached baselines. The following screenshot displays a host in compliance with the attached critical and non-critical patch baselines:

Compliance example in VUM

7. Remediate the hosts or VMs that are not in compliance.

How it works...

VUM supports an embedded or external database. Microsoft SQL Express is included with the VUM installation media. The embedded Microsoft SQL Express database is suitable for small deployments of five hosts and 50 virtual machines. Larger deployments require a Microsoft SQL or Oracle DB, which can be installed on the same server or an external one.

VUM cannot be deployed on the same server as the VCSA. VUM can be installed on the same server as a Windows vCenter Server, as long as sufficient resources are allocated. The following table lists the minimum requirements for VUM:

Component	vCPUs	Memory
VMware Update Manager (VUM)	2	2 GB

The disk space required to support VUM will depend on the size of the environment. VMware provides a VUM Sizing Estimator for vSphere 6.7, which can be downloaded from `https://docs.vmware.com/en/VMware-vSphere/6.7/vsphere-update-manager-documentation-671.zip`

Patch and upgrade baselines contain patches (or groups of patches). These baselines can be fixed or dynamic. Critical and non-critical patch baselines are included by default. These are dynamic baselines that are regularly updated. Baselines can be attached to a virtual machine, a group of virtual machines, a host, a group of hosts, a cluster, or a data center. Hosts, clusters, and data centers can be scanned against the attached patch baseline, and then remediated.

There's more...

The default preconfigured dynamic patch baselines poll an external, internet-accessible repository for updates and to download the updates that are required for remediation. For vSphere environments without access to the internet, the **Update Manager Download Service (UMDS)** can be used to download the patches and updates and then export the updates and patch information to a repository that's accessible by the isolated network.

5
vSphere Storage Design

Storage is an essential component of vSphere design and provides the foundation for the vSphere environment. A solid storage design that addresses capacity, performance, availability, and recoverability is the key to a successful vSphere design. The following diagram displays how a storage design is integrated into the design process:

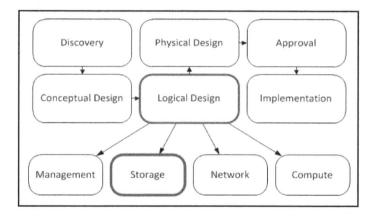

Storage design phase of in the vSphere design workflow

Several storage options and protocols are supported in the vSphere environment. The architecture that's chosen for a vSphere deployment depends on the capabilities and features needed to meet the design requirements.

This chapter will cover calculating the storage capacity and performance requirements, sizing datastores, and selecting a storage protocol. The calculations for the recipes in this chapter will be based on the following requirements that were identified in `Chapter 3`, *The Design Factors*:

- There are 100 application servers.
- Each application server is configured with 100 GB of disk space. The peak disk capacity usage of a single application server is approximately 65 percent of the total or 65 GB. The average disk performance of a single application server is 65 IOPS with an IO profile of 90 percent read and 10 percent write.
- Provide capacity to support growth for 25 additional application servers over the next 5 years.

Several new storage features are available with the release of vSphere 6.7. These new storage features include improvements to **Virtual SAN (VSAN)** and **Virtual Volumes (VVOL)**, and support for **Persistent Memory (PMEM)** and **Remote Direct Memory Access (RDMA) over Converged Ethernet (RoCE)**. This chapter will also provide an overview of these new storage options so that they can be incorporated into a vSphere 6 design.

In this chapter, we will cover the following recipes:

- Identifying RAID levels
- Calculating storage capacity requirements
- Determining storage performance requirements
- Calculating storage throughput
- Storage connectivity options
- Storage path selection plugins
- Sizing datastores
- Designing VSAN for virtual machine storage
- Designing **Virtual Volumes (VVOL)** for virtual machine storage
- Incorporating storage policies into a design
- NFS v4.1 capabilities and limits
- Using persistent memory to maximize VM performance

Identifying RAID levels

A **Redundant Array of Independent Disks (RAID)** combines multiple physical disks into a single unit of storage. The advantages in speed, reliability, and capacity can be realized, depending on which RAID level is selected. RAID provides the first level of protection against data loss due to a disk failure.

How to do it...

To select the proper RAID level to support the virtual workloads, you need to perform the following steps:

1. Identify the different RAID levels and capabilities
2. Select an appropriate RAID level to support a virtualized workload based on capacity and performance requirements

How it works...

RAID0 stripes disks together to appear as a single disk with a capacity equal to the sum of all the disks in the set. RAID0 provides excellent performance and capacity efficiency, but offers no data protection. If a disk fails in a RAID0 set, the data is lost and must be recovered from a backup or some other source. Since this level offers no redundancy, it is not a good choice for production or mission-critical storage.

The following diagram illustrates the disks in a RAID0 configuration:

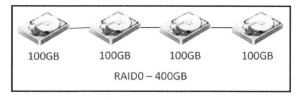

RAID 0

RAID1 duplicates or mirrors data from one disk to another. A RAID1 set consists of two disks and data is written on both the disks, which can then be read from either disk. If one of the disks fails, the mirror can be rebuilt by replacing the disk. The following diagram illustrates disks in a RAID1 configuration:

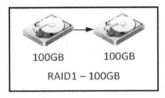

RAID 1

RAID1+0, RAID1/0, or RAID10 is a stripe of multiple mirrors. RAID10 provides excellent redundancy and performance, making this the best option for mission-critical applications. RAID10 is well-suited for applications with small, random, write-intensive IOs, such as high transaction applications, large messaging applications, or large transactional database applications. A RAID10 set can recover from multiple drive failures, as long as two drives in the same mirror set do not fail.

Both RAID1 and RAID10 have a capacity efficiency of 50 percent, since half of the disks in a RAID1 or RAID10 set are used to store the mirrored data. The following diagram illustrates disks in a RAID10 configuration:

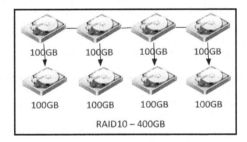

RAID 10

In RAID5, data is striped across several drives and parity is written equally across all the drives in the set. This parity allows for recovery from a failure of a single drive in the set. This level offers a balance of performance and capacity and is suitable for storing transactional databases, web servers, application servers, file servers, and mail servers. The following diagram illustrates disks in a RAID5 configuration:

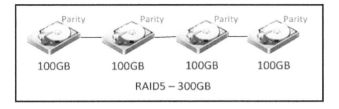

Parity distribution in RAID 5

The capacity efficiency of a RAID5 set is calculated using the formula *[(n - 1) / n] * 100*, where *n* is equal to the number of disks in the set. For example, a RAID5 set containing four 100 GB disks would provide 75 percent of the total capacity, or 300 GB:

$$[(4-1)/4]*100 = 75\%$$

$$(100GB * 4) * .75 = 300GB$$

RAID6 is similar to RAID5, except that the two parity blocks are written and distributed equally across all the drives in the set. The second parity increases the write penalty but protects against two drive failures in the set. File archiving and file servers are common workloads that are hosted on RAID6.

The capacity efficiency of a RAID6 set is calculated using the formula *[(n - 2) / n] * 100*, where *n* is equal to the number of disks in the set. A RAID6 set containing six 100 GB disks would provide approximately 67 percent of the total capacity, or 400 GB:

$$[(6 - 2) / 6] * 100 = {\sim}67\%$$

$$(100GB * 6) * .67 = {\sim}400GB$$

There's more...

To increase the redundancy of a RAID set, hot spares should be configured in the array. Hot spares are used to automatically replace a failed drive in a RAID set temporarily, until the failed drive can be replaced. A single hot spare can be configured to provide protection for multiple RAID sets.

Calculating storage capacity requirements

Capacity is typically measured in **gigabytes** (**GB**) or **terabytes** (**TB**). Capacity should include the total space needed to support the current requirements, the space needed to support growth, the space needed for virtual machine swapfiles, and the additional slack space for snapshots, logs, and other virtual machine data.

How to do it...

To calculate the storage capacity requirements, you need to perform the following steps:

1. Determine the capacity required to support the current workloads
2. Determine the capacity required to support future growth

How it works...

Capacity is calculated to support the current and future growth based on the design requirements, as follows:

Current capacity = 100 virtual machines x 100 GB = 10 TB

Growth capacity = 25 virtual machines x 100 GB = 2.5 TB

20% slack space = 12.5 TB x .20 = 2.5 TB

Capacity = 12.5 TB + 2.5 TB = 15 TB

Each virtual machine will have a swapfile or .vswp file that is created when the virtual machine is powered on. The size of the .vswp file for each virtual machine is equal to the size of the allocated memory, minus the memory reservation:

vSwap capacity = (100 virtual machines + 25 future virtual machines) x 8 GB of memory = 1 TB

The total capacity needed to support these requirements is 16 TB.

There's more...

The application servers are configured with 100 GB of disk space, but the maximum space that is actually consumed by a server is only 65 GB. Resizing the virtual machine disk or using thin provisioning can reduce the required amount of storage capacity significantly.

Since only the actual used space is consumed, thin provisioning virtual machine disks allows for the disk capacity to be over- allocated, which means that more capacity can be allocated to the virtual machine disks than what is actually available on the datastore. This increases the amount of management oversight required to monitor the capacity. vCenter datastore alarms can be configured to monitor over-allocation and datastore usage to assist in capacity management.

Determining storage performance requirements

Storage performance is an important factor of storage design. The storage must be designed to meet not only the capacity requirements but also the performance requirements for writes and reads to disk. Disk performance is measured in **Input/Output per Second (IOPS)**. One disk read request or one disk write request is equal to one IO. The storage performance must support the current requirements and growth.

How to do it...

The IOPS required to support an application is calculated based on the percentage of read IO, the percentage of write IO, and the write penalty of the RAID level the workload will be hosted on.

To calculate the IOPS requirements, perform the following steps:

1. Determine the number of IOPS a workload requires
2. Identify the percentage of read IO to write IO for the workload
3. Determine the write penalty of the RAID level that will host the workload
4. Calculate the IOPS the storage must be capable of providing to support the workload

How it works...

To get the total amount of required IOPS, multiply the number of workloads by the number of functional application IOPS:

*Total IOPS = (100 current workloads + 25 future workloads) * 65 IOPS = 8125 IOPS*

To calculate the functional IOPS required for a specific workload, use the following formula:

*Functional workload IOPS = (workload IOPS * %reads) + ((workload IOPS * %writes) * write penalty)*

The write penalty is based on the number of IO operations a specific RAID configuration requires for a single write request. Writing data to multiple disks in mirror or parity calculations in a RAID5 or RAID6 configuration adds IO operations to the write request. The write request is not completed until the data and parity are written to the disks.

The following table illustrates the write penalty based on the RAID levels:

RAID	Write penalty
0	1
1	2
5	4
6	6
10	2

Based on the requirements of 65 IOPS per workload with 90 percent reads and 10 percent writes on the storage configured in RAID5, the actual workload IOPS would be 85 IOPS:

*Functional application IOPS = (65 * .90) + ((65* .10) * 4) = ~85 IOPS*

Each disk in a storage array is able to provide a number of IOPS. The number of IOPS a single disk can deliver is calculated from the average latency and the average seek time of the disk. The formula to calculate disk performance is as follows:

IOPS = 1 / (average latency in milliseconds + average seek time in milliseconds)

The following table lists some approximate IOPS provided, based on the spindle speed and the drive type:

Drive speed	~ IOPS
SSD	> 2500
15k SAS/FC	175
10k SAS/FC	125
7,200 NL-SAS/SATA	75
5,400 SATA	50

Based on the number of IOPS required, there will be a need of *47 15k SAS drives* to support the workload:

8125 IOPS / 175 IOPS per drive = 46.4 or 47 15k SAS drives

The same workload on drives configured in RAID10 sets would require *52 15k SAS drives* to provide the required IOPS:

Functional workload IOPS = (65 * .90) + ((65* .10) * 2) = 72 IOPS

Total IOPS = (100 current workloads + 25 future workloads) * 72 IOPS = 9,000 IOPS

9,000 IOPS / 175 IOPS per Drive = 51.4 or 52 15k SAS drives

There's more...

Many arrays provide a caching mechanism using memory or SSD disks to increase the number of IOPS the array can deliver. This allows a few slow drives to deliver a higher number of IOPS. This caching can greatly reduce the number of drives needed to deliver the same number of IOPS by writing to a faster cache instead of writing directly to disks. Fast cache of EMC and flash cache of NetApp are examples of vendor-specific SSD caching technologies that can be used to increase storage IO performance.

Calculating storage throughput

The data transfer rate or throughput is the rate at which data can be read from or written to the storage device and is typically measured in MB/s. Storage adapters, connectivity, and array controllers will need to support the storage throughput requirements.

How to do it...

Throughput should be calculated to ensure that the storage controllers and disk can support the required data transfer rates. Throughput is also used to correctly size the storage connectivity bandwidth.

To calculate storage throughput requirements, perform the following steps:

1. Determine the IO size of the workload
2. Determine the number of IOPS required to support the workload
3. Calculate the throughput required

How it works...

Throughput is calculated by multiplying the IO size of the workload by the number of IOPS. Transactional databases and application servers typically have an IO size between 4 k and 64 k, whereas file archiving applications, backup applications, and media streaming applications typically have larger IO sizes from 64 k to 1,024 k.

To calculate the throughput, the following formula is used:

$$Throughput = functional\ workload\ IOPS * IO\ Size$$

Using the functional workload IOPS from the previous recipe and an IO size of 8 k, the throughput required can be calculated as follows:

$$Throughput = 9,000 * 8k = 72\ MB/s$$

Network interface card bandwidth is usually expressed in Mbps. To convert MB/s to Mbps, simply multiply by *8*:

$$Bandwidth\ Mbps = 72\ MB/s * 8 = 576\ Mbps$$

The array would need to support a throughput of at least 72 MB/s, and the connectivity bandwidth would need to be sufficient enough to support at least 576 Mbps.

Storage connectivity options

vSphere supports multiple storage protocols and connectivity options. Storage can be directly connected to a host, or storage can be centralized and shared with multiple hosts. Shared storage is required when implementing many vSphere features, such as VMware **High Availability (HA)**, VMware **Fault Tolerance (FT)**, and VMware **Distributed Resource Scheduling (DRS)**.

How to do it...

To determine the storage connectivity requirements, perform the following steps:

1. Identify the supported storage protocols and connectivity options.
2. Select the storage protocol and connectivity that supports the design requirements.

How it works...

Performance, availability, and costs are all factors that should be considered when choosing a storage connectivity option. The following table provides a quick overview of the different storage connectivity options and how they compare with each other in terms of performance, availability, and costs:

Protocol	Performance	Availability	Costs
Local storage	Good	Fair	Low
Fibre channel	Excellent	Excellent	High
iSCSI	Good	Excellent	Medium
NFS	Good	Good	Low
FCoE	Excellent	Excellent	High

Direct attached or local storage is storage directly attached to a host. Since this storage is not shared, many VMware features will not be available for virtual machines hosted on the local storage.

Best practices when using direct attached or local storage are as follows:

- Configure RAID to provide protection against a hard disk failure
- Use a hardware RAID controller that is on the VMware HCL

Fibre Channel (FC) is a block-level, low latency, high-performance storage network protocol that is well-suited for workloads with high I/O requirements. The FC protocol encapsulates the SCSI commands into the FC frames. A Fibre Channel **Host Bus Adapter (HBA)** is required to connect the host to the storage network or fabric. FC HBAs can provide a throughput of 2, 4, 8, or 16 Gbps, depending on the capabilities of the HBA and the FC network. FC uses zoning and LUN masking to configure which hosts can connect to which targets on the SAN.

The cost of deploying FC-connected storage can be significantly higher than other options, especially if an existing FC infrastructure does not already exist.

The best practices when using FC are as follows:

- Use multiple HBAs in the host to provide multiple paths from load balancing and redundancy.
- Ensure all HBAs and switches are configured for the same speed. Mixing the speed of HBAs and switches can produce contention at the FC switch and SAN.
- Use single-initiator single-target zoning. A single HBA, the initiator, is zoned to a single array target, the target. A separate zone is created for each host HBA.
- Mask LUNs are presented to ESXi hosts from other devices.
- Ensure firmware levels on FC switches and HBAs are up-to-date and compatible.

iSCSI provides block-level storage access by encapsulating SCSI commands in TCP/IP. iSCSI storage can be accessed with the iSCSI software initiator, which is included with ESXi through a standard network adapter, or using a dependent or independent iSCSI HBA:

- A dependent iSCSI adapter depends on VMware networking and iSCSI configuration for connectivity and management.
- An independent iSCSI HBA provides its own networking and configuration for connectivity and management. Configuration is done directly on the HBA through its own configuration interface.

Throughput is based on the network bandwidth, the speed of the network interface card (1 Gbps or 10 GbE), and the CPU resources required to encapsulate the SCSI commands into TCP/IP packets.

The cost of implementing iSCSI is typically significantly lesser than implementing FC. Standard network adapters and network switches can be used to provide iSCSI connectivity. Using dedicated iSCSI HBAs not only increases performance, but also increases cost. The price of 10 GbE switches and 10 GbE adapters continues to drop as the deployment of these becomes more widespread.

The best practices when using iSCSI are as follows:

- Configure multiple vmks bound to multiple vmnics to provide load balancing and redundancy for iSCSI connections.
- Use network cards with **TCP/IP Offload Engine** (**TOE**) enabled to reduce the stress on the host CPU.
- Use a physically separate network for iSCSI traffic. If a physically separate network is not available, use VLANs to separate iSCSI traffic from other network traffic.
- Enable jumbo frames (MTU 9000) on the iSCSI network.

The **Network File System** (**NFS**) **protocol** can be used to access virtual machine files stored on a **Network Attached Storage** (**NAS**) device. Virtual machine configuration files, disk (VMDK) files, and swap (.vswp) files can be stored on the NAS storage. vSphere 5.5 supports NFS Version 3 over TCP, and vSphere 6 added support for NFS v4.1. The capabilities and limitations of NFS v4.1 will be discussed in a separate recipe later in this chapter.

Throughput is based on the network bandwidth, the speed of the network interface card (1 Gbps or 10 GbE), and the processing speed of the NAS. Multiple paths can be configured for high availability, but load balancing across multiple paths is not supported with NFS.

The cost of implementing NFS connectivity is similar to iSCSI. No specialized network hardware is required. Standard network switches and network adapters are used and there is no need for specialized HBAs.

The best practices when using NFS-connected storage are as follows:

- Use a physically separate network for NFS traffic. If a physically separate network is not available, use VLANs to separate NFS traffic from other network traffic.
- Hosts must mount NFS version 3 shares and non-Kerberos NFS version 4.1 shares with root access.
- Enable jumbo frames (MTU 9000) on the NFS network.

Fibre Channel of Ethernet (**FCoE**) encapsulates Fibre Channel in Ethernet frames. A **Converged Network Adapter** (**CNA**) that supports FCoE is required, or a network adapter with FCoE capabilities can be used with the software FCoE initiator included with ESXi.

A common implementation of FCoE is with Cisco UCS blade chassis. The connectivity for TCP/IP network and FCoE storage traffic is converged between the chassis and the Fabric Interconnects. The Fabric Interconnects splits out the traffic and provides the connectivity paths to the TCP/IP network and storage network fabrics.

The best practices when using FCoE are as follows:

- Disable the **Spanning Tree Protocol** (**STP**) on the switch ports connected to FCoE adapters
- Ensure that the latest microcode is installed on the FCoE network adapter
- If the FCoE network adapter has multiple ports, configure each port on a separate vSwitch

Storage path selection plugins

Mutlipathing allows more than one physical path to be used to transfer data between the ESXi hosts and the storage array. In the event of a failure in a storage path, the host or hosts can switch to another available path. Multipathing also provides load balancing by distributing the storage IO across multiple physical paths.

How to do it...

To determine the multipathing policy, perform the following steps:

1. Identify the different native multipathing policies available and the capabilities of each policy.
2. Select a multipathing policy based on the number of paths and the array type used.
3. Change the default multipathing policy using the `esxcli` command.
4. Configure the multipathing policy on the storage devices presented to the ESXi host.

How it works...

The VMware **Native Multipathing Plugin** (**NMP**) is the built-in multipathing plugin for ESXi. It only supports storage arrays listed on the **Hardware Compatibility List** (**HCL**). The NMP automatically detects the type of storage array used and sets the appropriate path selection policy by associating a set of physical paths with a storage device or LUN.

The **Storage Array Type Plugin (SATP)** monitors the available storage paths, reports changes in the path status, and initiates failover between paths when needed. The **Path Selection Plugins (PSP)** determine which available path to use for IO. There are three native multipathing PSPs available:

- **Fixed**: The host always uses a preferred path if the preferred path is available. If the preferred path fails, another available path is selected and used until the preferred path becomes available. This is the default policy for active/active storage devices.
- **Most Recently Used (MRU)**: The host uses the most recently used path. If the current path fails, another path is selected. IO does not revert to the previous path when it becomes available. This is the default policy for active/passive storage devices.
- **Round Robin (RR)**: IO is rotated through all active paths. This provides load balancing across all physical paths available to the hosts. This PSP can be used on active/passive or active/active arrays.

Array vendors may provide their own path selection plugins to provide storage multipathing. The use of third-party MPPs will depend on array-and-vendor best practices. The NMP can be used for any supported array.

The optimal PSP to choose is dependent on the recommendations of the array vendor.

By default, a PSP is set based on the SATP used for the array. The SATP to use is identified by the **Pluggable Storage Architecture (PSA)** using a set of claim rules that base the selection on the vendor and model of the array. The SATP then determines the default PSP to be used.

The NMP PSP policies are as follows:

- VMW_PSP_MRU: For most recently used
- VMW_PSP_FIXED: For fixed
- VMW_PSP_RR: For round robin

The default PSP for an SATP can be changed using the following esxcli command:

```
esxcli storage nmp satp set —default-psp=<psp policy to set>
--satp=<SATP_name>
```

Using the command line changes the default PSP for all new devices identified by the SATP. The PSP for an individual device or LUN can also be changed. This can be done in the vSphere Client or vSphere Web Client by managing the paths for a single storage device on a host.

To change the PSP of a device using the vSphere Client, navigate to **Host and Clusters** | **Hosts** | **Configuration** | **Storage Adapters** and select the storage adapter that services the paths you want to modify. In the **Details** section of the **Storage Adapters** window, right-click on the device you want to modify the PSP on and select **Manage Paths**.

From the **Manage Paths** window, select the **Path Selection** with the dropdown menu and click on **Change**.

The following screenshot displays how to select and change the path selection policy for a device using the vSphere Client:

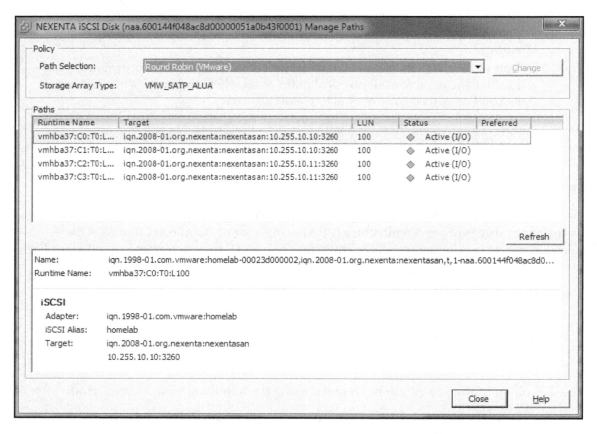

Path Selection Policy in the vSphere Client

Changing the default PSP for an SATP or the PSP for a device can be done without impacting normal operations. A change that's made to the PSP for a single device takes effect immediately. Changing the default PSP for the SATP changes only the settings of newly discovered devices and not the PSP settings of the current devices.

Sizing datastores

A datastore is a logical representation of storage that's presented to an ESXi host where virtual machine files are stored. A datastore can be a VMFS formatted volume, an NFS export, a **Virtual Volume (VVOL)** datastore, a **Virtual SAN (VSAN)** datastore, or a path on the local ESXi filesystem.

How to do it...

Design requirements, virtual machine disk size, IOPS, and recovery are all factors that can determine the number of virtual machines to store on a single datastore. The size of the datastore is calculated based on the number of virtual machines per datastore and the size of the virtual machines:

1. Determine the number of virtual machines per datastore based on the capacity, performance, and recovery requirements
2. Understand the impact the SCSI reservations may have on datastore sizing
3. Understand how recovery time impacts datastore sizing

How it works...

A design factor that was identified in `Chapter 3`, *The Design Factors*, specified that no more than 20 application servers should be affected by a hardware failure. Applying the same requirement to datastore sizing would mean that no more than 20 application servers should be hosted on a single datastore:

*Number of VMs per datastore * (VM disk size + .vswp size) + 20% = Minimum datastore size*

The datastore size for 20 application server workloads, each with 100 GB of disk storage and 8 GB of RAM with no reservations, plus 20 percent for slack, would be approximately 2.5 TB:

*20 * (100 GB + 8GB) + 20% = 2,592 GB or ~ 2.5 TB*

The storage backing the datastore has to provide enough IOPS to support the virtual machines running on it. If a virtual machine generates 50 IOPS and there are 20 virtual machines on the datastore, the storage must be able to support 1,000 IOPS.

The maximum size of a VMFS6 datastore is 64 TB.

Block storage formatted as a VMFS volume is susceptible to SCSI reservations or locking of the entire LUN for a very short period of time by a single host. A few operations that cause SCSI reservations to occur are as follows:

- Creating a VMFS datastore
- Expanding a VMFS datastore
- Powering on a virtual machine
- Creating a template
- Deploying a virtual machine from a template
- Creating a virtual machine
- Migrating a virtual machine with vMotion
- Developing a virtual machine disk
- Creating or deleting a file

With the introduction of VMFS5, along with the **vStorage APIs for Array Integration (VAAI)** hardware-assisted locking feature, the impact of SCSI reservations is minimized. If an array does not support the VAAI hardware-assisted locking feature, then the number of virtual machines per datastore may need to be decreased to reduce the impact of LUN locking for SCSI reservations.

The **Recovery Time Objective (RTO)** must also be taken into account when determining the size of a datastore. If the datastore is lost or becomes inaccessible, how long will it take to restore the virtual machines that were running on it?

Size of datastore / GBs recovered per hour <= RTO

If 500 GB is to be recovered per hour, the time to recover a failed datastore can be calculated as follows:

2.5 TB / 500 GB = 5 hours to recover

If the RTO for the applications or workloads running on the datastore is less than 5 hours, the datastore would need to be resized to ensure that recovery would take place within the defined RTO.

There's more...

Multiple datastores can be aggregated to create a datastore cluster. A datastore cluster is a collection of the member datastore resources with a shared management interface. vSphere Storage DRS manages the datastore cluster resources to determine the initial placement and ongoing balancing of virtual machine VMDKs across the datastores in the cluster. Datastore clusters are supported for both VMFS and NFS datastores.

A few recommended practices when using datastore clusters and Storage DRS are as follows:

- Cluster datastores with similar IOs and capacity characteristics
- Use separate datastore clusters for replicated and nonreplicated datastores
- Do not mix NFS and VMFS datastores in the same datastore cluster
- Do not place datastores shared across multiple data centers in a datastore cluster

When a virtual machine is placed on a datastore cluster, Storage DRS determines which datastore in the cluster the files will be stored in, based on space utilization and/or performance. The following diagram is a logical representation of the virtual machines placed on a datastore cluster:

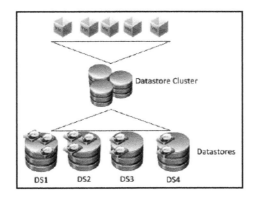

Virtual machines in a datastore cluster

The best practices when using datastore clusters are as follows:

- Datastores in a cluster should have similar performance capabilities
- Keep similar virtual machine IO workloads together on the same cluster
- Do not mix replicated and nonreplicated datastores in the same cluster
- Do not mix NFS and VMFS datastores in the same datastore cluster
- Use VMDK affinity rules to keep virtual machine disk files together on the same datastore within the datastore cluster
- Use VM anti-affinity rules to ensure that virtual machines run on different datastores within the datastore cluster

The *VMware vSphere Storage DRS Interoperability* whitepaper can be found at http://www.vmware.com/files/pdf/techpaper/vsphere-storage-drs-interoperabili ty.pdf. This whitepaper provides an overview of the datastore cluster best practices and interoperability of datastore clusters, along with other VMware products.

Designing VSAN for virtual machine storage

VMware **Virtual SAN (VSAN)** is integrated into the ESXi hypervisor. VSAN virtualizes and aggregates the local direct-attached disks in ESXi hosts. This creates a single pool of storage resources from the local disks with each host that is shared across all hosts in the VSAN cluster, as shown in the following diagram:

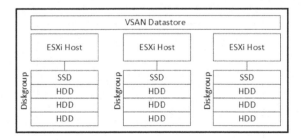

VSAN diskgroups

How to do it...

To use VSAN for storage in a vSphere virtual infrastructure design, follow these steps:

1. Identify the hardware requirements to support VSAN
2. Verify that the disks and controllers are on the VSAN **Hardware Compatibility List** (HCL)
3. Size VSAN to support performance and availability
4. Enable VSAN on the vSphere Cluster

How it works...

VSAN presents shared storage to ESXi hosts across a vSphere Cluster. Each host providing storage to the VSAN cluster requires the following:

- **Solid-State Disks (SSD)** to provide performance
- **Hard Disk Drives (HDD)** or SSDs to provide capacity
- A disk controller
- Network connectivity between hosts

As with all hardware in a vSphere environment, the hardware supporting VSAN must be verified on the **Hardware Compatibility List (HCL)** located at `http://www.vmware.com/resources/compatibility/search.php?deviceCategory=vsan`. Compatibility of the SSD, HDD, and disk controller, including the firmware, should all be validated on the HCL. Many server hardware vendors offer VSAN-ready nodes that have been preconfigured with supported hardware/firmware.

VSAN can be deployed as a hybrid, SSD and HDD disks, or as All-Flash. VSAN requires network connectivity between hosts. A 10 GbE network should be used for VSAN to provide the best performance, but 1 GbE is supported in a hybrid VSAN. 10 GbE is required for an All-Flash VSAN. A VMkernel is configured and enabled for VSAN traffic, as shown in the following screenshot:

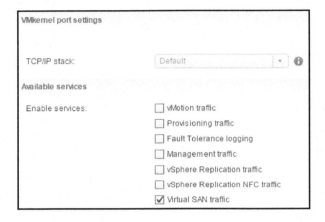

Enabling VSAN traffic

VSAN is enabled on a vSphere Cluster. ESXi hosts participating in VSAN, regardless of whether the host is providing storage or consuming storage, must be in the same cluster. The VSAN storage cannot be directly consumed by hosts outside the cluster. VSAN is enabled by simply turning on VSAN for a vSphere Cluster, as shown in the following screenshot:

Enabling VSAN

When enabling VSAN, the disk can be automatically or manually claimed. Disks are claimed to be used by VSAN and placed into disk groups. A disk group must contain at least one flash (SSD) disk and one or more HDDs. A single host can be configured with up to five disk groups and each disk group, can contain up to eight disks, one SSD, and seven HDDs. All Flash disk groups are also supported. In a VSAN disk group, the Flash disk provides performance and the HDD disk provides capacity. Claiming disks for VSAN is shown in the following screenshot:

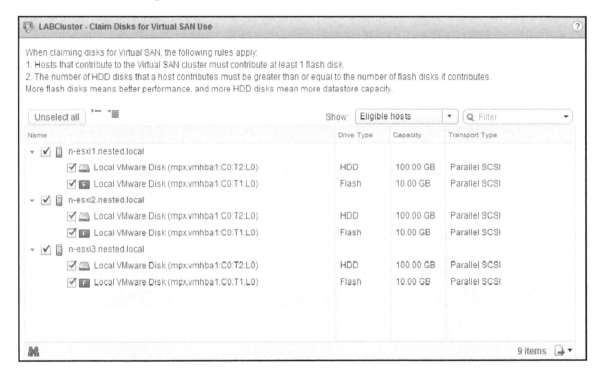

Claiming disks for VSAN

When sizing VSAN, VMware recommends the SSDs be sized to 10 percent of the HDD capacity in a disk group. For example, if there is 1 TB of HDD capacity, the SSD should be at least 100 GB. The capacity of the disk group is the sum of the HDD capacity. If there are three 1 TB HDDs in the disk group, the group will provide 3 TB of capacity storage. The size of the VSAN in the datastore is the aggregate of all disk groups claimed by VSAN across all hosts.

Three hosts, participating in a VSAN cluster, each with a disk group of three 1 TB HDDs to provide capacity, will present a VSAN datastore with approximately 9 TB of usable capacity.

When sizing VSAN, it is important to take into account **Failures To Tolerate** (**FTT**) and Fault Domain policies for virtual machines. A virtual machine consuming 100 GB of storage stored on a VSAN datastore with the FTT policy configured to 1 will consume 2 x the capacity, or 200 GB. This is due to the virtual machine storage being duplicated across two hosts so that the virtual machine disks will be available in the event that a single host fails. If the FTT is set to 2, then a virtual machine will consume 3 x the capacity. We will take a deeper look at storage policies later in this chapter.

There's more...

VMware's latest version of VSAN, 6.7 Update 1, includes a number of significant features and improvements, including the following:

- Guided workflows for VSAN cluster creation and node additions
- VMware Update Manager firmware and driver updates for ReadyNodes
- Automated UNMAP and guest integration

VMware continues to develop and improve the capabilities, efficiencies, and performance of VSAN storage, making it a suitable alternative to traditional storage for virtual machine workloads. More details on VSAN design and sizing can be found in the *VMware VSAN Design and Sizing Guide* at https://storagehub.vmware.com/t/vmware-vsan/vmware-r-vsan-tm-design-and-sizing-guide-2/http://www.vmware.com/files/pdf/products/vsan/VSAN_Design_and_Sizing_Guide.pdf.

Using VMware Virtual Volumes

Virtual Volumes (**VVOL**) is a virtual disk management and array integration framework that was introduced with vSphere 6. VVOL enables policy-based storage for virtual machines. A datastore is presented as backed by raw storage supporting multiple different capabilities, such as snapshotting, replication, deduplication, raid level, performance, and so on. These capabilities are exposed to the vSphere environment. Policies are created and assigned to virtual machines. When a virtual machine is placed on a VVOL datastore, the placement on the array is based on requirements that are defined in the policies.

How to do it...

To successfully incorporate VVOL as part of a vSphere infrastructure design, perform the following steps:

1. Identify the components and characteristics of VVOL
2. Identify the limitations and interoperability of VVOL with other vSphere components
3. Create a new storage provider in vCenter
4. Add a VVOL datastore

How it works...

The following table outlines the different components that are required to make up a VVOL environment:

Component	Description
vSphere APIs for Storage Awareness (VASA)	The VASA provider is a software component that was developed by the storage array vendor. The VASA provider provides the storage capability awareness to vCenter and the ESXi hosts.
Storage Containers (SC)	A pool of storage capacity and storage capabilities on the array. A storage container represents a virtual datastore.
Protocol Endpoint (PE)	A logical IO proxy that provides a data path from virtual machines to the virtual volumes.
VVOL Objects	Encapsulation of virtual machine files and disks. Objects are stored natively on the array storage containers.

VVOL differs from other vSphere storage in the fact there is no filesystem. The storage container is comprised of raw storage capacity grouped by capabilities. This storage container is presented as a datastore to the vSphere environment through the protocol endpoint. The protocol endpoint provides a data path and supports IP-based (iSCSI, NFS, FCoE) and FC connectivity. The VASA provider communicates with vCenter and the ESXi hosts to expose the storage capabilities of VVOL.

The following diagram provides a logical overview of VVOL and the connectivity between the components:

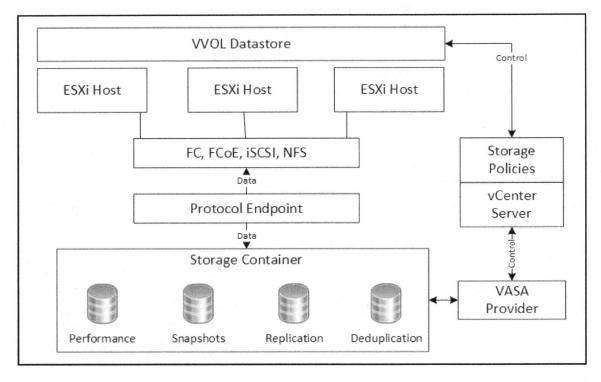

Entity relationships with VVOLs

VVOL is a new feature that has only just been introduced with vSphere 6. There are still a number of limitations regarding the features and products that are supported. For example, features such **Storage IO Control (SIOC)**, IPv6, **Fault Tolerance (FT)**, and **Raw Device Mapping (RDM)** are not supported on VVOL. Products such as **vSphere Data Protection (VDP)** and VMware **Site Recovery Manager (SRM)** do not currently support using VVOL, although VMware has committed to supporting this combination in a future release. At the moment, if a vSphere design requires these features or products, VVOL will likely not be a viable choice to provide storage to the environment. For a full list of supported/unsupported features and products up to 6.5, refer to this VMware Knowledge Base article: `https://kb.vmware.com/kb/2112039`.

To create a new storage provider, the name of the provider, the URL for the VASA 2.0 provider, and a username and password or a certificate for authentication are required. Storage providers are configured per vCenter server, as shown in the following screenshot:

Creating VVOL storage providers

Once the storage provider has been configured, the VVOL datastore is added by using the **New Datastore** wizard and by selecting the **VVOL** datastore type, as shown in the following screenshot:

Creating a VVOL datastore

When VVOL is selected as the type in the **New Datastore** wizard, the available storage containers will be displayed. Enter a **Datastore name** and select the **Backing Storage Container**, as shown in the following screenshot:

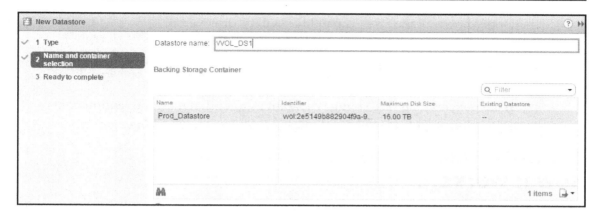

Naming a VVOL datastore

Once complete, the datastore will be created, presented to the hosts in the environment, and available for virtual machine storage.

Incorporating storage policies into a design

Storage policies are configured to simplify the provisioning of virtual machines on storage. Storage policies ensure that service levels are met for storage performance, protection, and availability. For **Software Defined Storage** (SDS), including VSAN and VVOL, these policies are a key component that are required for determining virtual machine placement during provisioning and throughout a virtual machine's life cycle.

How to do it...

When incorporating storage policies into a vSphere design, perform the following steps:

1. Determine the storage services and capabilities that are required by virtual machine workloads:
    - What data protection service may be required for virtual machines?
    - Are capabilities such as encryption at rest, deduplication, or compression required?
    - Are different tiers of storage required?

2. Identify how storage array capabilities will be discovered:
   - Is a VASA provider available to provide awareness of storage capabilities?
   - Will tags be used to manually tag datastores based on capabilities?

3. Create policies mapping storage capabilities to virtual machine requirements.
4. Assign storage policies to virtual machines and virtual machine disks.

How it works...

VM storage policies are created and managed through the vSphere Web Client, as shown in the following screenshot:

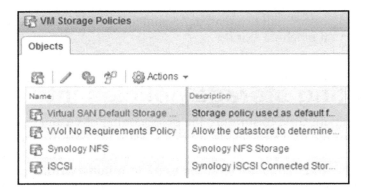

VM Storage Policies in the vSphere Web Client

VM storage policies contain a rule or a set of rules. These can be based on tags or on data services. Tag-based rules are created from tags that the administrator creates for storage capabilities and then manually assigns them to datastores. Data services based rules are created from capabilities that are discovered from a data service provider (for example, for a VASA provider on a VVOL-enabled array). A rule set can be based on data services, as shown in the following screenshot:

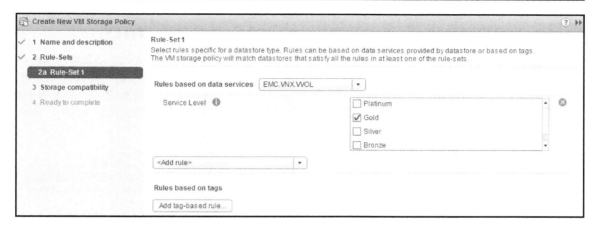

Creating rule-sets for a VM Storage Policy

VM storage policies can be assigned to a virtual machine or to individual virtual machine disks. The **Manage VM Storage Policies** dialog for a virtual machine is displayed in the following screenshot:

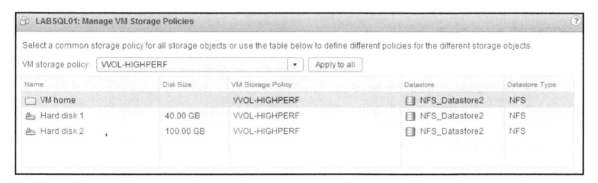

Assigning a VM Storage Policy to a VM

This is based on the requirements for the virtual machine. For example, a virtual machine running SQL may require different storage capabilities for the disks containing the OS, the logs, the tempDB, and the databases. Policies can be assigned to each virtual disc to ensure correct placement of the disks and ensuring compliance through the virtual machine's life cycle.

NFS version 4.1 capabilities and limits

vSphere 6 added support for NFS version 4.1. NFS clients for both NFS version 3 and NFS version 4.1 are included as part of ESXi. Using NFS version 4.1 provides additional features and functionality over NFS version 3, but there are some significant caveats and limitations that must be accounted for when using NFS version 4.1 in a vSphere design.

How to do it...

To determine how NFS version 4.1 can be incorporated into a vSphere 6 design, you must do the following:

- Identify the capabilities of NFS version 4.1
- Determine what design requirements will NFS version 4.1 satisfy
- Determine the limitations of NFS version 4.1
- Identify the requirements for configuring a NFS version 4.1 datastore

How it works...

NFS version 4.1 in vSphere 6 provides the following capabilities:

- Multipathing support for NFS datastores
- Non-root user access when using Kerberos
- Stateful server-side locking
- Better error recovery

These features provide enhancement to performance, security, and availability. There are still a number of limitations that will have an impact on using NFS version 4.1 in a vSphere design. These limitations include the following:

- No support for vSphere FT, VMware SRM, VVOL, or SIOC
- IPv6 is only supported for non-Kerberos datastores
- NFS version 3 datastores cannot be upgraded to NFS version 4.1
- No VAAI-NAS hardware acceleration

Features including vSphere High Availability (DRS), vSphere vMotion, and vSphere **Distributed Resource Scheduler (DRS)** are all supported when using NFS version 4.1 datastores.

Presenting both NFS version 3 and NFS version 4.1 datastores is supported. ESXi includes separate NFS clients to support each version. However, a single NFS share should not be accessible by both protocol versions, as this will likely result in data corruption.

The NFS server providing storage must support NFS version 4.1 and, as with all IP-connected storage, VMkernel interfaces are required on each ESXi host to support the storage connectivity.

NFS Kerberos Credentials provides a significant security improvement. It allows non-root access to the NFS export. NFS Kerberos Credentials are configured for each host. Only a single credential can be created. **NFS Kerberos Credentials** is created and managed from the **Authentication Services** settings on a host, as displayed in the following screenshot:

Entering NFS Kerberos credentials

NFS version 4.1 datastores are mounted to ESXi hosts using the **New Datastore** wizard. A datastore name and the folder location of the NFS share are required, just like NFS version 3. Multiple NFS servers can be added to provide multiple paths to the NFS version 4 share.

Using persistent memory to maximize VM performance

Persistent memory (PMEM) is a new technology that adds a storage layer between **Solid State Drives (SSDs)** and **Dynamic Random Access Memory (DRAM)**, and takes the best of both technologies. Recall that SSDs are devices that store data in dense, non-volatile, Flash memory and are much faster than spinning hard drives that store data on magnetic disks. DRAM is typical server memory, which is very fast but is volatile, meaning that data is only stored when power is applied. When power is lost, the data in DRAM is lost as well. PMEM, also referred to as a **Non-Volatile Dual Inline Memory Module (NVDIMM)**, is a technology that is as fast as DRAM, hundreds of times faster than SSDs, but non-volatile, like SSDs, and provides a useful function in a vSphere environment. VMs don't even have to be PMEM-aware. Legacy applications and operating systems can utilize PMEM technology in vSphere 6.7. PMEM-based storage can be presented as a virtual disk to legacy operating systems or directly to PMEM-aware operating systems.

How to do it...

Follow these steps to use PMEM storage in vSphere:

1. Install a supported PMEM device in your ESXi host
2. Present the PMEM device as a datastore
3. Create and attach virtual disks (vPEMDisk) to legacy VMs, ensuring that the VM storage policy is set to **Host-local PMem Default Storage Policy**
4. For VMs that have PMEM-aware operating systems and applications, add a new NVDIMM device from **Edit Settings....**

How it works...

Hardware vendors with early support for PMEM include Dell EMC and HPE. Their solutions are a combination of battery-backed DRAM, some with NAND-Flash modules, and logical PMEM implementations that use DIMMs and NVMe drives.

The virtualization overhead that PMEM uses is nominal at 3 percent, according to VMware, and the benefits include up to eight times increased bandwidth and latency of less than 1 microsecond. The best performance can be achieved when applications are modified to use the PMEM device in a byte-addressable manner.

vSphere Network Design 6

To effectively design a virtual network infrastructure, a design architect must understand the virtual network architecture, including which features are available and how they are configured. This chapter will contain recipes that a design architect can use to design a virtual network architecture that provides the capacity and availability required to support the virtual infrastructure.

The logical network design includes calculating the network capacity (or bandwidth) required to support the virtual machines and determining the capacity that's required to support VMware technologies, such as vMotion and Fault Tolerance. If IP-based storage connectivity is required, the design must account for the networking that's necessary to support storage traffic, as well:

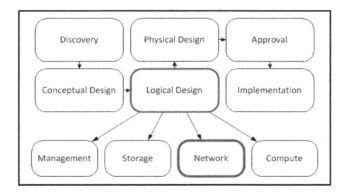

Network design in the vSphere design workflow

In this chapter, we will discuss the different virtual network switch technologies that are available in vSphere, and the different features that are available in each. This chapter will also cover how load balancing and teaming are used to improve network utilization efficiency and to increase availability. Network capacity resource management with traffic shaping, jumbo frames, and network I/O control will also be covered.

In this chapter, we will cover the following recipes:

- Determining network bandwidth requirements
- Standard or distributed virtual switches
- Providing network availability
- Network resource management
- Using private VLANs
- IP storage network design considerations
- Enabling jumbo frames
- Designing for VMkernel services
- Creating custom TCP/IP stacks
- vMotion network design considerations
- Using 10 GbE Converged Network Adapters
- IPv6 in a vSphere design
- Remote Direct Memory Access options

Determining network bandwidth requirements

Bandwidth refers to the capacity of the network, and it is measured in either **Gigabits per second (Gbps)** or **Megabits per second (Mbps)**. The bandwidth that's required is based on the amount of data transferred or the throughput required by the virtual machines. Most modern networks are capable of transferring data at 1 Gbps or 10 Gbps. Network adapters that support 40 and 100 Gbps have recently become available.

The number of physical network adapters in each host that are required to support a solution is dependent on the amount of bandwidth required to support virtual machine network traffic, the number of virtual switches required, and the network redundancy requirements.

The following information from the case example in `Chapter 3`, *The Design Factors*, is used to help calculate the network bandwidth requirements:

- Cisco switches are used for network connectivity. Separate VLANs exist for management connectivity and production application connectivity

- No more than 20 application servers (or 200 customers) should be affected by hardware failure
- Currently, each physical server contains a single gigabyte network interface card. Peak network usage is 10 Mbps

How to do it...

Refer the following steps to determine bandwidth requirements.

1. Calculate the total amount of bandwidth required to support virtual machine network traffic using the following formula:

Total Number or Virtual Machines x Bandwidth per Virtual Machine (Mbps) = Total Bandwidth Requirement (Mbps)

2. Calculate the amount of bandwidth required per host. This is dependent on the maximum number of virtual machines that can be run on a single host.
3. Determine the network requirements for other vSphere services and features, such as vMotion, iSCSI, NFS, and Fault Tolerance.
4. Select the type and number of network adapters to provide the network connectivity that's required to support the design requirements.

How it works...

The physical network infrastructure must be capable of supporting the total throughput requirement of the environment. The total throughput requirement is calculated by multiplying the number of virtual machines by the throughput that's required by a single virtual machine:

100 Virtual Machines x 10 Mbps = 1,000 Mbps Total

The throughput that's required for a single host is calculated by multiplying the number of virtual machines that will run on a host by the throughput that's required by a single virtual machine:

20 Virtual Machines x 10 Mbps = 200 Mbps per Host

Network adapters are generally capable of delivering throughput equal to approximately 80 percent of the adapter speed, for example, 800 Mbps for a 1 Gbps network adapter. A single gigabit Ethernet connection would provide sufficient bandwidth to support the virtual machine throughput requirements that were calculated previously. An additional network adapter would be required to support failovers.

There are also network bandwidth requirements to support VMkernel interface network connectivity for management, vMotion, IP storage, and Fault Tolerance. The minimum bandwidth requirements for VMkernel network connectivity are as follows:

- Management: 100 MB
- vMotion: 1 GB
- IP storage: This is dependent on the amount of storage throughput required, but is limited to the bandwidth of a single path
- Fault Tolerance: 1 GB (10 GB required for multi-vCPU FT)

Sufficient physical network connectivity and bandwidth must be included in the design to support these services.

Network connectivity can be provided by using multiple 1 GB network adapters, or 10 GbE Converged Network Adapters (CNAs) can be used to carry multiple network traffic types, including virtual machine network traffic and VMkernel (management, vMotion, FT, and IP storage) network traffic on a single 10 GbE network adapter, as shown in the following diagram:

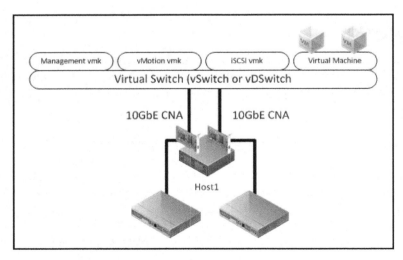

Using 10GbE CNAs for multiple traffic types

When CNAs are used to provide physical uplink connectivity to virtual switches, traffic shaping or **Network I/O Control** (**NIOC**) may be configured to ensure that sufficient network bandwidth is available to each traffic type serviced by the CNAs.

There's more...

For a virtual machine with very high network I/O requirements, DirectPath I/O allows a physical network adapter to be passed through directly to the virtual machine.

The following screenshot shows how a virtual machine is provided direct access to a physical network card with DirectPath I/O:

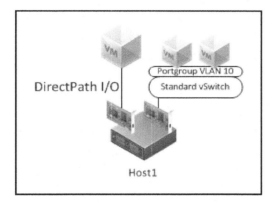

DirectPath I/O for a VM

When DirectPath I/O is used, the network adapter is only made available to the virtual machine that it is passed to, and cannot be shared with other virtual machines. The full bandwidth capacity of the network adapter is available to the virtual machine. Because a virtual machine with DirectPath I/O configured is dependent on the physical network card in the host, it cannot be moved to other hosts using vMotion, nor can it be protected using VMware HA.

Standard or distributed virtual switches

The connectivity of the virtual network to the physical network in a vSphere environment is accomplished by using one of two virtual switch technologies: the standard virtual Switch (vSwitch) or the virtual Distributed Switch (vDSwitch). VMware technologies like VMware HA, VMware DRS, and Fault Tolerance require that virtual switch configurations be consistent across all ESXi hosts in a cluster.

How to do it...

To determine whether to use standard or distributed virtual switches, follow these steps.

1. Identify the features and capabilities of virtual standard switches and distributed virtual switches
2. Based on the design requirements, determine which virtual switch technology should be selected to support them

How it works...

The virtual switch technology that's chosen is dependent on the connectivity, availability, and manageability requirements, and the features that are available on the virtual switch.

A vSwitch is configured and managed independently on each ESXi host and supports up to 1,024 virtual switch ports per vSwitch. Because vSwitches are configured on each individual host, it increases the administrative overhead required to support large environments. Advanced network features, such as port mirroring, NetFlow integration, and private VLANs, are not available when using standard virtual switches. vSwitches are available at all vSphere license levels.

Several networks can use the same vSwitch, or the networks can be separated across multiple vSwitches. Multiple physical uplinks can be associated with a vSwitch to provide redundancy and load balancing. vSwitches can be created with no physical uplinks to keep virtual machine network traffic isolated on a single host.

The following diagram depicts a common logical network design using standard virtual switches to provide virtual machine network connectivity:

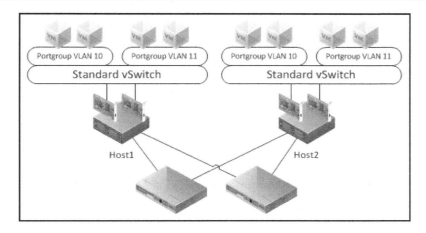

A typical virtual standard switch network design

vDSwitches are configured and managed by vCenter. A vDSwitch guarantees consistent network policy configurations and PortGroup configurations across all hosts, with uplinks that are connected to it. vSphere Enterprise Plus Licensing is required to use vDSwitches.

Multiple physical uplinks from each host can be associated with a vDSwitch, to provide redundancy and load balancing. A vDSwitch will not be available for use by a host without any physical uplinks associated with it. The following diagram depicts a logical virtual network design using a virtual distributed switch:

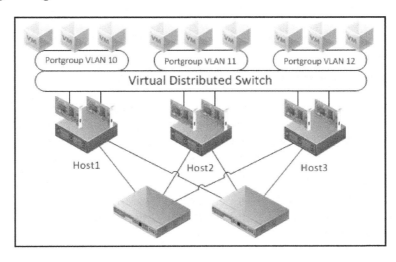

A typical virtual distributed switch network design

vCenter is required to manage vDSwitches. vCenter controls the configuration state and keeps track of virtual machine connection information for the vDSwitch. If the vCenter Server managing the vDSwitch is unavailable, new connections and modifications to the vDSwitch will not be possible.

The features that are available when using a vDSwitch are as follows:

- The central management of the virtual switch and virtual machine PortGroups
- Link Aggregation Control Protocol (LACP)
- Ingress and egress traffic shaping
- Load balancing based on the physical NIC load
- NetFlow integration
- Port mirroring
- Third-party virtual switches (Cisco Nexus 1000v)
- Private VLANs (PVLAN)
- Network I/O Control

There's more...

Third-party virtual switches, such as the Cisco Nexus 1000v, can be used to extend the functionality of a vDSwitch. They provide an interface for provisioning, monitoring, securing, and configuring the virtual network, using standard vendor network management tools.

Providing network availability

Network availability is obtained by minimizing Single Points of Failure (SPOF) and providing sufficient capacity. Multiple network ports, network adapters, and physical switches can be used to minimize single points of failure, and link aggregation can be used to provide load balancing across multiple network adapters.

vSphere virtual network configurations offer multiple NIC teaming and load balancing options. The options that are used are dependent on the number of network adapters available, the number of virtual machines connected, the physical network's topology, and the amount of bandwidth required.

How to do it...

Follow these steps to design for network availability.

1. Identify the availability options that are available on virtual switches and virtual switch PortGroups
2. Determine the load balancing policies to provide availability based on design requirements
3. Determine the network adapter teaming policies to provide availability based on design requirements

How it works...

Load balancing distributes the network load across multiple available adapters. Load balancing policies are configured as a part of the NIC Teaming and failover options on virtual switches, virtual machine PortGroups, and VMkernel interfaces.

The following screenshot illustrates the Edit Settings dialog for configuring the Teaming and failover options on the virtual machine PortGroup on a standard virtual switch:

Configuring Teaming and Failover options for a portgroup

The following load balancing policies can be applied to virtual switches or virtual PortGroups:

- Route based on originating virtual port: This is the default load balancing policy. When it is being used, the load is balanced based on the number of physical NICs and the number of virtual switch ports in use. Virtual port connections are distributed across the physical NICs available to the virtual switch. A virtual machine connected to the virtual port will always use the same physical NIC, unless the NIC becomes unavailable. This is usually the best load balancing method to use.

- Route based on IP hash: This load balancing policy uses a hashing algorithm that determines the physical path based on the source and destination IP addresses of the virtual machine traffic. A virtual machine's network traffic can use multiple available NICs. This policy is used when using either EtherChannel or the LACP link aggregation.

- Route based on source MAC hash: This load balancing policy is similar to the Route based on originating virtual port policy, except that the physical NIC used for virtual machine traffic is based on the virtual network adapter's MAC address and not the virtual port connection.

- Use explicit failover order: This policy is not really a load balancing policy, because network traffic always uses the physical NIC uplink that is configured as the highest ordered active physical uplink available.

- Route based on physical NIC load: This is an additional load balancing option offered by vDSwitches that is not available to vSwitches. It is the most efficient because it distributes the load across active uplinks, based on the actual workload of the physical NICs.

Redundancy in the virtual network is provided by configuring the Failover order. These configurations define the physical uplinks that are actively used to pass network traffic, and those that are available stand in the event of an active uplink failing.

The available adapters are as follows:

- **Active adapters**: These are adapters that are available for use by the virtual switch, a virtual machine network PortGroup, or a VMkernel interface.
- **Standby adapters**: These are adapters that only become active in the event that an active adapter becomes unavailable.
- **Unused adapters**: These adapters are unused. They will never be used by the virtual switch, a virtual machine PortGroup, or a VMkernel interface.

The following screenshot shows the adapters that are configured in Active and Standby. If the Active Adapter (vmnic0) fails, the Standby Adapter (vmnic1) will become active:

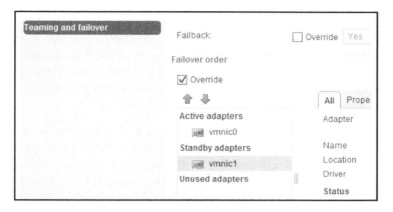

Active / Standby configuration of network adapters

The following diagram shows an example of an active/standby network configuration that's commonly used in small environments to provide connectivity and redundancy for the host management and vMotion networks:

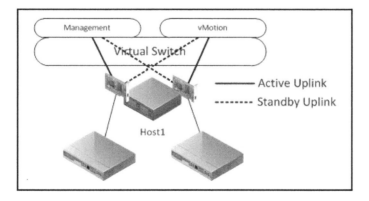

Logical view of an active / standby network configuration

Network Failover Detection and Failback are settings that control how a network failure is detected, and what happens when an active adapter is returned to service after a failure.

How network failure is detected is configured by using the Network Failover Detection option. Two failure detection options are available: Link Status Only and Beacon Probing. The Link Status Only option uses the link state (up or down) of the physical NIC to determine whether the uplink is available. The Beacon Probing option detects network failures by sending and receiving beacon probes out to all physical uplinks on the virtual switch, and it can detect link state and switch failures. At least three active uplinks are needed for beacon probing to work effectively. The VMware Knowledge Base article located at `http://kb.vmware.com/kb/1005577` provides more information on how beacon probing works with virtual switches.

The Failback setting defines whether an active adapter is returned to service if the adapter becomes available after a failure, based on the value set for Network Failover Detection. If a physical switch fails and Failback is enabled, with Link Status Only being used for Failover Detection, the adapter may become active and will be returned to service before the physical switch is available to pass traffic.

Network resource management

In a vSphere environment, physical network resources are shared across multiple virtual machines and services. The ability to ensure that sufficient capacity is available across shared resources is therefore important. If a single virtual machine or a VMkernel network service, such as vMotion or Fault Tolerance, saturates the available network capacity, other virtual machines and services, including host management services, may be adversely impacted.

How to do it...

Follow these steps to design a resource management scheme:

1. Identify the traffic shaping and network resource controls that are available on the virtual network switches.
2. Determine the network resources required for different traffic types: management, IP storage, vMotion, and virtual machine traffic.
3. Design traffic shaping, Network I/O Control policies, and Network Resource Pools to guarantee or limit network resources for the network traffic types, based on design requirements.

How it works...

Traffic shaping is used to limit the amount of bandwidth that's available to virtual switch ports. NIOC is used to apply limits and to guarantee traffic to different virtual network service types.

Traffic shaping can be configured on vSwitches, vDSwitch uplinks, VMkernel interfaces, and PortGroups to restrict the network bandwidth available to the network ports on the virtual switch. Traffic shaping is applied at all times, regardless of the amount of network capacity available. This means that if traffic shaping is enabled and configured on a virtual switch or PortGroup to limit the peak bandwidth to 1,048,576 Kbps (1 Gbps), only 1,048,576 Kbps of bandwidth will be used, even if more bandwidth is available.

The following bandwidth characteristics can be applied to the traffic shaping policy:

- Average bandwidth: This is the permitted average load, measured in kilobits/sec (Kbps)
- Peak bandwidth: This is the maximum allowed load, measured in kilobits/sec (Kbps)
- Burst size: This is the maximum number of bytes, measured in kilobytes, that can be burst over the specified average bandwidth

The traffic shaping policies on a vSwitch only apply to egress or outbound traffic. vDSwitch traffic shaping policies can be configured for both ingress (inbound) and egress (outbound) traffic.

The following is a screenshot of the configuration screen for applying Traffic shaping to a virtual machine PortGroup on a standard virtual switch:

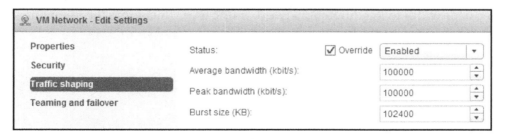

Configuring traffic shaping on a VSS portgroup

The following screenshot shows the Ingress traffic shaping and Egress traffic shaping settings that can be applied to a virtual machine PortGroup on a vDSwitch:

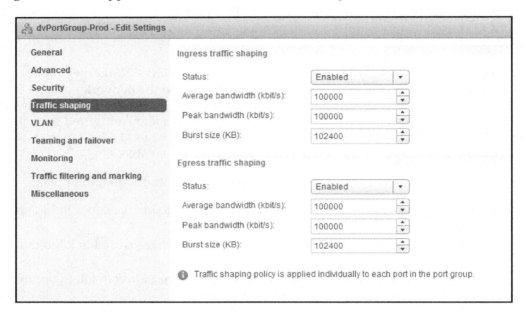

Configuring traffic shaping on a vDS portgroup

Unlike traffic shaping, Network I/O Control only provides control over the network bandwidth for specific network protocols during times of network contention. NIOC can only be enabled on vDSwitches.

Shares, limits, and reservations can be applied to network traffic types to limit and guarantee bandwidth to the different network traffic types, including the following:

- Management traffic
- vMotion traffic
- IP storage traffic (NFS/iSCSI)
- Virtual SAN traffic
- Fault Tolerance traffic
- vSphere replication traffic
- vSphere Data Protection backup traffic
- Virtual machine traffic

The System traffic screen in the vSphere Web Client provides information about the bandwidth capacity and the allocation of network resources across traffic types. The following screenshot illustrates the NIOC configurations of a vDSwitch:

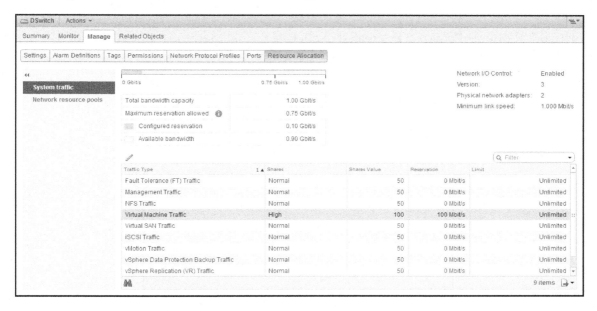

NIOC configuration on a vDS

Shares define the share of the available bandwidth on a physical NIC that's attached to the vDSwitch during a time of network bandwidth contention that a specific traffic type will receive. The Reservation is the Mbps guaranteed to a specific traffic type. The Limit is the Mbps limit that's applied to all hosts connected to the vDSwitch.

The percentage of bandwidth that a traffic type receives is based on the total number of shares available; for example, in the default configuration, the virtual machine traffic receives *100* shares of the *400 (50 + 50 + 50 + 50 + 100 + 50 + 50)* shares available. The formula for this is as follows:

Shares Value / Total Available Shares = Percentage of Physical Network Bandwidth

Therefore, 100 / 400 = 25%

The amount of bandwidth that's available to vMotion would be calculated based on the 50 shares allocated to the vMotion traffic, as follows:

$$50 / 400 = 12.5\%$$

Network Resource Pools can be created to allocate virtual machine traffic reservations across distributed PortGroups. For example, if 100 Mbps is reserved for virtual machine traffic, this reservation can be applied across different PortGroups. In the following screenshot, a New Network Resource Pool is created, allocating 90 Mbps of the 100 Mbps reservation to a pool named CriticalVMs:

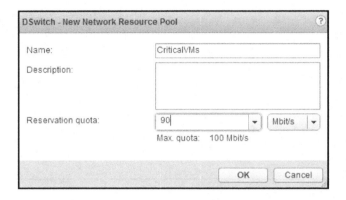

Configuring a network resource pool

Notice that the Reservation quota is the bandwidth that the Network Resource Pool will be guaranteed out of the overall reservation. The Reservation quota cannot be set to a value higher than the total reservation that's allocated to virtual machine traffic.

The Network resource pool is then assigned to a PortGroup on the virtual distributed switch, as shown in the following screenshot:

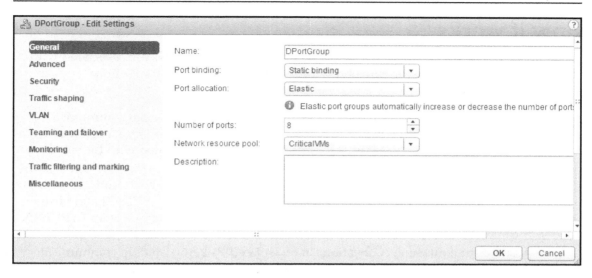

Assigning a network resource pool to a vDS portgroup

This allocates the reservation from the CriticalVMs network resource pool to the DPortGroup port group.

Using private VLANs

Private VLANs are an extension of the VLAN standard. PVLANs can be configured on virtual distributed switches to isolate traffic between virtual machines in the same VLAN.

How to do it...

Refer the following steps to design a private VLAN scheme:

1. Identify the types of private VLANs that are available and the functionality of each
2. Determine the use cases for the PVLANs and identify whether the PVLANs can be used to satisfy the design requirements
3. Design the PVLANs to meet the design requirements

How it works...

A primary PVLAN is created on a vDSwitch, and secondary PVLANs are associated with the primary PVLAN. There are three types of secondary PVLANs: Promiscuous, Community, and Isolated:

- The virtual machine connections in a Promiscuous PVLAN can communicate with all of the virtual machine connections in the same primary PVLAN. When a primary PVLAN is created, a Promiscuous PVLAN is created with the same PVLAN ID as the primary PVLAN.
- Virtual machine connections in a Community PVLAN can communicate with other virtual machine connections in the same Community PVLAN and virtual machine connections in the Promiscuous PVLAN. Multiple Community PVLANs can be associated with a single primary PVLAN.
- The virtual machine connections in an Isolated PVLAN can only communicate with the virtual machine connections in the Promiscuous PVLAN. Only one Isolated PVLAN can exist per primary PVLAN.

Private VLANs are created by editing the settings of a vDSwitch, as follows:

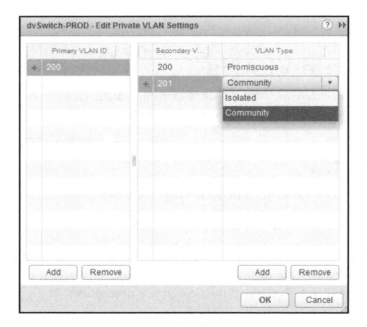

Editing a private VLAN

Once the PVLAN has been configured on the vDSwitch, a virtual machine network PortGroup is created with the PVLAN type and ID assigned, as follows:

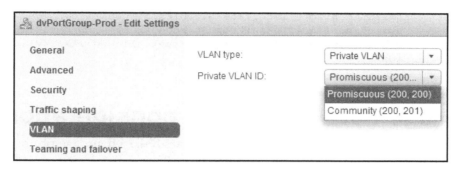

Configuring a private VLAN on a vDS portgroup

There's more...

For PVLAN traffic to be passed between ESXi hosts connected to a vDSwitch, the physical switch must be PVLAN-aware and properly configured to support PVLANs. The process to configure the PVLANs on a physical switch will vary from vendor to vendor. The following process shows the steps that are necessary to configure PVLANs on a Cisco IOS switch:

1. Enter the Cisco switch configuration mode:

    ```
    switch# configure terminal
    ```

2. Enable the PVLAN feature on the switch:

    ```
    switch(config)# feature private-vlan
    ```

3. Create the PVLAN on the switch and set the PVLAN type:

    ```
    switch(config)# vlan <vlan-id>
    switch(config-vlan)# private-vlan primary
    ```

4. Associate the secondary PVLANs with a primary VLAN:

    ```
    switch(config-vlan)# private-vlan association <secondary pvlan>
    ```

5. The switch ports that are connected to the vDSwitch uplinks need to be configured to allow for the PVLAN traffic:

```
switch(config)# interface GigabitEthernet1/1
switch(config-if)# switchport mode trunk
switch(config-if)# switchport trunk allowed vlan <vlan/pvlan
ids>
```

IP storage network design considerations

iSCSI, NFS, and **Fiber Channel over Ethernet (FCoE)** are IP-based storage protocols that are supported in a vSphere environment. This recipe will cover the design considerations for designing the IP networks that will be used for storage traffic.

How to do it...

Refer the following steps to design an IP storage network:

1. Identify the network connectivity and virtual switch configurations that are required for IP-connected storage
2. Determine the best practices for providing connectivity for IP-connected storage
3. Design the IP storage connectivity to meet design requirements

How it works...

IP storage traffic should be separated from other IP traffic. This separation can be provided by either using physically separate hardware (network adapters and physical switches) or by using separate VLANs for IP storage traffic. The networks associated with IP storage should be directly connected and non-routable.

Multiple network paths to storage should be configured to provide redundancy and load balancing. Single points of failure should be minimized so that the loss of a single network path does not result in the loss of storage connectivity.

Software iSCSI, NFS, and Software FCoE each require a VMkernel interface to be created on a virtual switch. The VMkernel interfaces that are used for iSCSI and FCoE must be bound to a single physical active adapter. Having more than one active adapter, or a standby adapter, is not supported with Software iSCSI or Software FCoE.

NFS v3 over TCP does not provide support for multipathing. Using link aggregation will only provide failover, and not load balancing. NFS will always use a single physical network path, even if multiple VMkernels are configured. To manually load balance NFS traffic, create separate VMkernel ports that are connected to separate networks and mount separate NFS v3 datastores.

NFS v4.1 supports multipathing for NFS servers, which support session trunking. Multiple VMkernel ports can be configured to provide access to a single NFS volume that's been configured with multiple IP addresses. This provides load balancing and resiliency for NFS v4.1.

The VMkernel port binding for Software iSCSI is configured in the properties of the Software iSCSI adapter. Only VMkernel ports that are compliant will be available for binding, as shown in the following screenshot:

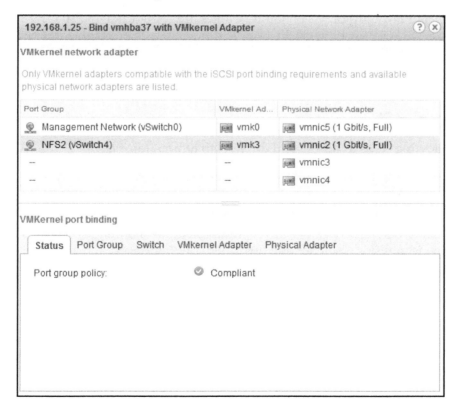

Port-binding compliant VMkernel ports

To enable the Software FCoE adapter, an NIC that supports FCoE offloads must be installed on the host. If a supported NIC is not installed, the ability to add the software FCoE adapter will not be available.

Physical network binding for FCoE is done when enabling a Software FCoE adapter. Compliant and supported physical adapters are available when adding the Software FCoE adapter. Separate FCoE adapters should be enabled and connected to each storage network fabric. A single ESXi host can support up to four software FCoE adapters. Each software FCoE adapter requires a dedicated VMkernel port bound to a dedicated physical adapter.

Using jumbo frames

Enabling jumbo frames on the networks that's used for vMotion or IP storage can increase performance and throughput. When jumbo frames are configured, iSCSI or NFS packets can be transferred over the network in a single frame; there is no fragmentation. This decreases the amount of CPU overhead that's necessary to encapsulate (and de-encapsulate) IP storage packets.

How to do it...

Refer the following steps to design and implement jumbo frames:

1. Determine the use cases for enabling jumbo frames
2. Configure the jumbo frames on virtual switches
3. Configure the jumbo frames on VMkernel ports
4. Ensure that jumbo frames are configured end to end on the physical network, that is, physical switches and array network interfaces
5. Test the network for proper end-to-end jumbo frame configuration

How it works...

Jumbo frames must be supported and enabled on the network from end to end; this includes the physical network infrastructure as well. In vSphere, jumbo frames are enabled either in the vSwitch configuration or on the vDSwitch uplinks by setting the value **Maximum Transmission Unit (MTU)** to 9000. Jumbo frames must also be enabled on VMkernel interfaces by setting the value of MTU for the PortGroup to 9000.

To enable jumbo frames, set the value of MTU (Bytes) on the vSwitch to 9000, as shown in the following screenshot:

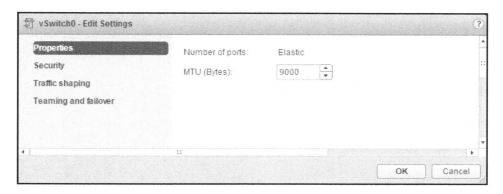

Editing the MTU of a VSS

If you are using a vDSwitch, the MTU (Bytes) is set to 9000 in the Advanced settings to enable jumbo frames:

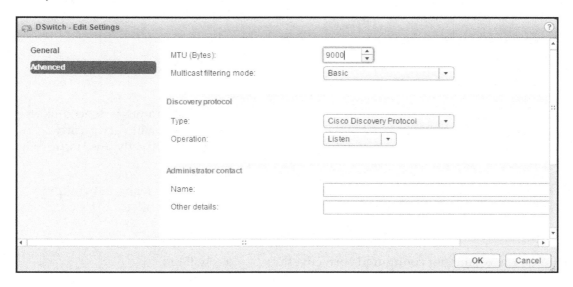

Editing the MTU of a vDS

The MTU setting must also be changed to 9000 on a VMkernel interface on the vSwitch or vDSwitch to enable jumbo frames, as shown in the following screenshot:

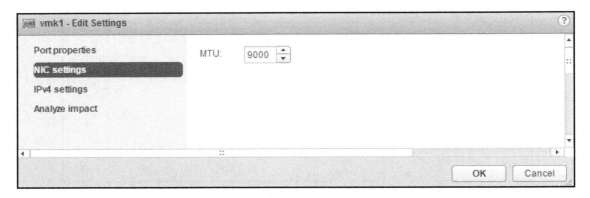

Editing the MTU of a VMkernel port

When you are using jumbo frames, the physical switch must also be configured to support the MTU. This will vary, depending on the switch vendor and version. To enable jumbo frames on a Cisco Catalyst Series switch, use the following command:

```
Switch(config)# system mtu jumbo 9000
```

In this case, the switch must be reloaded for the setting to take effect. Other switches may allow (or require) per-port MTU configuration.

If you are using jumbo frames for the storage network, the jumbo frames will need to be enabled on the network interfaces of the array. The process for this will vary greatly between array vendors. If the array interfaces are not configured correctly, the traffic may not pass, or the performance will be significantly impacted.

The jumbo frame configuration can be tested from the ESXi shell by using the vmkping command, with the **Data Fragment (DF)** bit (-d) and size (-s) options set, as follows:

```
ESX1 # vmkping -d -s 8972 <IP_Address_of_IP_Storage_Array>
```

If jumbo frames are not configured correctly, the vmkping will fail.

Creating custom TCP/IP stacks

TCP/IP stacks provide flexibility in the VMkernel interface design by allowing you to apply specific DNS and default gateway configurations to a VMkernel interface on a host.

There are three preconfigured TCP/IP stacks, as follows:

- Default TCP/IP stack: Supports management traffic
- vMotion TCP/IP stack: Supports the live migration, vMotion, of virtual machines
- Provisioning TCP/IP stack: Supports the cold migration, cloning, and snapshot creation of virtual machines

Custom TCP/IP stacks can be used to handle the network traffic of other applications and services, which may require separate DNS and default gateway configurations.

How to do it...

Refer the following steps to implement custom a TCP/IP stack:

1. Create a custom TCP/IP Stack on an ESXi host
2. Configure DNS, default gateway, and advanced settings on the TCP/IP Stack
3. Assign the TCP/IP Stack to a VMkernel adapter

How it works...

Using TCP/IP stacks for VMkernel network traffic provides the following benefits:

- It separates VMkernel routing tables
- It provides a separate set of buffers and sockets
- It isolates traffic types to improve performance and security

Currently, a custom TCP/IP stack cannot be created in the Web Client interface. A custom TCP/IP stack is created by using esxcli on the ESX host, as follows:

```
ESX1 # esxcli network ip netstack add -N "Name_of_Stack"
```

The DNS configuration associated with the TCP/IP stack can then be configured. This can automatically be obtained from a VMkernel adapter by using DHCP, or it can be set manually, as shown in the following screenshot:

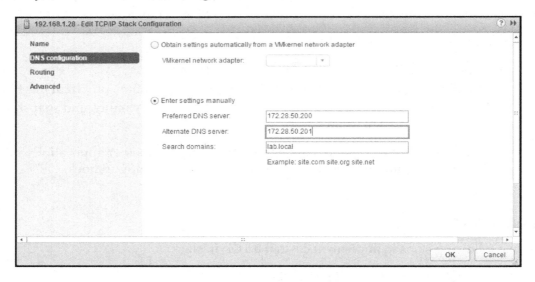

Editing the DNS servers of a TCP/IP stack

A VMkernel gateway can be assigned to the TCP/IP stack, as shown in the following screenshot:

Editing the gateway of a TCP/IP stack

Advanced TCP/IP stack settings include the maximum number of connections and the congestion control algorithm to use for the stack.

The TCP/IP stack is assigned to a VMkernel adapter when it is created, as shown in the following screenshot:

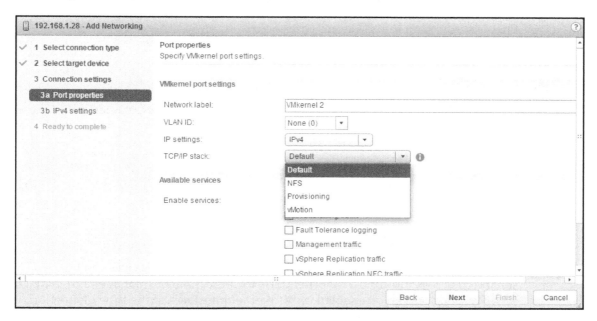

Assigning a TCP/IP stack to a VMkernel adapter

Designing for VMkernel services

VMkernel interfaces are configured to provide network connectivity for services in the vSphere environment. The VMkernels provide network paths for service connectivity. Multiple VMkernel interfaces can be created to provide a physical or logical separation for these services.

How to do it...

Refer the following steps to design and implement VMkernel services:

1. Identify services that require a VMkernel interface
2. Create a VMkernel interface to support the service
3. Enable services on the VMkernel interface

How it works...

Most vSphere services require a VMkernel interface to provide network connectivity. These services include the following:

- ESXi Management
- vMotion
- Fault Tolerance
- Virtual SAN
- vSphere Replication
- IP Storage (NFS, iSCSI, FCoE)
- Multiple services can share a single VMkernel port, or the services can be separated across multiple VMkernel ports for performance, management, and security. Services can be enabled on VMkernel interfaces at the time of creation, or by editing the Port properties, as shown in the following screenshot:

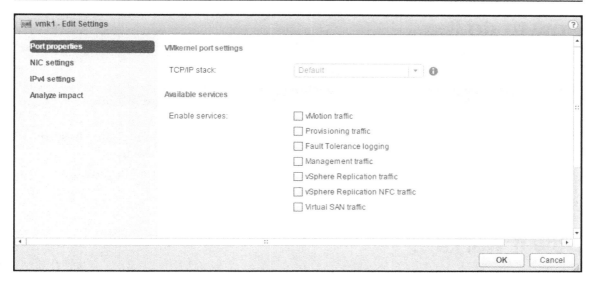

Services supported for VMkernel ports

Once the services have been enabled, the VMkernel interface will provide connectivity for the services that are selected. As we discussed in the previous recipe, TCP/IP stacks can be used to configure specific DNS settings and a default gateway for a service.

vMotion network design considerations

vMotion allows for the running state of a virtual machine to be transferred from one ESXi host to another. The network traffic that's required for the migration uses the VMkernel interfaces that have been enabled for vMotion. vMotion connectivity between ESXi hosts is required when using a **Distributed Resource Scheduler (DRS)** to balance the virtual machine load across hosts in a DRS-enabled cluster.

How to do it...

The following steps to design networking for vMotion:

1. Identify the vMotion network requirements
2. Determine the best practices for configuring the network connectivity that's required to support vMotion
3. Identify the benefits of keeping virtual machines together on the same host to minimize the network traffic that must transverse the physical uplinks
4. Design the vMotion network connectivity to support design requirements
5. Design DRS rules to support design requirements

How it works...

vMotion requires, at a minimum, a single, active, 1 GB network adapter. A second standby adapter should be configured to provide redundancy for the vMotion network.

A vMotion migration can consume all of the available network bandwidth. If the vMotion network is shared with other network traffic, traffic shaping or NIOC should be enabled to prevent vMotion from impacting other virtual network traffic. If possible, vMotion should be configured on a separate physical network or separate VLAN.

vSphere 5 introduced the ability to configure multiple adapters for use with vMotion. Multiple-NIC vMotion allows for the bandwidth of multiple physical NICs to be leveraged by vMotion to speed up the migration of virtual machines between hosts.

To configure Multiple-NIC vMotion, create multiple VMkernel interfaces with vMotion enabled. Configure each VMkernel interface to use a single active adapter, and configure other available adapters as standby adapters. When a virtual machine is vMotioned, either manually or by DRS, all available links will be used for the vMotion traffic. More information on Multiple-NIC vMotion can be found in the VMware Knowledge Base article at http://kb.vmware.com/kb/2007467.

There's more...

Network communications between virtual machines that are connected to the same virtual network on the same ESXi host will not use the physical network. All of the network traffic between the virtual machines will remain on the host.

Keeping virtual machines that communicate with each other together on the same host will reduce the load on the physical network; for example, keeping a web frontend server, application server, and database server together on the same host will keep the traffic between the servers internal to the host.

If the VMware DRS is configured on a vSphere Cluster, DRS rules can be configured on the cluster to keep virtual machines together on the same host.

In the following screenshot, a Virtual Machine Affinity Rule has been created to keep two virtual machines together on the same host:

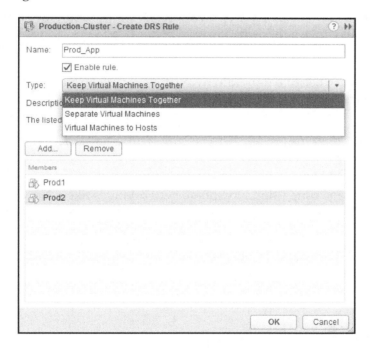

Creating a DRS rule

With DRS enabled, the virtual machines assigned to the DRS rule will be vMotioned to run on the same host.

Virtual machine anti-affinity rules (Separate Virtual Machines) can also be configured to ensure that virtual machines run on separate hosts. This can be used when service redundancy is provided by multiple virtual machines, such as with multiple virtual domain controllers. Keeping virtual machines separate will ensure that a host failure does not impact service redundancy.

Using 10 GbE converged network adapters

Computing has historically bounced between performance bottlenecks. When one technology evolves to perform better, it leaves an older technology to become the system's worst performing characteristic. Between memory caches, SSDs, high bandwidth networks, and software, the bottleneck constantly moves. With **10 Gb Ethernet** (**10 GbE**) networks today, we find it's usually not the result of too little bandwidth. But how can we ensure that we design our virtual data center with the highest performance when using 10 GbE **Converged Network Adapters** (**CNAs**)?

CNAs allow both Ethernet **Local Area Network** (**LAN**) traffic and **Fibre Channel over Ethernet** (**FCoE**) traffic to use the same physical network adapter, as opposed to using dedicated Ethernet and Fibre Channel adapters. Similar to how virtualization allowed for the maximum use of server hardware resources and reduced wasted resources, CNAs allow for the maximum use of bandwidth by pushing storage traffic over the same physical cable as LAN traffic. It's important to consider, however, how each type of traffic is managed on the physical link so that congestion is handled appropriately.

How to do it...

The best way to manage congestion in vSphere networking is likely Network I/O Control. Follow these steps to design a virtual data center with 10 GbE CNAs:

1. Identify all of your IP traffic types; for example, management, vMotion, Fault Tolerance, VM traffic, FCoE, and so on
2. Assign NIOC shares for each traffic type

How it works...

Choosing NIOC shares that ensure that storage traffic is not impacted is critical, because poor storage performance can ripple through an environment quickly, causing ill effects. Traffic types like vMotion and Fault Tolerance are important too, but their weight is less than that of storage or VM traffic. Their NIOC shares should reflect this.

IPv6 in a vSphere design

Internet Protocol version 6 (IPv6) was developed to replace **IP version 4 (IPv4)**. IPv6 addresses are 128-bit IP addresses, compared to the 32-bit addresses in IPv4. IPv6 is becoming more common in data center network environments, and vSphere has included support for IPv6 since vSphere 5.x.

How to do it...

Refer the following steps to design and implement IPv6:

1. Enable IPv6 on the ESXi host
2. Determine the vSphere features and services with IPv6 support
3. Configure the VMkernel interfaces to use IPv6

How it works...

By default, IPv6 support is enabled on ESXi hosts. If the IPv6 support is changed, disabled, or enabled, a host reboot is required. Enabling or disabling IPv6 is done on each ESXi host by editing the Advanced Network Settings from the Networking management tab for the host, as shown in the following screenshot:

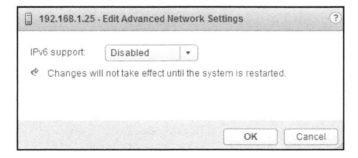

Enabling IPv6 support

Once enabled, IPv6 can be configured for supported vSphere features and services. The following vSphere features and services support IPv6:

- ESXi and vCenter management
- vMotion and vSphere DRS

- Fault Tolerance
- vSphere HA
- NFS v3 storage
- iSCSI (software or hardware)

IPv6 is not currently supported with the following vSphere features:

- Auto deploy
- DPM with IPMI/iLO
- Virtual volumes
- Virtual SAN
- Authentication proxy
- NFS v4.1

When IPv6 is enabled on an ESXi host, VMkernel interfaces can be created with IPv4, IPv6, or both IPv4 and IPv6 settings, as shown in the following screenshot:

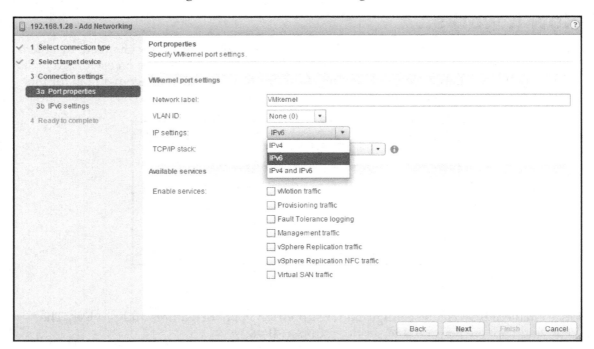

Choosing IP versions for a VMkernel port

IPv6 addresses can be configured automatically by using DHCP or router advertisement, or the IPv6 address can be a static address that is manually assigned.

Remote direct memory access options

Since vSphere 6.5, Remote Direct Memory Access (RDMA) over Converged Ethernet (RoCE) has been supported. RoCE provides extremely low latency and high throughput communication over an Ethernet network, and allows one VM to access the memory contents of another VM directly, without the involvement of the hosts' CPU. This is usually reserved for network-intensive applications. Like FCoE, it requires a lossless network. RoCE requires hardware support in the form of Host Channel Adapters (HCAs) when VMs communicate across different ESXi hosts. RDMA is built into ESXi, and therefore, HCAs are not required when VMs reside on the same ESXi host. As of vSphere 6.7, only some Linux distributions support RoCE, such as guest operating systems running virtual hardware version 13 or later. The RoCE support in vSphere 6.5 (and later) is named **Paravirtual RDMA (PVRDMA)**.

How to do it...

Refer the following steps to implement RDMA in vSphere:

1. Install a supported Host Channel Adapter
2. Configure PVRDMA on each host with an HCA
3. Assign a PVRDMA network adapter to a VM

How it works...

When configured with PVRDMA adapters, VMs with network-intensive applications can communicate over RDMA. When two VMs need to communicate across ESXi hosts and each host has an HCA installed, PVRDMA communication is enabled. If two VMs with PVRDMA adapters need to communicate on the same ESXi host, the HCA, if installed, is not used, and traffic is kept within the VMkernel itself. If a VM with RDMA enabled needs to communicate with a VM that does not support RDMA, the communication falls back to TCP/IP.

vSphere Compute Design 7

This chapter will cover logical compute design. **Compute** refers to the processor and memory resources required to support the virtual machines running in the vSphere environment. Calculating the required CPU and memory resources is an important part of the design process and ensures that the environment will be able to support the virtual machine workloads. Design decisions like scaling up, scaling out, and clustering hosts will be covered. The following diagram displays how the compute design is integrated into the design process:

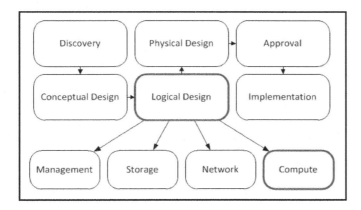

Compute design in the vSphere design workflow

In a physical environment where a single operating system or a single application is installed on a dedicated physical hardware, compute utilization usually averages as 10-20 percent of the available resources. The majority of the memory and CPU resources are idle and wasted. In a virtual environment, the resources that are available are utilized by multiple operating systems and applications. It is not uncommon to see a usage of 65-80 percent of the available resources.

We will take a look at the clustering hosts' resources to take advantage of the advanced VMware features: vSphere **High Availability (HA)**, vSphere **Distributed Resource Scheduler (DRS)**, and vSphere **Fault Tolerance (FT)**. Ensuring that significant resources are available for failover and provide vMotion compatibility are key factors of cluster design. Methods to reserve or limit resources and for providing flash-based caching will also be covered.

In this chapter, we will cover the following recipes:

- Calculating CPU resource requirements
- Calculating memory resource requirements
- Transparent page sharing
- Scaling up or scaling out
- Determining the vCPU-to-core ratio
- Clustering compute resources
- Reserving HA resources to support failover
- Using distributed resource scheduling to balance cluster resources
- Ensuring cluster vMotion compatibility
- Using resource pools
- Providing Fault Tolerance protection
- Leveraging host flash

Calculating CPU resource requirements

There are several factors that must be considered when calculating CPU resource requirements, such as the amount of CPU resources that are required to support the current workloads, the amount of CPU resources required to support future growth, and the maximum CPU utilization threshold.

The following information from Chapter 3, *The Design Factors*, will be used to calculate the CPU requirements:

- Currently, there are 100 physical servers, each hosting a single application. Each application services 10 customers.
- The business expects to add 50 new customers over the next year.

- Support growth over the next five years.
- Each application server is configured with two dual-core 2.7 GHz processors. The peak usage of a single application server is approximately 10 percent of the total, or approximately 1 GHz.

How to do it...

Refer the following steps to calculate CPU resource requirements:

1. Determine the amount of CPU resources required to support the current workloads:

   Number of Workloads x CPU Speed in MHz or GHz = Current CPU Resources Required

2. Determine the maximum utilization threshold. This is the maximum percentage of available resources that should be consumed.
3. Determine the amount of growth in CPU resources that the environment should support.
4. Calculate the amount of CPU resources required:

Current Workload CPU Resources + Future Growth + Maximum Utilization Threshold = Total CPU Resources Required

How it works...

Calculating the required CPU resources that are necessary to support the current workload is straightforward and uses the following formula:

Number of Workloads x CPU Speed in MHz or GHz = Current CPU Resources Required

100 x 1 GHz = 100 GHz

To determine the total CPU resources required, the amount required to support future growth must also be calculated. The amount of CPU resources required for future growth will be determined by the design requirements. Based on the requirements identified in Chapter 3, *The Design Factors*, the environment should be designed to support a growth of 25 additional virtual machines over the next five years.

A maximum utilization threshold must also be determined and accounted for in CPU resource requirements. This threshold determines the maximum percentage of total CPU resources that will be consumed. It is unlikely that the environment would be configured to consume 100 percent of the CPU resources available. If the maximum utilization threshold is 75 percent, an additional 25 percent of CPU resources will be added to calculate the total CPU resources required:

Current CPU Resources Required + Future Growth = Total CPU Resources Required

100 GHz + (25 x 1 GHz) = 125 GHz

When the maximum utilization threshold is 75%, the calculation will be as follows:

125 GHz * (100/75) = ~167 GHz

The environment must be designed to support the 167 GHz of CPU resources that are, in turn, required to support the current workloads and future workloads, and to provide for a maximum utilization threshold of 75 percent.

Calculating memory resource requirements

There are several factors that must be considered when calculating memory requirements; these factors include the amount of memory required to support the current workloads, the amount of memory required to support future growth, the amount of memory required for virtual machine memory overhead, and the maximum memory utilization threshold.

Like the CPU requirements, information from Chapter 3, *The Design Factors*, will also be used to calculate the memory requirements:

- Currently, there are 100 physical servers, each hosting a single application. Each application services 10 customers.
- The business expects to add 50 new customers over the next year.
- Support growth over the next five years.
- Each application server is configured with 8 GB of memory. The peak usage of a single application server is approximately 65 percent, or around 5.2 GB.

How to do it...

Refer the following steps to calculate memory resource requirements:

1. Determine the amount of memory resources required to support the current workloads:

   Number of Workloads x Memory Usage = Current Memory Required

2. Determine the memory overhead required.
3. Determine the maximum utilization threshold. This is the maximum percentage of available resources that should be consumed.
4. Determine the amount of growth in the memory resources that the environment should support.
5. Calculate the amount of memory resources required:

Current Workload Memory Usage + Memory Overhead + Future Growth + Maximum Utilization Threshold - TPS Savings = Total Memory Resources Required

How it works...

To calculate the amount of memory required to support the current workloads, the following formula is used:

Number of Workloads x Memory Usage = Current Memory Required

100 x 5.2 GB = 520 GB

The memory overhead of a virtual machine must also be accounted for when calculating memory requirements. The amount of memory required for an overhead depends on the configuration of the virtual machine.

The number of vCPUs allocated to the virtual machine, the amount of memory allocated to the virtual machine, and the virtual hardware configured for the virtual machine, will all have an impact on the amount of memory required for overhead:

Memory overhead example

Typically, the memory overhead required for a virtual machine is between 20 MB and 150 MB. Memory overhead estimations based on the amount of RAM and the number of vCPUs can be found in the vSphere documentation, as follows:

- **vSphere 6.0**: https://pubs.vmware.com/vsphere-60/topic/com.vmware.vsphere.resmgmt.doc/GUID-B42C72C1-F8D5-40DC-93D1-FB31849B1114.html
- **vSphere 6.5/6.7**: https://docs.vmware.com/en/VMware-vSphere/6.7/com.vmware.vsphere.resmgmt.doc/GUID-4954A03F-E1F4-46C7-A3E7-947D30269E34.html?hWord=N4IghgNiBcILYFM4HsBOBPABMgbg1AFgmACYgC+QA

This may seem like a small amount of memory, but over dozens (or even hundreds) of virtual machines, it can have a significant impact on the amount of total memory required:

(Number of Workloads x Memory Usage) + (Number of Workloads x Memory Overhead) = Current Memory Required

(100 x 5.2 GB) + (100 x 50 MB) = 525 GB

To calculate the total memory required, future growth must be considered. When memory is calculated for growth, the memory overhead that's required to support the additional virtual machines must also be considered.

The maximum utilization threshold must also be determined for memory resources. This threshold defines the maximum percentage of the total memory resources that will be consumed. If the maximum utilization threshold is 75%, an additional 25% of memory resources will need to be added to calculate the total memory resources required:

*Current Memory Required + Future Growth * (100/Maximum Threshold%) = Total Memory Resources Required*

*525 GB + [(25 x 5.2 GB) + (25 x 50 MB)] * (100/75) = ~875 GB*

875 GB of memory is required to support the current workloads, the future growth, and a maximum utilization threshold of 75%.

Transparent page sharing

Transparent Page Sharing (TPS) is a memory saving technology used by vSphere that allows for duplicate memory pages to be shared between virtual machines. To address security concerns about sharing memory between virtual machines across security domains, TPS can be disabled, enabled across groups of virtual machines with the same salt settings, or enabled across all virtual machines in the environment.

How to do it...

Refer the following steps to design and implement TPS:

1. Identify the different options for sharing duplicate memory pages within a virtual machine and across groups of virtual machines
2. Configure TPS to meet requirements for the security and performance of the environment
3. Configure salt values on virtual machines to enable or disable page sharing between virtual machines

How it works...

TPS de-duplicates pages of memory both within a virtual machine (Intra-VM) and across virtual machines (Inter-VM). By default, Inter-VM TPS is disabled due to security concerns about sharing memory pages between virtual machines that cross security boundaries (for example, virtual machine guests within the DMZ and virtual machine guests in the production environment). TPS can be configured to allow for Inter-VM sharing between all virtual machines, or only across certain groups of virtual machines, by adding a salt value to the virtual machines. The VMware KB article at `http://kb.vmware.com/kb/2097593` provides more information about changes and enhancements to TPS.

The host advanced configuration option, `Mem.ShareForceSalting`, can be set to configure how TPS will be used. This setting is configured per ESXi host, as shown in the following screenshot:

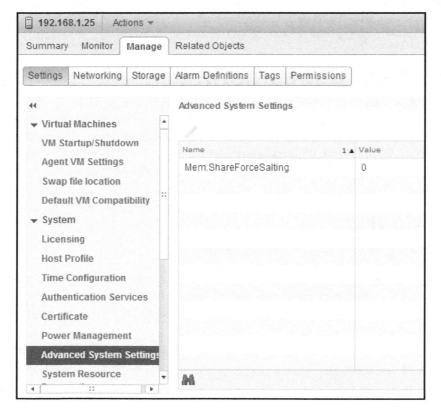

Enabling advanced settings for TPS

`Mem.ShareForceSalting` can be set to a value of 0, 1, or 2. Add the configuration parameter `sched.mem.pshare.salt` to a virtual machine to set the salt value. Page sharing can be configured to only share pages between virtual machines with the same salt values.

The following table outlines how Intra-VM and Inter-VM page sharing is impacted based on the `Mem.ShareForceSalting` setting:

`Mem.ShareForceSalting` settings	Inter-VM sharing	Intra-VM sharing
0	Yes, between all virtual machines on the host. Virtual machine salt value is ignored.	Yes
1	Sharing between virtual machines with the same `sched.mem.pshare.salt` setting. Sharing between virtual machines where `sched.mem.pshare.salt` is not present.	Yes
2 (default)	Only among virtual machines with the same `sched.mem.pshare.salt` setting. The virtual machine `vc.uuid` is used as the salt value by default.	Yes

The following screenshot displays the memory utilization for a specific virtual machine, showing the amount of shared memory:

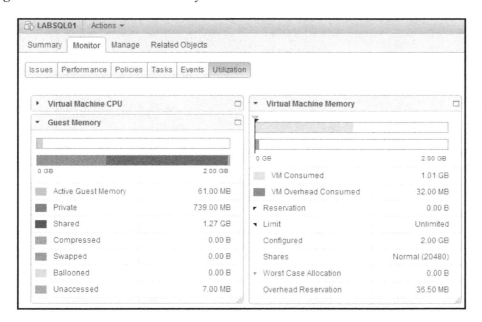

VM memory utilization and shared memory

Notice the savings that the shared memory provides compared to the VM consumed memory, which is the amount of physical memory consumed on the host. The following screenshot shows the TPS savings across a vSphere cluster:

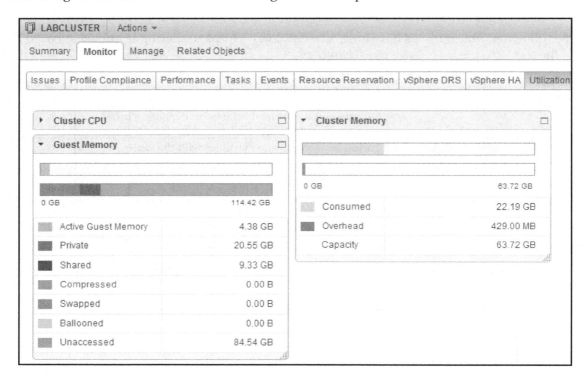

TPS savings on a vSphere cluster

There's more...

When large memory pages are used, TPS only provides a benefit when there is memory pressure on the host. When the memory utilization on a host reaches 95%, large pages are broken down into small pages to enable TPS. Large memory pages can be disabled on the ESXi hosts. This is done by setting `Mem.AllocGuestLargePage` to 0. This configuration must be done on each host. Disabling large pages will increase sharing and decrease the amount of physical memory required, but it can have a performance impact, especially with memory-intensive workloads.

Scaling up or scaling out

Once the total CPU and memory resource requirements have been calculated, the amount of resources per host must be determined. Host resources can be designed based on two resource-scaling methodologies: scaling up or scaling out.

When scaling up, fewer, larger hosts are used to satisfy the resource requirements. More virtual machines run on a single host; because of this, more virtual machines are also affected by a host failure.

When scaling out, many smaller hosts are used to satisfy the resource requirements. Fewer virtual machines run on a single host, and fewer virtual machines will be affected by a host failure.

How to do it...

Refer the following steps to design for scaling up or scaling out:

1. Determine whether the host in the environment should scale up or scale out.
2. Determine the number of virtual machine workloads per host.
3. Based on the number of virtual machines per host, calculate the number of hosts that are required. This should also include the number of hosts required to support growth and failover:

(Number of Workloads / Number of Workloads per Host) + (Number of Future Workloads / Number of Workloads per Host) + Number of Failover Hosts = Number of Physical Hosts Required

4. Using the identified CPU requirements, calculate the CPU resources required per host:

Total CPU Resources Required / (Number of Physical Hosts Required - Failover Hosts) = CPU Resources per Host

5. Using the identified memory requirements, calculate the memory resources that are required per host:

Total Memory Resources Required / (Number of Physical Hosts Required - Failover Hosts) = Memory Resources per Host

How it works...

Many CPU and memory resources were calculated in the earlier recipes in this chapter, and are as follows:

- The total number of CPU resources required is 167 GHz
- The total number of memory resources required, taking into account a 25% savings for transparent page sharing, is 657 GB

Based on the design factors, the determination can be made on whether a host should be designed to scale up or scale out. In this case, the following design information provides what is needed to size the individual host resources:

- Currently, there are 100 physical servers, each hosting a single application. Each application services 10 customers
- No more than 20 application servers (or 200 customers) should be affected by a hardware failure
- The business expects to add 50 new customers over the next year
- Support growth over the next five years

Based on the requirements, the total number of hosts that are required to support the current workloads, the future workloads, and the redundancy requirements can be calculated as follows:

Total Hosts Required = (100 physical servers / 20 virtual servers per host) + [((50 new customers x 5 years) / 10) / 20] + 2 failover hosts = 8.25 = 9 Physical Hosts Required

Use the following equation to determine the number of CPU resources that are required per host (the failover hosts are not included here because these resources are effectively reserved for failover):

167 GHz / 7 = 23.8 GHz CPU per Host

Use the following equation to determine the number of memory resources that are required per host (as with CPU resources, the failover hosts are not included in the calculation):

657 GB / 7 = ~94 GB Memory per Host

Each physical host will need to be sized to support 20 virtual machines, and will require 23.8 GHz of CPU resources and 94 GB of memory resources.

There's more...

The requirements from `Chapter 3`, *The Design Factors*, are very specific about the maximum number of virtual machines that can be run on a host. This simplifies the scale-up or scale-out design decision. The following are a couple of other possible design requirements to work through to demonstrate the impact that scaling up and scaling out will have on resources:

- What if a requirement was to virtualize the environment using three hosts? What resources would be required for each host? If there are 100 virtual machines, how many will be impacted during a host hardware failure?
- What if the requirement was that each host should be configured with resources to support no more than 10 virtual machines? How will that change the number of resources required for each host? If there are 100 virtual machines, how many will be impacted during a host hardware failure?

Determining the vCPU-to-core ratio

The number of virtual machine vCPUs allocated compared to the number of physical CPU cores available is the vCPU-to-core ratio. Determining this ratio will depend on the CPU utilization of the workloads.

If the workloads are CPU-intensive, the vCPU-to-core ratio will need to be smaller; if the workloads are not CPU-intensive, the vCPU-to-core ratio can be larger. A typical vCPU-to-core ratio for server workloads is about 4:1—four vCPUs allocated for each available physical core. However, this can be much higher if workloads are not CPU-intensive.

A vCPU-to-core ratio that is too large can result in high CPU ready times—the percentage of time that a virtual machine is ready but is unable to be scheduled to run on the physical CPU—which will have a negative impact on the virtual machine's performance.

How to do it...

Refer the following steps to determine the vCPU-to-core ratio:

1. Determine the number of vCPUs that are required, as follows:

vCPUs per Workload x Number of Workloads Per Host = Number of vCPUs Required

2. Determine the vCPU-to-core ratio based on the CPU utilization of the workloads. If the workloads are CPU-intensive, the vCPU-to-CPU-core ratio will be lower; for less CPU-intensive workloads, the ratio will be higher. The ratio of 4:1 is generally a good starting point for server workloads.

3. Calculate the number of CPU cores that are required to support the vCPU-to-CPU-core ratio:

Number of vCPUs / vCPU-to-core ratio = Number of Cores Required

How it works...

The vCPU-to-core ratio is calculated based on the number of vCPUs allocated and the number of physical CPU cores available. For example, if two vCPUs are allocated to each virtual machine, the following applies:

2 vCPUs allocated to each virtual machine x 20 virtual machines = 40 vCPUs

In a design with 40 vCPUs that requires a 4:1 vCPU-to-core ratio, a minimum of 10 physical cores would be required.

If dual 8-core processors are used, the vCPU-to-core ratio can be calculated as follows:

2 x 8 Cores = 16 Total Cores

40 vCPUs and Physical 16 Cores = 2.5 vCPUs to each physical core, or a 2.5:1 vCPU-to-core Ratio

Clustering compute resources

A **vSphere cluster** is a group of ESXi hosts. The CPU, memory, storage, and network resources of each host are combined to form a logical set of cluster resources. A vSphere cluster is required to facilitate the use of features such as vSphere HA, vSphere DRS, and Fault Tolerance.

A single vSphere 5.x cluster can contain up to 32 hosts. For vSphere features such as vSphere HA and DRS to work correctly, the configurations must be consistent across all hosts in the cluster. The consistency of shared storage and network configurations is a necessity.

How to do it...

Refer the following steps to create a vSphere cluster:

1. Using the vSphere Web Client, create a new vSphere cluster
2. Enable vSphere High Availability on the cluster
3. Enable vSphere Distributed Resource Scheduling on the cluster

How it works...

A new cluster is created by using either the vSphere Web Client or the vSphere Client. Right-click on the data center object in which you want the cluster to be created and select **New Cluster**. The **New Cluster** dialog will open, as shown in the following screenshot:

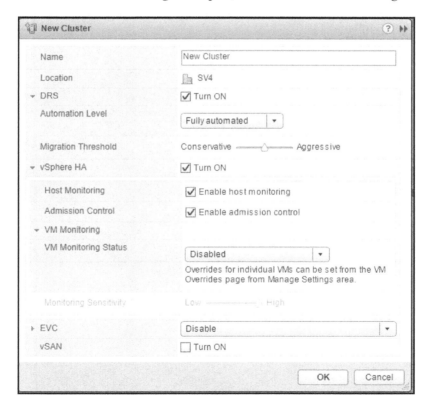

Creating a new cluster

A name must be provided for the cluster. Other cluster options, such as enabling DRS and vSphere HA, can be configured during the new cluster creation, or can be configured at a later time by editing the properties of the cluster.

Once the cluster has been created, hosts can be added to the cluster. New hosts are added to the cluster with the **Add Host** wizard if you right-click on the cluster and select **Add Host**. Existing hosts can be added to the cluster by dragging and dropping the host inventory object into the new cluster. The cluster's **Summary** tab displays the available cluster resources, the cluster resource usage, and details about the vSphere DRS and vSphere HA configurations:

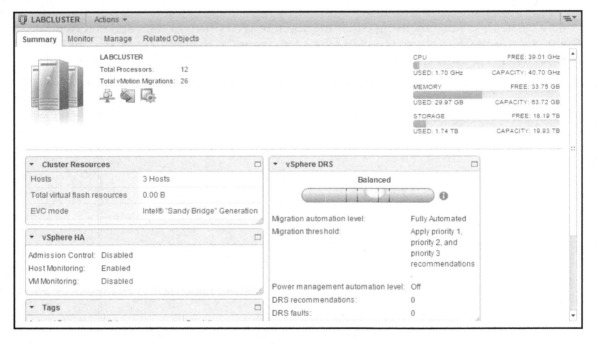

Cluster summary tab

Hosts within a cluster should be configured with similar compute resources. In a cluster where the VMware DRS is enabled, processor compatibility is required. Checking for processor compatibility will be covered later in this chapter.

Reserving HA resources to support failover

When vSphere **High Availability** (**HA**) has been enabled on a vSphere cluster, the virtual machines running on the cluster are protected from a host hardware failure or virtual machine guest operating system crash.

In the event that a host suffers a hardware failure, or if ESXi crashes, the virtual machines are restarted on the surviving hosts in the cluster. Resources must be reserved in the cluster to guarantee that the necessary resources are available to restart the virtual machines.

How to do it...

Refer the following steps to reserve HA resources to support failover:

1. Edit the settings of the vSphere cluster to enable high availability
2. Enable the HA Admission Control policy
3. Select the HA Admission Control policy that should be applied to the cluster
4. Define the failover settings that are required, based on the HA Admission Control policy that's selected

How it works...

VMware HA Admission Control ensures that enough physical resources are available to meet the CPU and memory reservation requirements needed to restart the virtual machines on surviving hosts, in case there is a host failure:

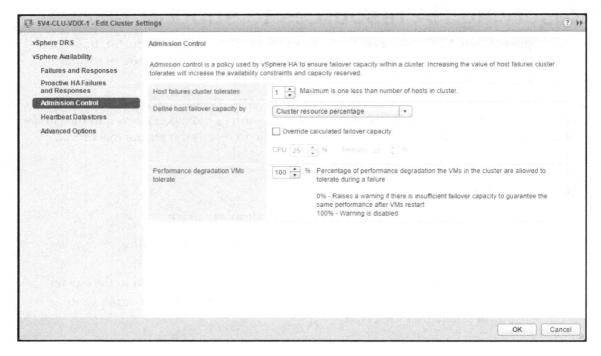

Configuring cluster admission control settings

When HA Admission Control is enabled, virtual machines cannot be powered on if there are insufficient resources to meet the reservation requirements for the virtual machines that are protected in the HA cluster. The resource requirements are calculated based on the HA Admission Control policy that's selected.

In vSphere 6.7, there are three HA admission control policies:

- Define failover capacity by static number of hosts
- Define failover capacity by reserving a percentage of the cluster resources
- Use dedicated failover hosts

The **Define failover capacity by static number of hosts** policy (for vSphere client: **Host failures cluster tolerates**) reserves failover resources based on the slot size. The slot size is determined by the largest CPU and memory reservation for a virtual machine that has been powered on. The number of slots available in the cluster and the number of slots to be reserved based on the failover capacity selection are calculated by HA.

A single virtual machine with a large memory or CPU reservation will have an impact on the number of slots available. The value of **Fixed slot size**, which can be configured using the vSphere Web Client, defines the amount of CPU and memory resources that make up a slot. In the versions of vSphere prior to 5.1, the slot size could be configured with the vSphere Client by setting the HA advanced options as `das.slotCPUInMHz` for CPU resources and as `das.slotMeminMB` for memory resources.

Using the **Define failover capacity by reserving a percentage of the cluster resources** policy (for vSphere Client: **Percentage of cluster resources reserved as failover spare capacity**) allows for a percentage of the memory and CPU resources to be reserved to accommodate a host failure. This reservation is distributed across all hosts in the cluster. To guarantee resource availability in the event of a host failure, the percentage should be set to reserve the CPU and memory resources equal to a single host in a cluster; for example, for a five-host cluster, 20 percent of cluster resources should be reserved. This will guarantee that enough resources are available to support a single host failure.

The **Use dedicated failover hosts** policy (for vSphere Client: **Specify failover hosts**) reserves a configured host to be available for failover. The hosts that are specified as failover hosts will not provide resources to virtual machines during normal operations. The host is a hot spare, and virtual machines will only be started on the hosts.

If HA Admission Control is disabled, virtual machines can be powered on, even if there are not enough resources available to ensure failover capacity. If the surviving hosts are not able to provide the resources with the necessary reservations to start the virtual machines, the virtual machines will not be restarted when a host fails.

Using distributed resource scheduling to balance cluster resources

The vSphere DRS determines the initial placement of virtual machines and balances resources across available host resources in a vSphere cluster. Virtual machine resources can be guaranteed or limited. Rules can be applied to keep virtual machines together on the same host, or to ensure that virtual machines run on separate hosts.

How to do it...

Refer the following steps to implement and configure DRS:

1. Edit the settings of the vSphere cluster to enable vSphere DRS
2. Select a value for the **DRS Automation Level** that should be applied to the DRS-enabled cluster
3. Select a value for the **Migration Threshold** that should be applied to the DRS-enabled cluster

How it works...

vSphere DRS can be enabled when creating a new vSphere cluster, or by editing the settings of an existing cluster:

Enabling vSphere DRS

When DRS is enabled, the **DRS Automation Level** and **Migration Threshold** are set to determine how DRS will place and migrate virtual machines between hosts in the cluster to balance the resources across all hosts in the cluster.

If the **Automation Level** is set to **Manual**, vCenter will make suggestions for initial virtual machine placement and virtual machine migrations. When a virtual machine is powered on, DRS makes a suggestion for the initial placement of the virtual machine based on the balance of cluster resources, but this must be acknowledged by (or can be changed by) the administrator. Migrations will not be performed unless they are acknowledged by an administrator.

Setting the **Automation Level** to **Partially Automated** will make vCenter automatically select a cluster host to place the virtual machine at power-on, but it will only make recommendations for virtual machine migrations. Migrations are not performed unless they are acknowledged by an administrator.

When the **Automation Level** is set to **Fully Automated**, it allows vCenter to automatically determine the initial placement of virtual machines. This setting also causes vCenter to automatically migrate virtual machines between the hosts in the cluster, in order to balance resource usage across all cluster hosts. When the **Automation Level** is set to **Fully Automated**, virtual machines will also automatically be migrated to other hosts in the cluster when a host is placed in the maintenance mode.

 The default DRS migration threshold will typically provide the best balance for most clusters. If the cluster resources are not balanced or if too many DRS migrations are being invoked, the migration threshold can be adjusted to be either more conservative or more aggressive.

The **Migration Threshold** determines how the cluster will be balanced when the **Automation Level** is set to **Fully Automated,** or how DRS recommendations will be generated when the **Automation Level** is set to **Manual** or **Partially Automated**.

A conservative migration threshold setting will only cause virtual machines to migrate if the migration will result in a significant improvement in the balance of resources. Setting the migration threshold to be more aggressive will cause the virtual machines to migrate if any benefit can be realized from the migration. Setting the migration threshold to be too aggressive can result in unnecessary virtual machine migrations, or virtual machines constantly migrating in an attempt to aggressively balance the resources.

Ensuring cluster vMotion compatibility

vMotion allows running virtual machines to be migrated between vSphere hosts. To facilitate live vMotion, the processors between hosts must contain the same CPU features and present the same instruction sets. **Enhanced vMotion Compatibility (EVC)** masks compatibility issues between the hosts in a cluster.

> Enabling EVC on a cluster ensures that hosts that are added to the cluster in the future will not have vMotion compatibility issues.

Processors must be from the same manufacturer; EVC does not provide vMotion compatibility between Intel and AMD processors. EVC is not required to support HA across different processor types and only supports live vMotion between hosts.

How to do it...

Refer the following steps to enable EVC:

1. Edit the settings of the vSphere cluster
2. Change the value of **EVC Mode** to **Enable EVC** and select an EVC mode baseline

How it works...

The EVC mode is enabled on the cluster when the cluster is created, or by editing the properties of the cluster. The EVC baseline is selected based on the processor manufacturer (EVC for AMD hosts or EVC for Intel hosts). The selected baseline compatibility is validated against all hosts in the cluster.

The following screenshot shows the EVC mode enabled for Intel hosts and the mode set to **Intel "Sandy Bridge" Generation**:

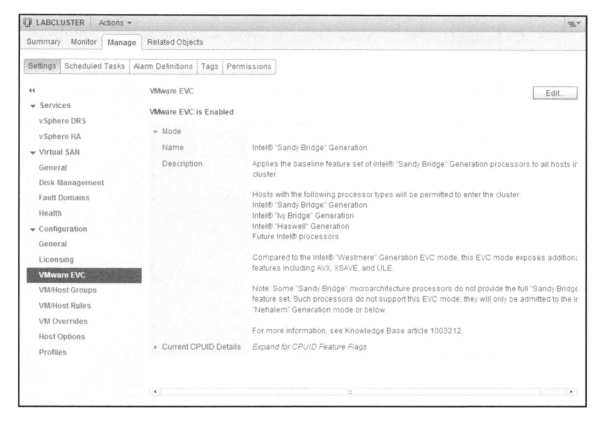

Example EVC configuration

The EVC baseline configuration and the processor supported for each EVC baseline can be found in the *VMware Knowledge Base* at `http://kb.vmware.com/kb/1003212`.

Using resource pools

Resource pools are logical abstractions of resources that can be grouped into hierarchies to reserve or limit CPU and memory resources to virtual machines and subordinate resource pools. Shares, limits, and reservations can be applied to a pool, and can be expanded from child pools to parent pools.

How to do it...

Refer the following steps to configure resource pools:

1. Understand how resource pool shares, reservations, and limits are applied.
2. Create and configure resource pools to reserve or limit resources to virtual machines. The following screenshot shows how a resource pool is created and configured with **Shares**, **Reservations**, and a **Limit** for **CPU** and **Memory** resources:

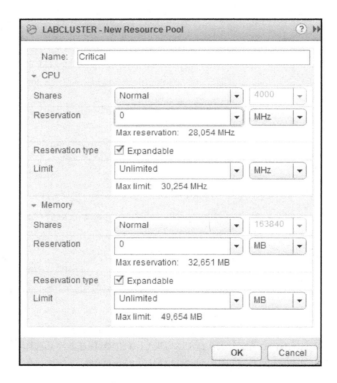

Example resource pool configuration

How it works...

Resource pools are used to define how CPU and memory resources are shared between virtual machines during times of contention, to guarantee CPU and memory resources to a group of virtual machines, and to limit the amount of resources available to virtual machines.

When you are creating a resource pool, the following resource allocations can be applied:

- **Share**: This is used during the time of CPU or memory contention to determine how virtual machines will be scheduled against available CPU and memory resources. Access to the resources is relative to the number of shares allocated. Each virtual machine in a resource pool receives a percentage of the shares that are available to the pool.
- **Reservation**: The CPU and memory resources that are guaranteed to the resource pool. Reservations can be set to expandable, which means that if there are not enough resources in the pool to meet the reservation, it can expand into the parent. If resources are not available to meet the reservation, virtual machines cannot be powered on.
- **Limit**: The upper limit of CPU and memory resources that are available to the resource pool. If a limit is configured, the resource pool will not exceed this limit, even when additional resources are available.

Resource pools can be configured in a hierarchy of parents and children. This can be helpful in delegating shares, reservations, and limits to multiple applications or departments. The following diagram provides a logical example of how resource pools can be used to allocate available resources between **CriticalVM** workloads and **DEV/TEST** environments:

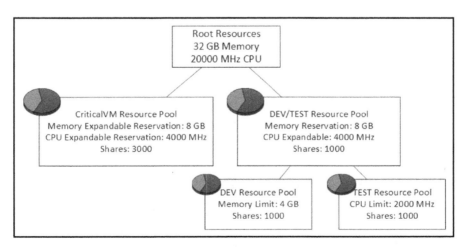

Resource pool shares example

The resources that are available and consumed by virtual machines in a resource pool can be viewed in vSphere Web Client, as shown in the following screenshot:

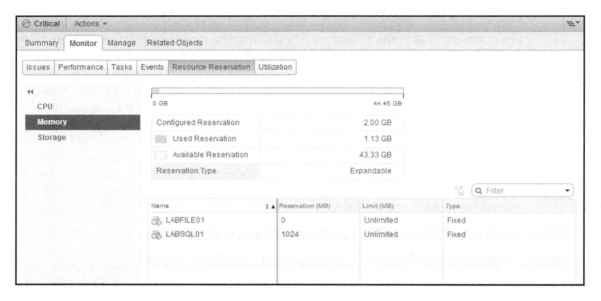

Resource pool monitoring

Notice that the **Configured Reservation** of the pool is set to **2.00 GB**, but the **Available Reservation** is 43.33 GB. Since the **Reservation Type** is set to **Expandable**, the memory resources in the parent resource pool, in this case, the cluster, are available to this resource pool.

Resource pools add complexity to a design and should only be used if necessary. Do not use resource pools for the organization of virtual machines.

Providing Fault Tolerance protection

vSphere **Fault Tolerance** (**FT**) provides protection from a host or storage hardware failures for critical virtual machines by enabling a secondary running copy of the virtual machine, running on a separate host and stored in a different datastore. The secondary virtual machine is identical to the primary protected virtual machine, and failover is instant and transparent:

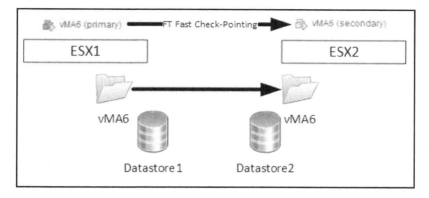

Fault Tolerance example

vSphere FT Fast Checkpointing keeps the primary and secondary virtual machines in sync to allow the secondary virtual machine to instantly take over, should the primary virtual machine be impacted by a host or storage failure.

How to do it...

To configure Fault Tolerance, refer the following steps:

1. Identify the use cases for vSphere FT
2. Identify the requirements for enabling vSphere FT
3. Enable vSphere FT for a virtual machine
4. Test vSphere FT for an enabled virtual machine

How it works...

FT protects critical virtual machines against host and storage hardware failures. Prior to vSphere 6, FT only supported a single vCPU virtual machine. Support for **vSMP (Symmetric Multi-Processing)** now provides more use cases for utilizing FT to protect virtual machines, including the following:

- Protecting critical virtual machines with up to 4 vCPUs and 64 GB memory.
- Reducing the complexity of other clustering services.
- Protecting applications sensitive to the loss of TCP connections. FT failover maintains TCP connections between clients and the protected virtual machine.

The requirements for enabling FT protection for a virtual machine are as follows:

- 10 GbE network connectivity between hosts when protecting multi-vCPU virtual machines.
- vSphere 6 FT supports virtual disks provisioned as thin, thick, or eager-zeroed thick.
- Up to four FT protected (primary or secondary) virtual machines, with up to 8 vCPUs total per host. For example, across two hosts, four virtual machines, with two vCPU each, can be protected.
- All virtual machine allocated memory will be reserved for both the primary and secondary virtual machines when FT is enabled.
- NFS v3 and block storage are supported. VSAN, VVOLS, and NFS v4.1 datastores are not supported for primary or secondary FT protected virtual machines.

FT requires 10 GbE to protect virtual machines with multiple vCPUs. If it is protecting a single vCPU virtual machine, 1 GbE can be used. The Fault Tolerance logging service must be enabled on a VMkernel port, as shown in the following screenshot:

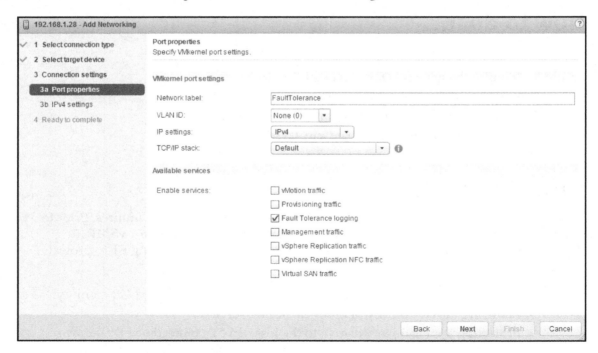

Configuring VMkernel port for Fault Tolerance networking

To enable FT for a virtual machine, select the virtual machine in the inventory, right-click it, and, from the **Fault Tolerance** menu, **Turn On Fault Tolerance**, as follows:

Turning on Fault Tolerance

The **Turn On Fault Tolerance** wizard will prompt for a host to run the initial secondary virtual machine and the datastore to store the secondary virtual machine configuration file, VMDK files, and tie breaker file. These should be stored in a separate datastore from the primary virtual machine, but can be stored together on the same datastore; this will not provide protection against a storage outage.

When FT is enabled, a secondary virtual machine is created on a different host from the primary virtual machine and the virtual disks are copied to the selected datastore. Once enabled, the vSphere Web Client displays the **Fault Tolerance status**, **Secondary VM location**, and the **Log bandwidth usage** for the FT protected virtual machine on the virtual machine's **Summary** page, as shown in the following screenshot:

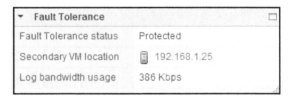

Viewing Fault Tolerance summary

Once FT has been enabled on a virtual machine, it can be tested by selecting **Test Failover** from the **Fault Tolerance** menu of the virtual machine, as follows:

Test Failover option for Fault Tolerance

When testing failover, the secondary virtual machine becomes the primary virtual machine, and a new secondary virtual machine is created.

Leveraging host flash

Virtual Flash enables the use of **Solid State Disks** (**SSD**) or PCIe-based flash storage in ESXi hosts to accelerate the performance of virtual machines by providing read caching and host swapping.

How to do it...

Refer the following steps to leverage host flash:

1. Configure local SSDs or flash devices as a Virtual Flash Resource
2. Configure **vSphere Flash Read Cache** (**vFRC**) for virtual machine disks
3. Allocate Virtual Flash capacity for the host swap cache

How it works...

Configuring local SSDs for use as a Virtual Flash Resource is done from the ESXi host settings' **Virtual Flash Resource Management** menu. Adding capacity will display the flash devices that are eligible to be used as Virtual Flash Resources, as shown in the following screenshot:

Adding a virtual flash resource

Flash devices that are selected as Virtual Flash cache are formatted with a **Virtual Flash File System** (**VFFS**), and the capacity can only be used for Virtual Flash Resource.

Once flash capacity has been added, the virtual machines are configured to consume the Virtual Flash Resource as vFRC. vFRC is configured per virtual machine disk.

Configuring the flash read cache for a virtual machine is done by using **Edit Settings**. Select the virtual machine hard disk to configure for **Virtual Flash Read Cache**, **Enable virtual Flash Read Cache**, and allocate the amount of cache to reserve and the **Block Size** for the virtual machine, as shown in the following screenshot:

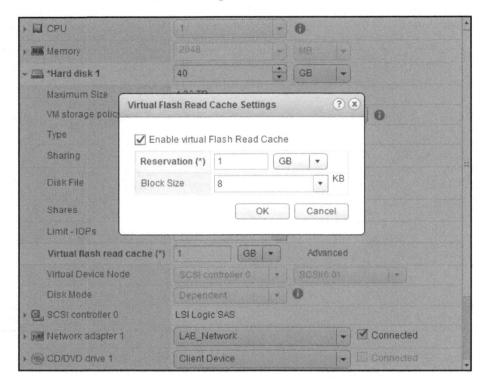

Enabling virtual Flash Read Cache

A portion of Virtual Flash Resource capacity can be reserved for the host swap cache. This cache can be shared by all virtual machines running on the host and provides low-latency caching for virtual machine swap files. Using Virtual Flash Resources for host caching will reduce the performance impact on the virtual machines, should VMkernel swapping occur.

vSphere Physical Design 8

The vSphere physical design process (as shown in the following diagram) includes choosing and configuring the physical that's hardware required to support storage, network, and compute requirements:

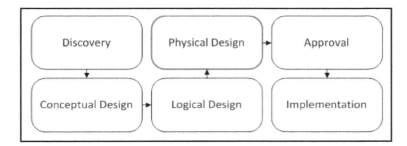

Physical design in the vSphere design workflow

During the physical design process, the hardware and configuration choices should map to the logical design and satisfy the functional and nonfunctional design requirements.

A design architect should answer the following questions about each design decision:

- Does the design meet the requirements of the logical design?
- Does the design satisfy the functional and nonfunctional requirements?
- Is the selected hardware supported?

There will often be more than one physical solution that will meet the design requirements. The job of the architect is to choose hardware to provide the resources that are required while meeting the design requirements and constraints.

This chapter will contain recipes for using VMware's Hardware Compatibility List, the physical design of storage, network and compute resources, creating a custom ESXi image, and the best practices for BIOS settings on a server running ESXi. This chapter will also provide an overview of methods for upgrading existing ESXi hosts.

In this chapter, we will cover the following recipes:

- Using the VMware **Hardware Compatibility List (HCL)**
- Understanding the physical storage design
- Understanding the physical network design
- Creating the physical compute design
- Creating a custom ESXi image
- The best practices for ESXi host BIOS settings
- Upgrading an ESXi host

Using the VMware Hardware Compatibility List

VMware's Hardware Compatibility List is a database of all of the tested and supported physical hardware. The physical hardware that's chosen to support the created design must be checked against the HCL to ensure that it will be supported. This includes storage devices, I/O devices, and servers. It is important to ensure not only that the hardware vendor and model are supported, but also that the firmware version of the hardware is supported.

Verifying support against the HCL is important not only for new designs, but also when upgrading a design from one version to another in vSphere. Legacy hardware is often removed from the HCL when new versions of vSphere are released.

How to do it...

To verify whether a certain hardware device is supported in the current version of vSphere, perform the following process:

1. Visit `http://www.vmware.com/go/hcl/`.

2. Select the type or category of device to determine its compatibility by selecting it using the **What are you looking for** drop-down menu. For example, if the compatibility of a **Network Interface Card** (**NIC**) is being determined, select **IO Devices**, as shown in the following screenshot:

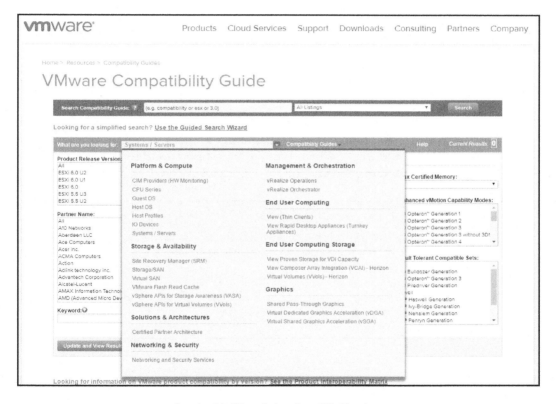

Screenshot of the VMware Hardware Compatibility List webpage

3. Select values for the **Product Release Version, Brand Name,** and **IO Device Type**, as shown in the following screenshot:

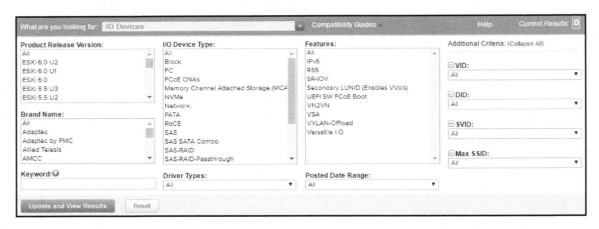

IO device options in the VMware HCL

4. Enter a value for **Keyword**, such as the model number. In this example, the search will be for NC364T, which is an HP quad port 1 GB server adapter, as shown in the following screenshot:

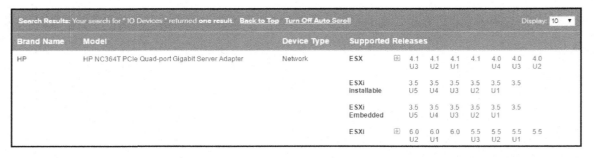

Example output of IO devices in the VMware HCL

5. Clicking on the device model will display details about the device, the firmware versions that are supported, and the device driver that's used by ESXi, as shown in the following screenshot:

Example output after choosing a device model in the VMware HCL

How it works...

The VMware HCL provides an easy-to-search online database of hardware that has been tested and is supported in a vSphere environment.

> Hardware that is not listed on VMware's Hardware Compatibility List may still work with vSphere. However, if the hardware is not listed on the HCL, it may cause issues in regards to obtaining support from VMware in the event of issues with the environment. Only hardware found on the HCL should be used in vSphere production environments.

Selecting the hardware type, VMware product and version, hardware vendor, device type, and supported features allows a design architect to quickly view and select supported hardware. Details about the supported firmware or BIOS versions, the availability of native drivers, and the requirements for third-party drivers can also be viewed quickly for hardware information on the HCL.

There's more...

VMware also provides compatibility guides. The compatibility guides can be accessed through a menu on the HCL page, located at `http://www.vmware.com/go/hcl`. These guides provide details about the features that are supported by a specific piece of supported hardware, and can be seen in the following screenshot:

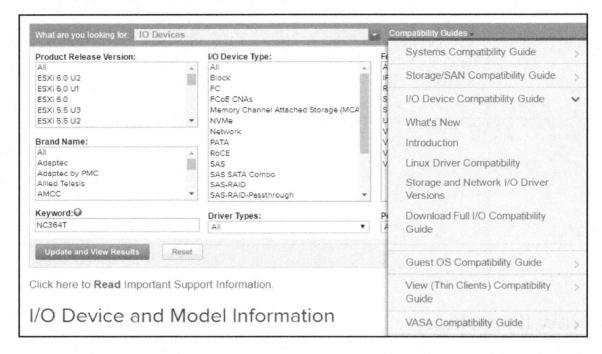

Listing the compatibility guides directly from the HCL webpage

The following screenshot is an excerpt from the **Storage/SAN Compatibility Guide**, showing the support details of the EMC VNX series arrays:

EMC	VNX5100	FC	VMW_SATP_ALUA_CX / VMW_PSP_FIXED *13, 34, 74 VMW_SATP_ALUA_CX *13, 34, 74, 80, 182, 24, 148, 158, 196, 76, 168, 187, 260, 171, 201, 202, 270, 243, 172, 271, 272, 273, 274, 275	DGC
EMC	VNX5200	FC	VMW_SATP_ALUA_CX *13, 34, 74, 80, 182, 24, 148, 158, 196, 76, 168, 187, 260, 171, 201, 202, 270, 243, 172, 271, 272, 273, 274, 275	RAID5
EMC	VNX5300	FC	VMW_SATP_ALUA_CX / VMW_PSP_FIXED *13, 34, 74 VMW_SATP_ALUA_CX *13, 34, 74, 80, 182, 24, 148, 158, 196, 76, 168, 187, 260, 171, 201, 202, 270, 243, 172, 271, 272, 273, 274, 275	DGC
EMC	VNX5400	FC	VMW_SATP_ALUA_CX *13, 34, 74, 80, 182, 24, 148, 158, 196, 76, 168, 187, 260, 171, 201, 202, 270, 243, 172, 271, 272, 273, 274, 275	RAID5
EMC	VNX5500	FC	VMW_SATP_ALUA_CX *13, 34, 74, 80, 182, 24, 148, 158, 196, 76, 168, 187, 260, 171, 201, 202, 270, 243, 172, 271, 272, 273, 274, 275 VMW_SATP_ALUA_CX / VMW_PSP_FIXED *13, 34, 74, 24	DGC

Example EMC VNX support output from the HCL

Another important guide to reference is VMware's *Product Interoperability Matrix*, located at `http://partnerweb.vmware.com/comp_guide2/sim/interop_matrix.php`. This guide provides interoperability information about vSphere products, databases, and host operating systems. If multiple VMware products will be used in the storage design, their interoperability must be checked against the matrix to determine which versions are compatible with which products.

For example, if the VMware **Site Recovery Manager (SRM)** is going to be used in a vSphere 6.7 design, the interoperability matrix can be checked to determine which versions of SRM are compatible with that version of ESXi 6.7:

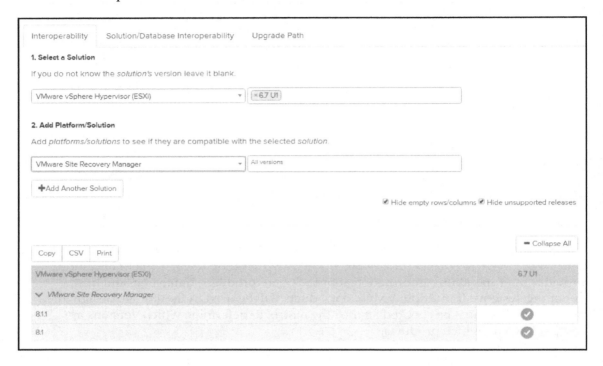

Example ESXi and SRM compatibility output from the VMware Product Interoperability Matrix

The VMware compatibility guides are also available from the **Product Interoperability Matrixes** page.

In addition to VMware interoperability pages, hardware vendors usually have their own interoperability pages that they require you to adhere to when running their hardware. For example, a common vSphere design includes VMware vSphere on Cisco UCS blade servers. If you call Cisco for technical support, one of the first things they'll do is verify on their own HCL whether they support your configuration. If not, they'll likely ask you to update your environment to a supported state before they'll put too much time into troubleshooting. The following screenshot shows Cisco's HCL:

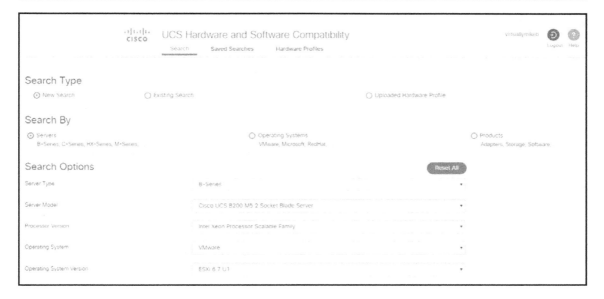

Cisco's UCS Hardware Compatibility List

Understanding the physical storage design

Storage is the foundation of any vSphere design. Properly designed storage is key for vSphere features like **High Availability (HA)**, **Distributed Resource Scheduling** (DRS), and **Fault Tolerance (FT)**, to operate.

How to do it...

Performance, capacity, availability, and recoverability are all factors that must be taken into account when determining the hardware and the configuration of the physical storage. The physical storage design requires that you follow these steps:

1. Select a storage hardware that satisfies the logical storage design. This includes the storage array, storage host bus adapters, and any switching, fiber channel, or Ethernet that may be required to support storage connectivity.
2. Verify the compatibility of each storage hardware component by using the VMware HCL.
3. Design the storage configuration to satisfy the design factors related to availability, recoverability, performance, and capacity.

How it works...

The physical storage design must meet the capacity and performance requirements that are defined by the logical storage design, and these requirements must be mapped back to the design factors.

The logical storage design identifies the capacity, IOPS, and throughput that are required to support the vSphere design. The design factors identify the functional requirements, such as availability and recoverability, and any constraints that may be placed on the physical design, such as using an array from a specific vendor or using a specific storage protocol.

The logical storage design specifications are as follows:

- **Storage capacity**: 16 TB
- **Storage IOPS**: 6,250
- **I/O profile**: 8 k
- **I/O size**: 90% Read/10% Write
- **Total storage throughput**: 55 MB/s
- **Number of virtual machines per datastore**: 20
- **Datastore size**: 2.5 TB

The factors that influence the physical storage design are as follows:

- Shared or local storage
- Block storage or file storage
- Array specifications, such as active/active or active/passive, the number of storage processors, and the cache
- Storage protocol that uses fiber channel, iSCSI, NFS, or **Fiber Channel over Ethernet (FCoE)**, as well as the type and number of disks and the RAID configuration
- Support for VMware integration: **vStorage APIs for Array Integration (VAAI)** and **vSphere APIs for Storage Awareness (VASA)**
- Support for advanced storage technologies: deduplication, tiering, and flash-based cache
- The **Recovery Point Objective (RPO)**, which is the amount of data that will not be lost in the event of a disaster, and the **Recovery Time Objective (RTO)**, which is the amount of time it takes to recover the system and data in the event of a disaster

The chief considerations when choosing a storage platform are IOPS, throughput, and support for features such as VAAI, VASA, SRM, and accelerated backups. The physical storage design should focus on both performance and capacity. The physical storage design must be able to meet the performance requirements of the design.

Meeting the design capacity requirements is typically easy to accomplish, but ensuring that the storage will meet the performance requirements takes a bit more work. The I/O profile of the workloads, the number of IOPS required, the types of disks used, and the RAID level that is selected all have an impact on the storage performance. It is good practice to first design the storage to meet the performance requirements, and then design it to meet the capacity requirements.

Understanding the physical network design

Network connectivity must be provided for both virtual machine network connectivity and VMkernel connectivity. Physical switches, uplinks, virtual switches, and virtual port groups are all components of the physical network design.

How to do it...

Performance, capacity, availability, and recoverability are all factors that must be taken into account when determining the hardware and the configuration of the physical network. The following steps are necessary to successfully complete the physical network design:

1. Select the network hardware that satisfies the logical network design, including physical network switches and network interface cards.
2. Verify whether the network I/O device hardware, such as network interface cards and **Converged Network Adapters (CNAs)**, are compatible and supported by using the VMware HCL.
3. Design the physical network topology and virtual network configuration to satisfy the design factors related to availability, recoverability, performance, and capacity.

How it works...

The physical network design must satisfy the performance and availability requirements that are defined by the logical network design, which, in turn, must support the design factors. The logical network design identifies the capacity requirements, and the design factors define the availability and recoverability requirements.

Aside from providing virtual machine connectivity, many vSphere features, such as High Availability, vMotion, and Fault Tolerance, have specific virtual and physical network connectivity requirements that must be taken into account when designing the physical network. If IP-connected storage like iSCSI or NFS is used, the physical network connectivity for these must also be included as part of the physical network design.

The logical network design specifications are as follows:

- **Total virtual machine throughput**: 1000 Mbps
- **Virtual machines per host**: 20
- **Virtual machine throughput per host**: 200 Mbps
- **IP storage**: iSCSI
- **Storage throughput**: 55 MB/s
- **vMotion/DRS**: Enabled

The factors that influence the physical network design include the following:

- The number and type of the physical switches
- The topology of the existing physical network
- Using either physically or logically separated (such as VLANs) networks
- The number of physical uplinks per host
- The physical adapter type: 1 GB or 10 GB
- Teaming and link aggregation
- Network bandwidth and throughput
- Failover and failback policies
- The quality of service and traffic shaping
- The type of virtual switches to use: virtual standard switches or virtual distributed switches
- The networks required for VMkernels to support management, vMotion, Fault Tolerance, and IP-connected storage

In the following diagram of an example virtual and physical network design, the VLANs and virtual standard switches have been configured to distinguish traffic types; single points of failure have been minimized by using multiple uplinks, and failover policies have been configured to provide redundancy and performance:

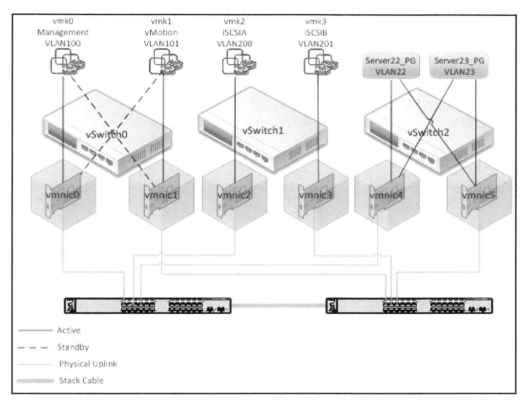

Example physical and virtual network design

Creating the physical compute design

The physical compute design selects the CPU and memory resources to meet the requirements of the design. Aside from the CPU and memory resources, the physical compute design also includes selecting the form factor to support the interface cards that are necessary to support the design.

How to do it...

Like with other parts of the physical design, the performance, capacity, availability, and recoverability are all factors to consider in the physical compute design. The following steps can be performed to create the physical compute design:

1. Select server hardware that satisfies the logical compute design
2. Verify the compatibility of each component of the compute hardware by using the VMware HCL
3. Configure compute resources to satisfy the design factors related to availability, recoverability, performance, and capacity

How it works...

The logical compute design defines the capacity and performance requirements for CPU and memory resources.

The logical compute design specifications are as follows:

- **Total CPU resources**: 167 GHz
- **Total memory resources (25% TPS savings)**: 657 GB
- **Number of virtual machines per host**: 20
- **Number of hosts required (N+2)**: 9
- **CPU resources per host**: 23.8 GHz
- **Memory resources per host**: 94 GB

The hardware that's selected for the physical compute design must satisfy the resource requirements of the logical compute design. These resources include the CPU and memory resources. The physical hardware that's selected must also be able to support the network and storage connectivity resources that are defined in the logical network and storage design.

Along with the design requirements and constraints, the factors that influence the physical compute design are as follows:

- The required CPU resources
- The required memory resources
- The vCPU-to-CPU-core ratio

- The processor manufacturer and model
- The number of hosts required: scale up or scale out
- The host form factor: rack or blade
- The number of PCI slots
- The number and type of network uplinks
- The number and type of **Host Bus Adapters** (**HBA**)
- Power, space, and cooling requirements

The following diagram is an example of a physical compute design that uses the Cisco UCS blade platform; the blades have been configured to support the logical requirements, and multiple chassis have been chosen to eliminate single points of failure:

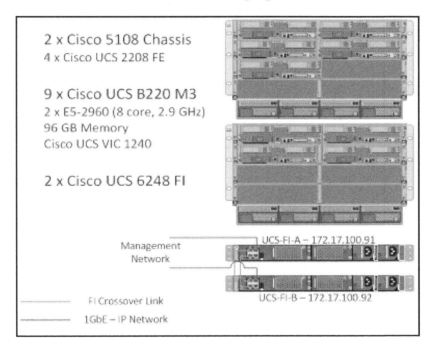

Example physical compute design

The following diagram is the rear view of the Cisco UCS blade solution and shows the supporting components, including the connectivity of the chassis to the fabric interconnects. The diagram also shows connectivity between the fabric interconnects and the network and storage. Multiple links to the chassis, network, and storage not only provide the capacity and performance that are required, but also eliminate single points of failure, as shown in the following diagram:

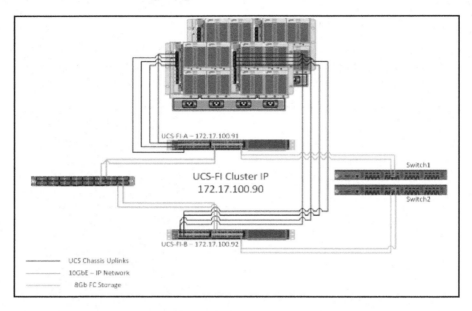

Example Cisco UCS physical compute solution

Creating a custom ESXi image

The drivers for some supported hardware devices are not included as part of the base ESXi image. These devices require that a driver be installed before the hardware can be used in vSphere.

How to do it...

Third-party drivers are packaged as **vSphere Installation Bundles** (**VIBs**). A VIB file is similar to a ZIP archive, in that it is a single file that includes an archive of the driver files, an XML descriptor file, and a signature file. VIB files have the .vib file extension.

The required drivers can be installed after ESXi has been installed using the `esxcli` command:

```
esxcli software vib install -v <path to vib package>
```

When installing from a bundle or ZIP file, the following `esxcli` command can be used:

```
esxcli software vib install -d <full path to vib zip bundle>
```

A custom ESXi image can also be created by using the Image Builder tools that are included with PowerCLI. PowerCLI can be downloaded from `https://www.vmware.com/support/developer/PowerCLI/`. Custom ESXi images can be used when deploying hosts using VMware Auto Deploy, or custom images can be exported to an ISO to be used for installation or upgrades. Perform the following steps to create a custom EXSi image:

1. Download the **ESXi Offline Bundle** from the **My VMware** portal. The following screenshot displays the **ESXi Offline Bundle** download link on the **My VMware** portal:

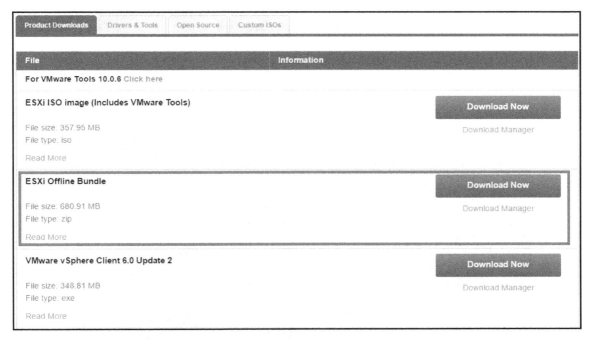

Download the ESXi Offline Bundle

2. Download the required third-party VIB files. This example uses the drivers of QLogic FC-FCoE, which were downloaded from the **My VMware** portal, as shown in the following screenshot:

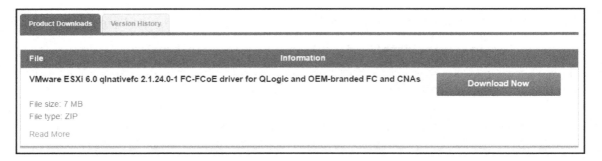

Example download of drivers to install in custom image

3. Use Image Builder PowerCLI to add the **ESXi Offline Bundle** and third-party VIB files as software depots, as follows:

```
Add-EsxSoftwareDepot <pathtoESXiOfflineBundel.zip> Add-
EsxSoftwareDepot <pathto3rdPartyVIB.zip>
```

The following screenshot illustrates adding the **Offline ESXi Bundle** and third-party software bundles by using the Add-EsxSoftwareDepot Image Builder PowerCLI command:

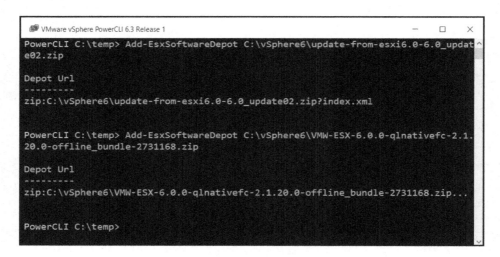

Adding the offline ESXi bundle and third-party software to software depot with PowerCLI

4. List the available software packages to locate the Qlogic drivers, and note the package names:

```
Get-EsxSoftwarePackage | where {$_.Vendor -eq "Qlogic"}
```

The following screenshot illustrates the use of the Get-EsxSoftwarePackage PowerCLI command to locate the package name of the third-party package that will be added to the new ESXi image:

```
VMware vSphere PowerCLI 6.3 Release 1                              —    □    ×

PowerCLI C:\temp> Get-EsxSoftwarePackage | Where {$_.Vendor -eq "Qlogic"}

Name                 Version                        Vendor    Creation
                                                              Date
----                 -------                        ------    ------------
qlnativefc           2.1.20.0-1OEM.600.0.0.2159203  QLogic    4/9/2015 ...


PowerCLI C:\temp>
```

Locating the package name of third-party packages using PowerCLI

5. List the available image profiles by using the following command:

```
Get-EsxImageProfile
```

The following screenshot illustrates the output of the Get-EsxImageProfile PowerCLI command that lists the available profiles:

```
VMware vSphere PowerCLI 6.3 Release 1                              —    □    ×
PowerCLI C:\temp> Get-EsxImageProfile

Name                     Vendor        Last Modified    Acceptance Level
----                     ------        -------------    ----------------
ESXi-6.0.0-20160301001s-no-... VMware, Inc.  3/4/2016 3:3... PartnerSupported
ESXi-6.0.0-20160302001-stan... VMware, Inc.  3/4/2016 3:3... PartnerSupported
ESXi-6.0.0-20160301001s-sta... VMware, Inc.  3/4/2016 3:3... PartnerSupported
ESXi-6.0.0-20160302001-no-t... VMware, Inc.  3/4/2016 3:3... PartnerSupported


PowerCLI C:\temp>
```

Example output of Get-EsxImageProfile in PowerCLI

6. Create a clone of an image profile to apply customization to. The clone will allow the profile to be manipulated without making changes to the original profile:

```
New-EsxImageProfile -CloneProfile <ProfiletoClone> -Name
<CustomProfileName> -Vendor Custom -AcceptanceLevel
PartnerSupported
```

The following screenshot illustrates the output of the `New-EsxImageProfile` PowerCLI command that creates a clone of an existing profile:

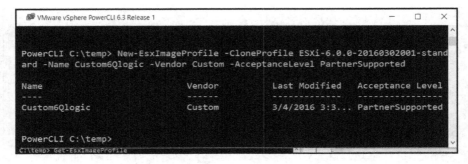

Creating a clone of an existing profile in PowerCLI

7. Add the software packages to the cloned image profile; this step is repeated for each package that needs to be added to the new image profile:

```
Add-EsxSoftwarePackage -ImageProfile <CustomProfileName> -
SoftwarePackage <SoftwarePackagetoAdd>
```

The following screenshot displays the output of the `Add-EsxSoftwarePackage` PowerCLI command when the third-party software package is added to the new ESXi image:

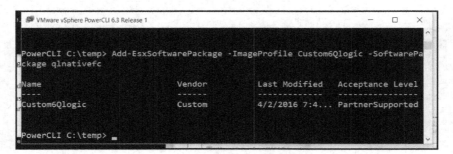

Adding a third-party software package using PowerCLI

8. Create an ISO from the cloned image profile by using the following command; the ISO will include the additional software packages:

```
Export-EsxImageProfile -ImageProfile <CustomProfileName> -
ExportToIso -filepath <Pathtonew.iso>
```

The following screenshot shows the `Export-EsxImageProfile` PowerCLI command. There will be no message output from the command if it completes successfully, but the ESXi image ISO will be created and made available in the provided path:

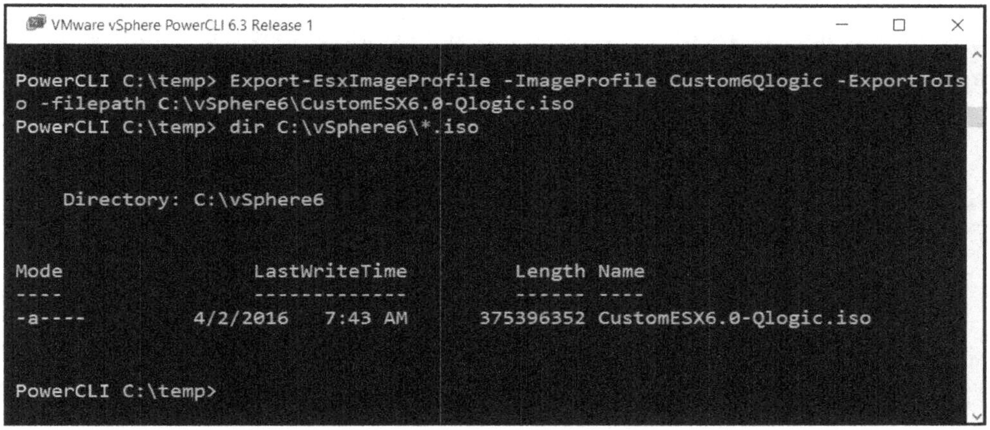

Exporting the new image in PowerCLI

The new ISO image includes the third-party VIB files, and it can be used to install ESXi.

How it works...

The Image Builder PowerCLI commands are used to create a custom image from the ESXi Offline Bundle and the vendor-provided bundle. To maintain the smallest footprint possible, not all supported hardware drivers are included with the native ESXi installation package.

The ESXi Offline Bundle contains multiple profiles: one that includes VMware tools (the standard profile) and one without VMware tools (the no-tools profile). A clone of the profile is created and the vendor software is added to it. When all of the necessary software has been added to the profile, it is exported to an ISO image that can be used to deploy ESXi hosts.

Custom image profiles that are created using the Image Builder PowerCLI commands are also used when using auto deploy to deploy stateless or stateful hosts. The procedure for creating a custom image profile to be used by Auto Deploy is the same, with the exception of the profile being exported to the custom ISO.

There's more...

Custom ESXi ISOs are also provided by manufacturers. Cisco, HP, Hitachi, Fujitsu, and other hardware manufacturers provide these custom ESXi ISO images, which can be downloaded from the **My VMware** portal using the **Custom ISOs** tab, as illustrated in the following screenshot:

Custom ISOs are available to download

These custom ISOs are preconfigured to include the drivers that are necessary for manufacturer-specific hardware.

The best practices for ESXi host BIOS settings

The BIOS settings will vary, depending on the hardware manufacturer and the BIOS version. Supported BIOS versions should be verified on the VMware HCL for the hardware selected. The following screenshot shows the HCL details of a Dell **PowerEdge R620**, with the supported BIOS versions:

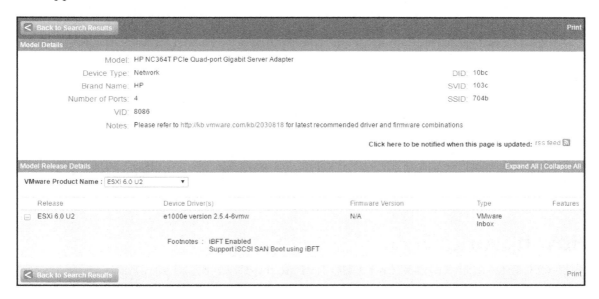

HCL details with supported BIOS versions

If the hardware is supported but the running BIOS version is not supported, the BIOS should be upgraded to a supported version.

How to do it...

The BIOS manufacturer and the BIOS version will determine the BIOS settings available for a particular server. The following settings are provided as a guideline for optimizing the BIOS for an ESXi installation. Ask the hardware vendor for recommendations on settings that are specific to the hardware and BIOS versions:

- Enable Intel VTx or AMD-V
- Enable Intel **Extended Page Tables** (**EPT**) or AMD **Rapid Virtualization Indexing** (**RVI**)
- Disable node interleaving if the system supports **Non-Uniform Memory Architecture** (**NUMA**)
- Enable Turbo Boost if the processor supports it
- Enable **Hyper-Threading** (**HT**) if it's supported by the processor
- Set Intel **Execute Disable** (**XD**) or AMD **No Execute** (**NX**) to **Yes**
- Set power saving features to **OS Control Mode**
- Enable the C1E halt state
- Disable any unnecessary hardware or features (floppy controllers, serial ports, USB controllers, and so on)

How it works...

Intel VTx, **Intel EPT**, **AMD-V**, and **AMD RVI** are hardware-based virtualization technologies that provide extensions to perform tasks that are normally handled by software to improve resource usage and enhance virtual machine performance. Enabling Intel VTx or AMD-V is required if the host will be running 64-bit guests.

If the design calls for disabling large memory pages to realize the advantages of **Transparent Page Sharing** (**TPS**) at times other than when there is memory contention, the Intel EPT or AMD RVI must be disabled. Enabling EPT or RVI will enforce large pages, even if they have been disabled in ESXi. This is not recommended for production environments, but can provide sufficient memory savings in lab or test environments.

If the system is NUMA-capable, the option to enable node interleaving, which will disable NUMA, may be available. Enabling NUMA by disabling node interleaving will provide the best performance. This ensures that memory that's accessed by a processor is local to that processor or in the same NUMA node as that processor.

Enabling Turbo Boost will increase efficiency by balancing CPU workloads over unused cores.

Intel Hyper-Threading allows for multiple threads to run on each core. When HT is enabled, the number of logical processors available is doubled. Each core is able to accept two concurrent threads of instructions.

Setting the power saving features to **OS Control Mode** will allow ESXi to manage power saving on the host. If **OS Control Mode** is not available or supported, power saving features should be disabled. Enabling the C1E halt state increases the power savings.

There's more...

If you're running Cisco UCS servers, it's useful to know that the default BIOS settings are already set to support ESXi out of the box. Therefore, important settings like hardware virtualization, no execute, NUMA, and others are already configured correctly. Other server vendors may be the same, but I encourage you to verify this. The default BIOS settings on UCS servers are a balance of performance and power management. For most workloads, you can expect these settings to perform well. If you expect to run **High-Performance Computing (HPC)**, select workloads like massive **Online Transaction Processing (OLTP)**, or similarly unique and performance-sensitive workloads, expect to dive deeply into the vendor documentation and white papers to tune your BIOS settings accordingly.

Upgrading an ESXi host

Many environments have already adopted some level of virtualization. A data center design will likely have to include upgrading the current infrastructure to leverage new features and functionality. Upgrading ESXi is a simple process, but it requires some planning to ensure compatibility and supportability. Chapter 4, *vSphere Management Design*, provides details about upgrading vCenter Server. This recipe will provide the details for planning an upgrade of ESXi hosts.

ESXi 5.x can be upgraded directly to ESXi 6.0 or 6.5. If you want to upgrade a host to 6.7 from 5.x, you'll first need an upgrade to 6.0 or 6.5, then another upgrade to 6.7.

How to do it...

When preparing to upgrade ESXi hosts, use the following steps:

1. Identify the methods that are available for upgrading ESXi
2. Verify hardware and firmware compatibility by using the VMware HCL, which can be found at http://www.vmware.com/go/hcl

How it works...

The following methods are available to upgrade ESXi:

- **Interactive upgrade**: An interactive upgrade can be performed from the ESXi console to upgrade ESXi from an ESXi image on a CD/DVD-ROM or USB drive. To perform an interactive upgrade boot to the image on the CD-ROM or USB drive, follow the onscreen wizard to upgrade ESXi.
- **Scripted upgrade**: ESXi upgrades can be scripted by using a kickstart file. The default kickstart file is located in /etc/vmware/ks.cfg. The ks.cfg file allows the upgrade to be performed from a CD/DVD-ROM, USB, FTP server, NFS server, or HTTP/HTTPS server. Details about creating a ks.cfg file and automating the ESXi upgrade can be found in the VMware vSphere documentation for installing or upgrading hosts by using a script, which is located
  at http://pubs.vmware.com/vsphere-60/topic/com.vmware.vsphere.upgrade.d oc/GUID-870A07BC-F8B4-47AF-9476-D542BA53F1F5.html.
- **The command line with** esxcli: esxcli can be used to upgrade ESXi from a depot or bundle by using the following command:

```
esxcli software vib install -d <FullPathToUpgradeDepot>
```

- **vSphere Update Manager** (**VUM**): Using VUM, an ESXi image is uploaded, an upgrade baseline is created, the baseline is applied to hosts, and the hosts are remediated against the baseline. The *Designing a vSphere Update Manager deployment* recipe in `Chapter 4`, *vSphere Management Design*, provides details about installing and using VUM to upgrade ESXi hosts.
- **vSphere Auto Deploy**: Hosts that are deployed using vSphere Auto Deploy can be reprovisioned by using a new image profile. Creating an ESXi 6 image profile is covered in the *Creating a custom ESXi image* recipe, from earlier in this chapter.

Any time that an ESXi upgrade is performed, it is important to verify compatibility on the VMware HCL. The host hardware and BIOS and the installed adapters should be verified with the list to ensure the stability of the host and the support of the environment. Verifying compatibility using the HCL is covered in the *Using the VMware Hardware Compatibility List* recipe, from earlier in this chapter.

Virtual Machine Design 9

Virtual machine design is just as important as physical hardware design, and it should be part of the physical design process. Correctly designing and configuring virtual machines with proper resource allocation will help to increase consolidation in the virtual environment and ensure that a virtual machine has access to the resources that it requires to run the workloads efficiently.

A few questions that should be answered as a part of virtual machine design are as follows:

- What resources will be assigned to individual virtual machines?
- What virtual hardware will be allocated to virtual machines?
- How will new virtual machines be deployed?
- How will multiple virtual machines supporting an application be grouped based on dependencies?
- How will virtual machines be placed on host resources to ensure the efficient use of resources and availability?
- How will physical servers be converted into virtual machines?

This chapter will cover right-sizing virtual machines to ensure that they have the resources they require without over-allocating resources. We will also cover allocating virtual hardware to virtual machines and how to create a virtual machine template to quickly deploy a standardized virtual machine.

Configuring the ability to add CPU and memory resources without taking the virtual machine out of production will also be covered, along with how to group virtual machines into applications, or vApps. We'll also discuss using affinity and anti-affinity rules on a DRS cluster to reduce the demand on a physical network, or to provide application availability in the event of a host failure. Finally, in this chapter, we will demonstrate how to convert a physical server into a virtual machine.

In this chapter, we will cover the following recipes:

- Right-sizing virtual machines
- Enabling CPU hot add and memory hot plug
- Using paravirtualized VM hardware
- Creating virtual machine templates
- Installing and upgrading VMware Tools
- Upgrading VM virtual hardware
- Using vApps to organize virtualized applications
- Using VM affinity and anti-affinity rules
- Using VMs to Hosts affinity and anti-affinity rules
- Converting physical servers with vCenter Converter Standalone
- Migrating servers into vSphere

Right-sizing virtual machines

Right-sizing a virtual machine means allocating the correct amount of CPU, memory, and storage resources that are required to support a virtual machine's workload. The optimal performance of the virtual machine and the efficient use of the underlying hardware are both obtained through right-sizing virtual machine resources.

In a physical server environment, it can be difficult and time-consuming to add resources:

1. Compatible parts will need to be identified
2. The parts will need to be ordered
3. You will likely need to wait weeks for the parts to arrive
4. Someone will need to be in the data center
5. The server will need to be shut down
6. The server will need to be removed from the rack and opened up
7. The parts need to be installed

Because of this, physical servers are often configured with more resources than are actually required to ensure that there are sufficient resources available if the need for resources increases. Typically, physical servers only use a small percentage of the resources available to them; this means that a great deal of resources are constantly kept idle or are wasted. Adding resources to a physical server also typically requires that the server be powered off, and possibly even removed from the rack, which takes even more time and impacts production.

In a virtual environment, it is much easier to add CPU, memory, and disk resources to a virtual machine. This eliminates the need to over-allocate resources. Virtual machines are configured with the resources that they require, and more resources can be added quickly and easily as the demand increases. If a virtual machine has been configured to use CPU hot add and memory hot plug, additional resources can be added without taking the virtual machine out of production.

How to do it...

Perform the following steps to right-size virtual machines:

1. Determine the CPU, memory, and storage resources required by the virtual machine

> When you are right-sizing virtual machine resources, start with the minimum requirements and add additional resources to the virtual machine as needed.

2. Adjust the virtual machine CPU, memory, and storage resource allocations to meet the requirements of the workload without over-allocating

How it works...

Tools like VMware Capacity Planner or Windows perfmon can be used to determine the actual resources that are required by an application running on a physical server. The resources that are used by a virtual machine can be examined by using the vSphere Client program. From the **Summary** tab on the summary page of a virtual machine, it is easy to determine what CPU, memory, and disk resources have been allocated to the virtual machine, along with the current usage of each of these resources, as shown in the following screenshot:

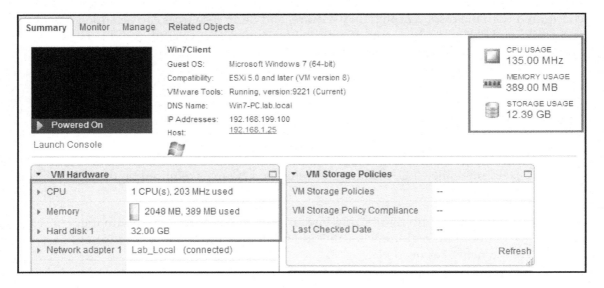

Viewing resources allocated to a VM

Performance charts can also be used to provide information about CPU and memory usage over time. The real-time advanced memory performance chart that's shown in the following screenshot shows the memory metrics of the **Win7Client** virtual machine:

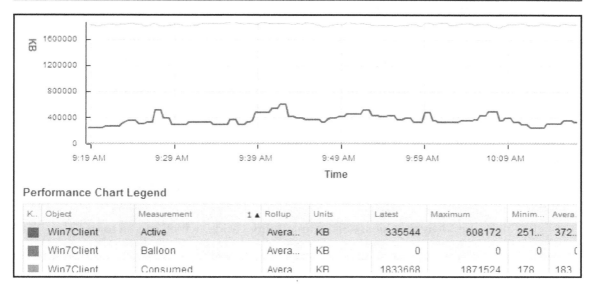

Performance Chart Legend

K..	Object	Measurement	1 ▲	Rollup	Units	Latest	Maximum	Minim...	Avera..
■	Win7Client	Active		Avera...	KB	335544	608172	251...	372..
■	Win7Client	Balloon		Avera...	KB	0	0	0	(
■	Win7Client	Consumed		Avera	KB	1833668	1871524	178	183

Viewing performance charts in the vSphere Web Client

The chart options can be adjusted to show metrics for the last day, week, month, or even year. These metrics can be used to determine whether a virtual machine has been allocated more memory than required.

Once the resource requirements have been identified, the virtual machine resources can be modified, or right-sized, to ensure that a virtual machine has not been allocated more resources than are required for the workload running on it.

vRealize Operations Manager (**vROps**) is a separate VMware product that can be used to monitor the resources that are used by a virtual machine, and it has capacity planning and efficiency monitoring that's specific to right-sizing virtual machines. More information on vROps can be found at `http://www.vmware.com/products/vcenter-operations-management/`.

Enabling CPU hot add and memory hot plug

Adding CPU and memory resources to a virtual machine is a simple process. The process to add resources to a virtual machine is to power down the virtual machine, increase the number of vCPUs or the amount of memory, and power on the virtual machine again.

In vSphere 4.0, two new features, CPU hot add and memory hot plug, were introduced to allow for virtual machine vCPUs and virtual machine memory to be increased without requiring that the virtual machine be powered off. CPU hot add and memory hot plug must first be enabled on the virtual machine, which does require it to be powered off. Once it is enabled, however, CPU and memory resources may be added dynamically; powering off the virtual machine is not necessary.

How to do it...

Perform the following steps to enable CPU hot add and memory hot plug for virtual machines:

1. Check the VMware Guest OS Compatibility Guide, which can be found at `http://partnerweb.vmware.com/comp_guide2/pdf/VMware_GOS_Compatibility_Guide.pdf`, to identify whether vCPU and memory hot-adding is supported for the virtual machine guest operating system. The following screenshot is from the VMware Guest OS Compatibility Guide and shows the **Hot Add Memory** and **Hot Add vCPU** support for **Windows Server 2012 Datacenter Edition R2**:

| Windows Server 2012 Datacenter Edition R2 | Workstation12.0, 11.0, 10.0
Fusion8.0, 7.0, 6.0
ESXi6.0 U2 [1,6,7,8,3], 6.0 U1 [1,6,7,8,3], 6.0 [1,6,7,8,3], 5.5 U3 [1,6,7,8,3], 5.5 U2 [1,6,7,8,3], 5.5 U1 [1,6,7,8,3], 5.5 [1,6,7,8,3]
ESXi5.1 U3 [1,2,6,7,8,3], 5.1 U2 [1,2,6,7,8,3], 5.1 U1 [1,2,6,7,8,3], 5.1 [1,2,6,7,8,3], 5.0 U3 [1,2,6,7,9,8], 5.0 U2 [1,2,6,7,9,8] | e1000e, VMXNET 3 (Recommended), IDE, LSI Logic SAS, SATA, VMware Paravirtual, Hot Add Memory, Hot Add vCPU, SMP, Tools Available on Media

e1000e, VMXNET 3 (Recommended), IDE, LSI Logic SAS, VMware Paravirtual, Hot Add Memory, Hot Add vCPU, SMP, Tools Available on Media |

Viewing hot-add support for guest operating systems

2. To configure CPU hot add or memory hot plug for a virtual machine, it must be powered off.
3. To enable CPU hot add on the virtual machine, edit the virtual machine settings and expand the *CPU settings. Select the **Enable CPU Hot Add** checkbox, as shown in the following screenshot:

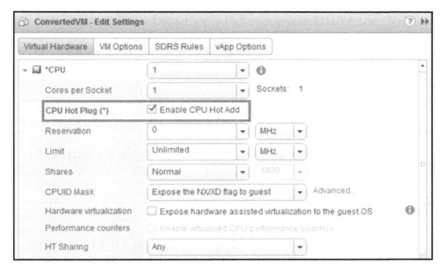

Enabling CPU Hot Add

4. To enable memory hot plug, expand the *Memory settings and select the Enable checkbox for Memory Hot Plug (*), as shown in the following screenshot:

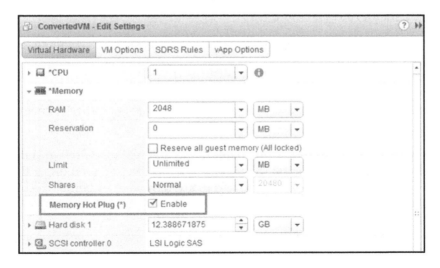

Enabling memory Hot Plug

5. Once CPU hot add and memory hot plug have been enabled for a virtual machine, the virtual machine can be powered back on.

6. vCPUs and memory can now be added to the running virtual machine without having to shut it down.

How it works...

Once CPU hot add and memory hot plug have been enabled on a virtual machine, it will not be necessary to power off the virtual machine to add additional vCPUs or additional memory.

Although vCPUs and memory can be added while the virtual machine is running, once Hot Add (or Hot Plug) has been enabled, some operating systems may require for the guest to be rebooted before the added vCPUs or memory are recognized by the operating system.

Enabling the CPU hot add and memory hot plug features does increase the virtual machine overhead reservation slightly. Also, remember that when a virtual machine's memory is increased, the virtual machine swap file (.vswp) also increases to the size of the allocated memory (minus any memory reservations). The swap file automatically grows when the virtual machine's memory is increased.

CPU resources do not have to be added in twos. If a virtual machine requires the resources that are associated with three CPUs, three vCPUs can be assigned to the virtual machine. It is also not necessary to allocate virtual machine memory in GB increments; a virtual machine can be allocated 1,256 MB of memory if that is what is necessary to meet resource requirements.

With CPU hot add and memory hot plug enabled, the removal of vCPUs and memory from a virtual machine will still require that the virtual machine be powered off or that the operating system be rebooted before the resources are removed, or before the removal of resources is recognized by the guest operating system.

Using paravirtualized VM hardware

Paravirtualization provides a direct communication path between the guest OS within the virtual machine and the ESXi hypervisor. Paravirtualized virtual hardware and the corresponding drivers that are installed with VMware Tools are optimized to provide improved performance and efficiency. This hardware includes the VMXNET network adapter and the PVSCSI storage adapter.

How to do it...

Adding paravirtualized hardware adapters to a virtual machine is done by using the following process:

1. Access the **Guest OS** compatibility section of the VMware HCL at `http://www.vmware.com/go/hcl` to determine guest OS support for paravirtual adapters. A screenshot of the **Guest OS** compatibility HCL, along with the **Networking** and **Storage** adapters highlighted in red boxes, is as follows:

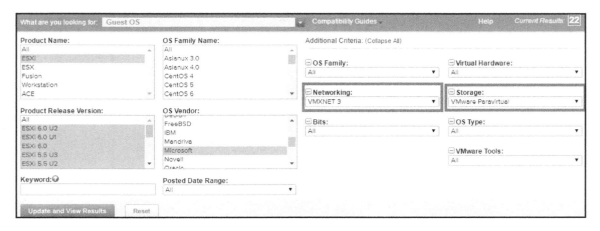

Verifying paravirtual network support for guest operating systems

2. Install VMware Tools in the virtual machine.

3. To install the paravirtualized network adapter, edit the virtual machine's **Virtual Hardware**, add a **New Network adapter**, and select **VMXNET3** for the **Adapter Type**, as shown in the following screenshot:

Adding a paravirtual network adapter to a VM

4. To install the paravirtualized SCSI adapter, edit the virtual machine's **Virtual Hardware**, add a **New SCSI controller**, and select **VMware Paravirtual** for the **Adapter Type**, as shown in the following screenshot:

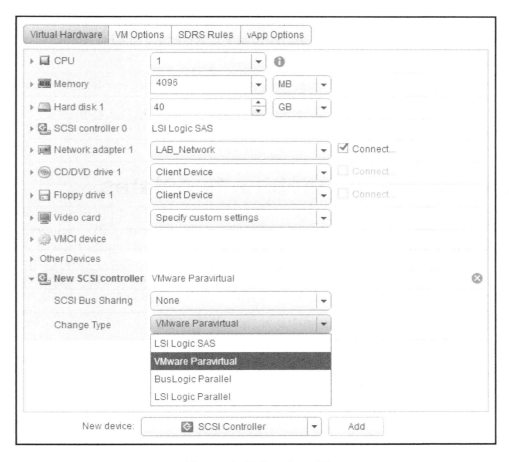

Adding a paravirtual SCSI controller to a VM

How it works...

Once the adapter has been configured, the optimized virtual hardware is presented to the virtual machine guest. The drivers for the paravirtualized hardware adapters are included with VMware Tools. The paravirtualized hardware can be added to a virtual machine before VMware Tools is installed, but the hardware will not be available for use by the guest OS until VMware Tools is installed.

The VMXNET3 adapter provides higher network throughput with less host CPU overhead.

The PVSCSI adapter is suitable for I/O intensive applications. Like the VMXNET3 adapter, the PVSCSI adapter increases storage throughput with minimal host CPU overhead.

Creating virtual machine templates

Virtual machines can be deployed quickly and in a standardized fashion by using pre-built templates. Virtual machine templates are configured with minimum CPU, memory, and storage resources. The guest operating system and any prerequisite applications are installed in the template. Instead of taking hours (or even days, in some cases) to install the operating system and prepare the server, once a template has been created, a new virtual machine can be deployed within minutes. Virtual machine templates not only allow for quick deployment, but also help to maintain consistency across virtual machines that are deployed in the environment.

How to do it...

The following steps are required to create a virtual machine template:

1. Create a virtual machine; configure the vCPU, memory, and storage resources; install the guest operating system; install the required applications; and apply any application or operating system updates or patches.
2. The virtual machine can be cloned to a template by using the **Clone to Template** wizard, as shown in the following screenshot:

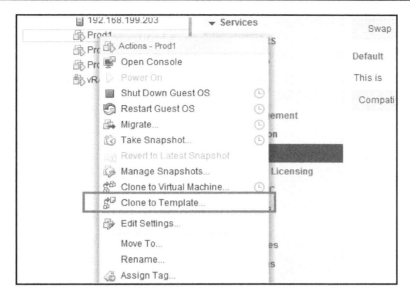

Context menu to clone a VM to template

3. The virtual machine can also be converted into a template by using the **Convert to Template** wizard, as shown in the following screenshot:

Context menu to convert a VM to template

4. Once the virtual machine template has been created, new virtual machines can be deployed from the template by using the **Deploy VM from this Template** wizard, as shown in the following screenshot:

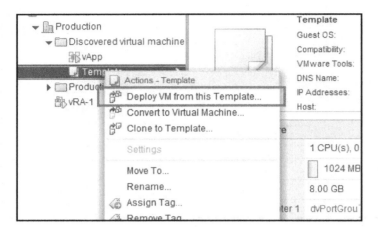

Context menu to deploy a VM from a template

How it works...

When cloning a virtual machine to a template, the **Clone to Template** wizard allows the administrator to choose the data center, cluster, and storage to create the new virtual machine template. Cloning a virtual machine to a template can be done while the source virtual machine is powered on.

When a virtual machine is converted into a template, the virtual machine is converted locally; the template will have the same inventory properties (data center, cluster, and storage) as the virtual machine that has been converted. The virtual machine configuration file (.vmx) is changed to a template configuration file (.vmtx) when a virtual machine is converted. The virtual machine needs to be powered off to be converted to a virtual machine template.

The following screenshot shows the virtual machine template files on a **datastore** (the virtual machine template configuration file has been boxed in red):

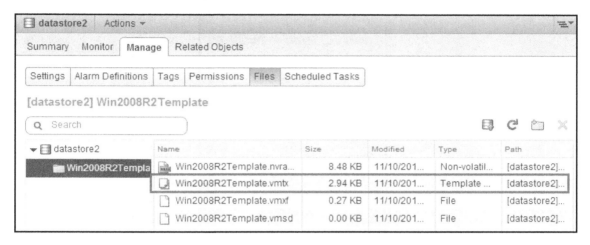

VM template files on datastore

The virtual machine template file is similar to the .vmx file, and it contains configuration information about the virtual hardware that's presented to the virtual machine or template.

There's more...

A guest customization specification can be applied to a virtual machine that is being deployed from a template. The customization specification allows for settings that are unique to the deployed virtual machine to be applied during the deployment process. These custom specifications include information such as the computer's name, the licensing, the IP address, and the domain membership.

The **New VM Guest Customization Spec** wizard is displayed in the following screenshot:

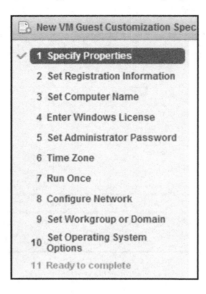

Sections of a VM guest customization specification

The customization specification can be saved so that it can be applied to future virtual machines that are deployed from templates. Guest customization specifications can also be applied when cloning a virtual machine.

Upgrading and installing VMware Tools

VMware Tools enhances the performance and improves the management of virtual machines. It does this by loading optimized drivers for virtual hardware and installing utilities to access virtual machine configurations and metrics. VMware Tools is not required, but for optimal virtual machine performance, it should be installed on all virtual machines in the environment.

The status of VMware Tools is displayed on the virtual machine's **Summary** page, as shown in the following screenshot:

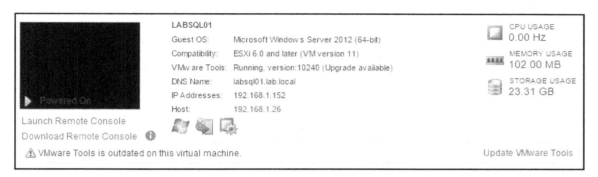

Status of VMware Tools on the VM summary tab

The drivers for the optimized paravirtual hardware, such as the VMXNET3 adapter and the PVSCSI adapter, are included in VMware Tools, and VMware Tools must be installed before the hardware is available for use within the guest. VMware Tools should be installed and kept up to date for every guest operating system.

How to do it...

There are multiple options available for upgrading VMware Tools:

1. If VMware Tools is out of date, a warning is displayed in the vSphere Client. VMware Tools can be updated from the VM's **Summary** page by using the **Update VMware Tools**, as shown in the following screenshot:

⚠ VMware Tools is outdated on this virtual machine.   Update VMware Tools

VMware Tools is out of date warning

2. Right-clicking on the virtual machine and selecting the **Guest OS** menu will allow you to **Install** or **Upgrade VMware Tools**, as shown in the following screenshot:

VM context menu to upgrade VMware Tools

3. If VMware Tools is not installed, the **Install VMware Tools** option will be available.
4. Update or install VMware Tools as required.

How it works...

When upgrading or installing VMware Tools on a virtual machine, a VMware Tools ISO image is connected to the virtual machine. If VMware Tools is already installed, the upgrade automatically runs to update the VMware Tools to the current version. If VMware Tools is not already installed, the installer must be manually run to install VMware Tools. A reboot of the virtual machine will be required once the VMware Tools installation has completed.

There's more...

Virtual machines can be configured to automatically upgrade VMware Tools to the current version. This is done by editing the virtual machine's settings and selecting the **Check and upgrade VMware Tools before each power on** in **VM Options**, as shown in the following screenshot:

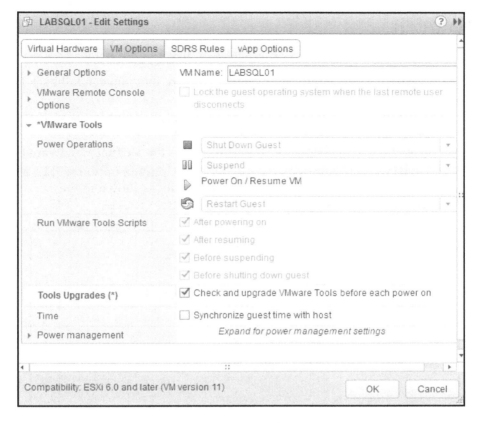

Option to automatically upgrade VMware Tools before each power on operation

Upgrading VM virtual hardware

The virtual machine hardware version or virtual machine compatibility specifies the version of virtual machine hardware that's presented to the virtual machines and the ESXi versions that the virtual machine is then compatible to run on. Updating the virtual machine hardware exposes new features that are available to virtual machines (for example, the ability to provision vmdks up to 62 TB) and ensures that the virtual hardware is optimized to the version of ESXi.

How to do it...

To upgrade the virtual hardware of a virtual machine, use the following steps:

1. Take a snapshot of the virtual machine to ensure that you can fall back to a known good state if the upgrade fails.
2. It's critically important to install or update VMware Tools in the virtual machine before the virtual hardware upgrade.
3. Edit the settings of a virtual machine and access the **Virtual Hardware** tab.
4. If a virtual hardware upgrade is available, the **Upgrade** option will be available. Select the **Schedule VM Compatibility Upgrade**, as shown in the following screenshot:

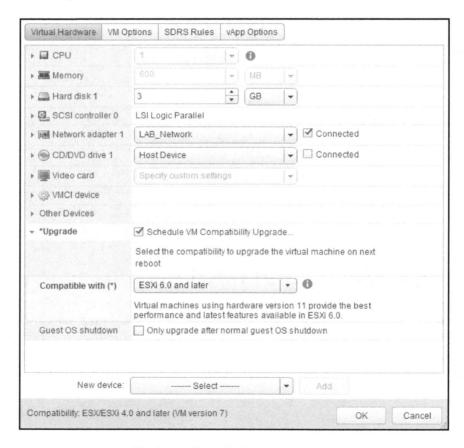

VM option to schedule virtual hardware upgrades on next reboot

5. Set the compatibility level that the virtual hardware should be upgraded to, as shown in the following screenshot:

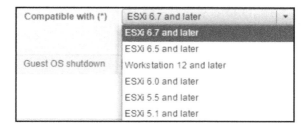

Selecting virtual hardware compatibility

6. Shut down and power on the virtual machine to upgrade the virtual machine hardware.

How it works...

The hardware compatibility maps to a virtual hardware version. The following table shows the relationships between the compatibility and the virtual machine hardware version:

Virtual Machine Hardware Version	Compatibility
VM version 14 (vmx-14)	ESXi 6.7 and later
VM version 13 (vmx-13)	ESXi 6.5 and later
VM version 11 (vmx-11)	ESXi 6.0 and later
VM version 10 (vmx-10)	ESXi 5.5 and later
VM version 9 (vmx-9)	ESXi 5.1 and later
VM version 8 (vmx-8)	ESXi 5.0 and later
VM version 7 (vmx-7)	ESX/ESXi 4.0 and later
VM version 4 (vmx-4)	ESX/ESXi 3.5 and later

When a virtual hardware upgrade is scheduled, the virtual hardware of the virtual machine is upgraded the next time the virtual machine is rebooted.

The virtual machine hardware version should be set to the compatibility of the lowest version of ESXi in the environment to ensure that the virtual machine can run on any host in the environment. For example, if a design includes both 6.0 and 6.7 hosts and a virtual machine's hardware is upgraded to vmx-14, the VM will no longer run on the ESXi 6.0 hosts.

There's more...

The default VM compatibility can be set on a vSphere data center or cluster. Setting the default virtual machine compatibility is done with the **Edit Default VM Compatibility** dialog, which can be accessed by right-clicking on the data center or cluster in the vCenter inventory. The **Edit Default VM Compatibility** dialog is shown in the following screenshot:

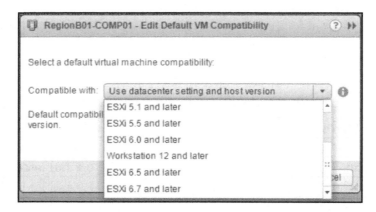

Choosing the default virtual hardware compatibility for a cluster

Once a default VM compatibility is set on a data center or cluster, the virtual machines that are deployed in the data center and cluster will be deployed with the default virtual machine hardware, based on the compatibility settings.

Using vApps to organize virtualized applications

vApps can be used to group individual virtual machines with interdependencies into a single application. A common use case for this would be a multi-tier web application that requires a web server frontend, an application server, and the supporting database server. The application can then be managed as a single inventory object.

How to do it...

Perform the following steps to use vApps to organize virtual machine workloads:

1. Create a new vApp by launching the **New vApp...** wizard, as shown in the following screenshot:

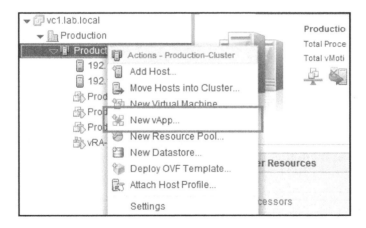

Context menu to create a new vApp

2. The method for creating the vApp (either creating a new vApp or cloning an existing vApp), the vApp **Name**, the **Folder** location, and the resource allocation settings, are configured in the **New vApp** wizard, as shown in the following screenshot:

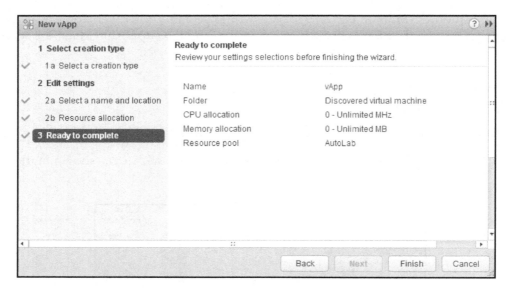

Completing the New vApp wizard

3. Once the vApp has been created, you can add virtual machines to the new vApp by dragging them into the vApp. The following screenshot shows a **vApp** containing the **Prod1** and **Prod2** virtual machines:

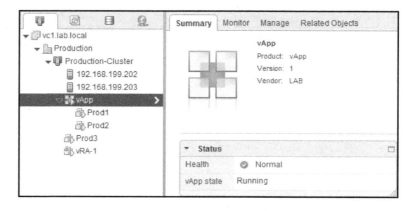

vApp summary tab

4. The settings of the vApp can be edited. In the following screenshot, the **Start order** is configured to start the virtual machines in the vApp in a specific order. The **Start order** ensures that virtual machines are started in order of their dependencies when the vApp is powered on:

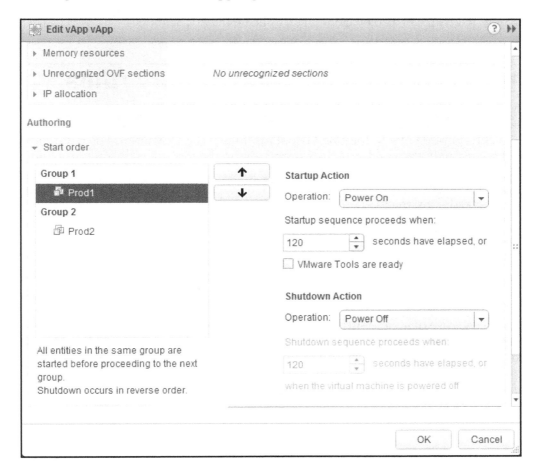

Editing a vApp for VM startup order

How it works...

A **vApp** is a container of the virtual machines that support an application. Once placed in a vApp, startup and shutdown can be configured based on application dependencies, resources can be reserved or limited, and the entire vApp can be exported in an OVA or OVF format. A vApp can also be cloned to duplicate the application.

Using VM affinity and anti-affinity rules

When virtual machines are powered on in a DRS cluster, vCenter determines where the virtual machines should be placed to balance resource usage across the cluster. The DRS scheduler runs periodically to migrate virtual machines using vMotion. The main purpose of DRS is to ensure that virtual machines are receiving the resources they request and to maintain a balance of resource usage across the cluster. Affinity or anti-affinity rules can be used to control where VMs are placed within a cluster. Affinity rules keep VMs on the same physical host, reducing the load on the physical network by keeping traffic between them from leaving the host. Anti-affinity rules keep VMs separated on different physical hosts, ensuring higher availability.

One use case of an affinity rule would be to keep all of the virtual machines supporting an application on the same host. This would ensure that the network communications between the virtual machines supporting the application do not traverse the physical network.

An example use case of an anti-affinity rule would be to keep multiple virtual Active Directory domain controllers running on separate hosts to ensure that not all of the domain controllers are affected by a single host failure.

How to do it...

The following steps are required to use VM affinity and anti-affinity rules:

1. DRS rules are created on the **Settings** page of a DRS-enabled cluster, as shown in the following screenshot:

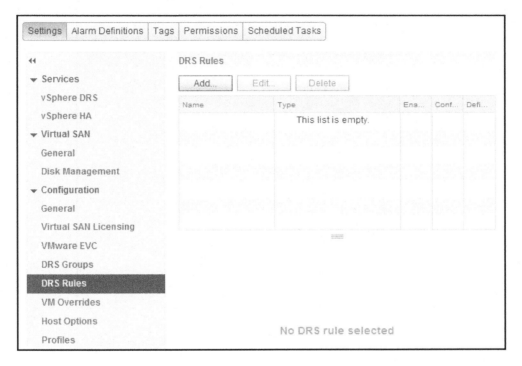

DRS rules section for a cluster

2. DRS rules can be created for three purposes: to **Keep Virtual Machines Together** on the same host, to **Separate Virtual Machines** across different hosts, or to assign **Virtual Machines to Hosts**, as shown in the following screenshot:

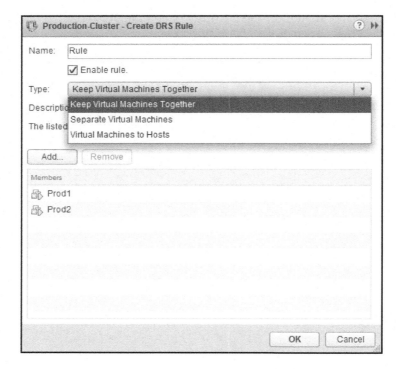

Types of DRS rules

How it works...

With the DRS rules configured, the distributed resource scheduler will apply the rules when determining the placement of virtual machines when they are powered on or when migrating virtual machines to other hosts to balance cluster resource usage.

When an affinity rule has been configured to keep several virtual machines together, if DRS migrates one of the virtual machines in the rule, all of the virtual machines that are configured will also be migrated to the new host. When an anti-affinity rule has been configured to keep virtual machines separated, DRS will not migrate a virtual machine to a host running another virtual machine that's been configured in the rule.

Using VM to Host affinity and anti-affinity rules

Virtual Machine to Hosts rules can be created to keep virtual machines on or off specific hosts (or groups of hosts). These types of DRS rules are useful for keeping the management of virtual machines, such as vCenter Server, on specific hosts to make those virtual machines easier to locate in the event of a failure. This also allows for virtual machines to be separated across different hosts in a rack or blade chassis to ensure that the loss of a rack or chassis does not impact all virtual machines; for example, to split the members of a Microsoft SQL Always On Availability Group across chassis.

How to do it...

The following process can be used to create **Virtual Machine to Hosts** affinity or anti-affinity rules:

1. From the cluster's **Settings** page, access the **VM/Host Groups** section to manage virtual machine and host groups, as shown in the following screenshot:

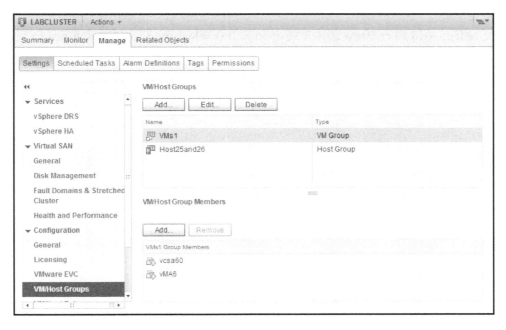

Managing VM / Host groups

2. Select **Add** to create a new host group and select the hosts to add to the group, as shown in the following screenshot:

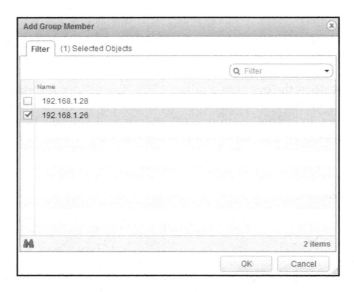

Adding a new host group

3. Select **Add** to create a new VM group, and select the virtual machines to add to the group, as shown in the following screenshot:

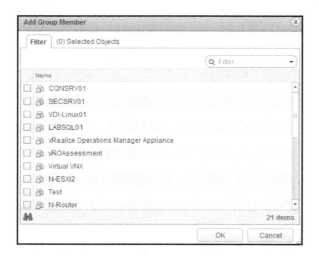

Adding a new VM group

4. From the **DRS Rules** menu, create a **VM/Host Rule** by providing a rule **Name**, setting the **Type** to **Virtual Machines to Hosts**, selecting the **VM Group** and **Host Group** to include in the rule, and selecting the required or preferential affinity/anti-affinity rules, as shown in the following screenshot:

Creating a VM / Host rule

5. Click on **OK** to create the **Virtual Machines to Hosts** rule.

How it works...

When creating **Virtual Machines to Hosts**, the affinity or anti-affinity rules can be set to be required or preferential, as shown in the following screenshot of the dropdown box from the **Create VM/Host Rule** wizard:

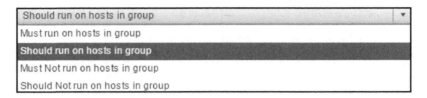

Should or Must DRS rule options

The VM/Host affinity and anti-affinity rules are as follows:

- **Must run on hosts in group**: This is a required VM to Host affinity rule, and the virtual machines must run on the specified hosts. This rule will not be violated, even in an HA event.
- **Should run on hosts in group**: This is a preferential VM to Host affinity rule, and the virtual machines will run on the selected host when possible. The virtual machines can run on hosts outside of the group if necessary (for example, in an HA event).
- **Must Not run on hosts in group**: This is a required VM to Host anti-affinity rule, and the virtual machines will not run on hosts within the group. This rule will not be violated, even in an HA event.
- **Should Not run on hosts in group**: This is a preferential VM to Host anti-affinity rule, and the virtual machines can run on hosts within the group if necessary (for example, in an HA or maintenance event).

Once the VM/Host rules have been created, vSphere DRS will apply the rules when managing virtual machine placement and resource balancing within the vSphere cluster.

Converting physical servers with vCenter Converter Standalone

There are two methods for virtualizing the workloads that are running on physical servers. The workloads can be migrated into the virtual environment by creating new virtual machines, loading a guest operating system, installing applications, and migrating the application data to the new virtual machines; or, physical servers can directly be converted into virtual machines by using VMware vCenter Converter Standalone, or similar third-party tools.

How to do it...

The following steps are required to use VMware vCenter Converter Standalone:

1. Download VMware Converter from
   http://www.vmware.com/web/vmware/downloads. VMware Converter can be installed as either a local installation or a client-server installation. More information on installing VMware Converter is available in the VMware vCenter Converter Standalone guide, at
   http://www.vmware.com/support/pubs/converter_pubs.html.

   The local installation is used to convert the physical machine on which the converter software is installed. When it is installed using the client-server installation, the local machine becomes a server that can be managed remotely, which uses the Converter Standalone client to convert the physical servers.

2. Once VMware Converter has been installed, the **VMware vCenter Converter Standalone** client is used to connect to the converter server, which is either local or installed on a remote machine. The **VMware vCenter Converter Standalone** login dialog is shown in the following screenshot:

VMware vCenter Converter connection page

3. To convert a machine, select **Convert machine** to start the conversion wizard, as shown in the following screenshot:

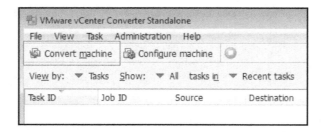

Convert machine option in vCenter Converter

4. The first step of the conversion is to select the **Source System** type. This is the type of system that will be converted into the virtual environment. The source type can be **Powered-on machine** (physical or virtual), **VMware Infrastructure virtual machine**, **Backup image or third-party virtual machine**, or **Hyper-V Server**.

5. Once the source type has been selected, specify the powered-on virtual machine's information. This is the machine that will be converted, and it can be either the local machine or a remote machine. To convert a remote machine, the **IP address or name** field must be filled in, along with administrator credentials and the **OS Family** field. When converting the local machine, the user running the converter must have administrator access to the local machine. The following screenshot shows a sample **Source System** configuration to convert a remote powered-on machine:

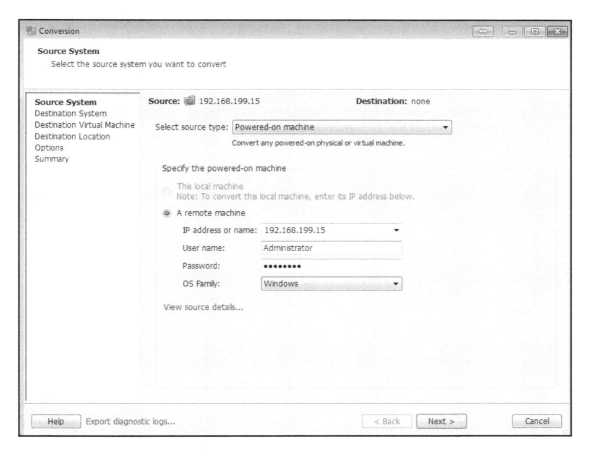

Configuring source system in a vCenter Converter job

6. Once the source system information has been provided, the Converter Standalone agent will be installed on the source system. Once the conversion has finished, the agent can be uninstalled automatically or manually:

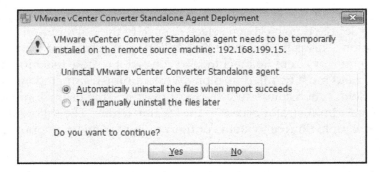

Choosing vCenter Converter uninstall option

7. Once the Converter Standalone agent has been successfully installed, the destination system where the source system will be converted will be configured. The destination type, the destination IP address, and the destination credentials will be configured. The following screenshot shows the configuration of a vCenter Server as the **Destination System**:

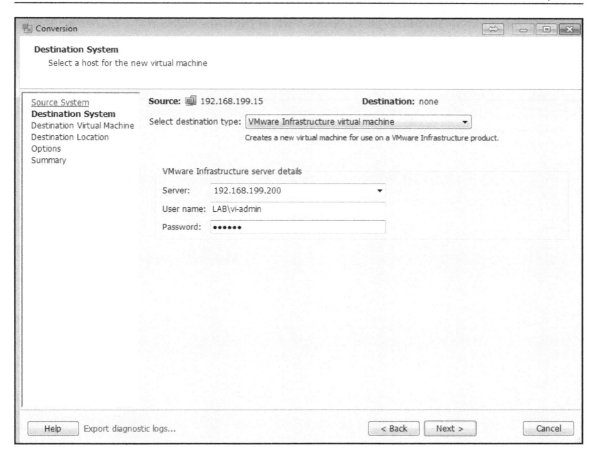

Choosing destination of vCenter Converter job

8. Information about the **Destination Virtual Machine**, such as the name and the virtual machine inventory placement, is then configured. The following screenshot shows the name and inventory placement for a physical-to-virtual conversion:

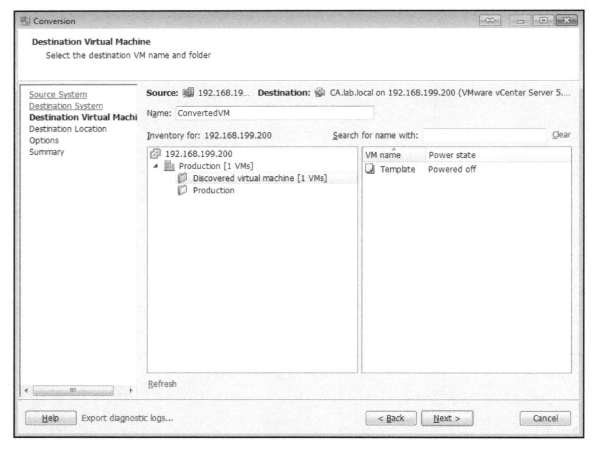

Configuring destination VM options in vCenter Converter

9. The **Destination Location** is then selected, as shown in the following screenshot. This location is the data center, cluster, or host that the converted machine will be deployed to. The datastore where the converted machine configuration file (.vmx) will reside and the virtual machine version to use are also configured here:

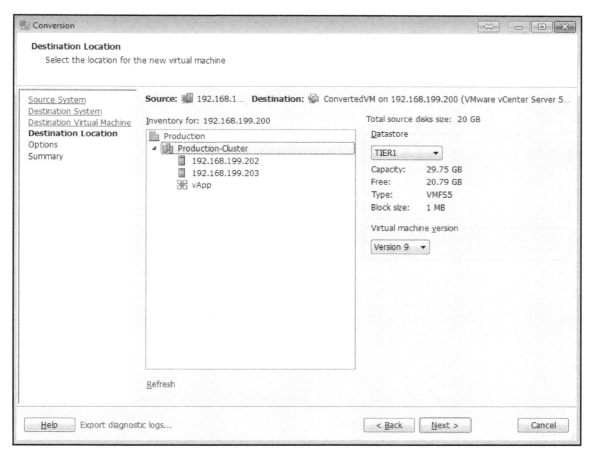

Choosing a destination for vCenter Converter job

10. A number of options can be configured for the converted machine, including what virtual machine network to connect to, what datastore to deploy the converted disk to (and in what format), and the device configuration. The following screenshot shows the **Options** configuration screen with the volume configuration for the machine that is being converted:

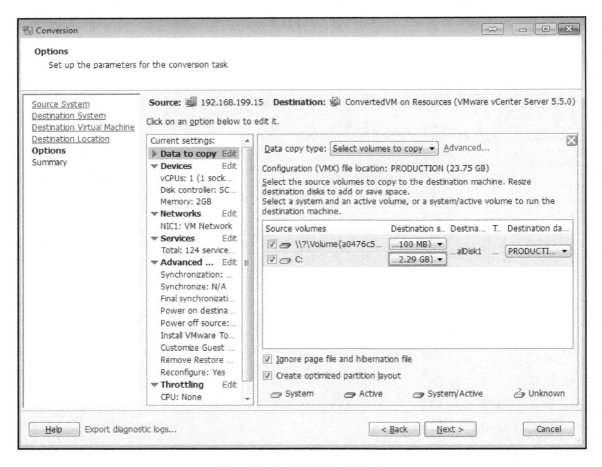

Options configuration screen in vCenter Converter

11. The **Summary** screen is then displayed, where the conversion options can be reviewed before starting the conversion process. An example **Summary** dialog is shown in the following screenshot:

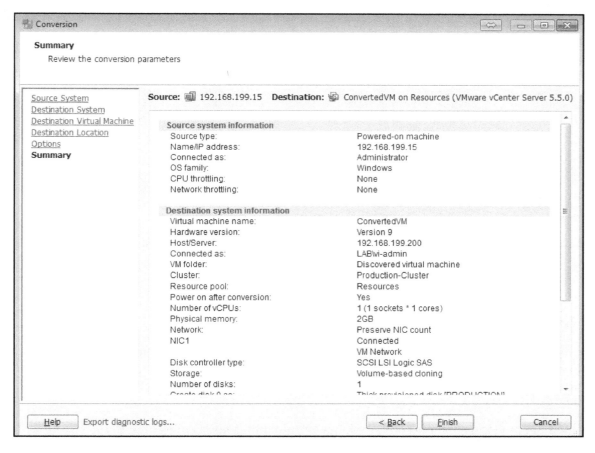

Summary screen of a vCenter Converter job creation

12. Once the conversion starts, the progress can be monitored in the **VMware vCenter Converter Standalone** client, as shown in the following screenshot. The client allows for multiple conversions to be configured and run simultaneously:

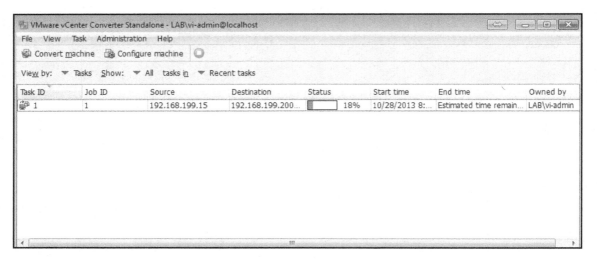

Monitoring vCenter Converter job progress

How it works...

When a physical server is converted using vCenter Converter Standalone, the physical server is cloned into the virtual environment. This creates a copy of the physical server as a virtual machine containing a duplicate of the operating system, applications, and data from the physical server.

When the physical server is converted, new virtual hardware is presented to the virtual machine. The physical hardware that was associated with the virtual machines is no longer present, and references to it should be removed. In Windows, this is done by using the Device Manager.

During the physical-to-virtual conversion, the physical hardware is replaced with virtual hardware. During the conversion, references to the physical hardware and the associated drivers are not removed from the operating system. To remove non-present hardware from a Windows Server, set the environment variable `devmgr_show_nonpresent_devices` to `1`. This will enable non-present devices to be visible in the Device Manager.

An old but useful tool to help clean up the effects of **Physical-to-Virtual (P2V)** conversions, such as non-present devices, is called the VM Advanced ISO, by Kendrick Coleman. The ISO itself is a compilation of tools, but one in particular should be used to clean up a P2V conversion. You'll find it in the `P2v Clean-Up` directory of the ISO. It's a script called remove non-present devices. You can download the VM Advanced ISO from `http://kendrickcoleman.com/index.php/Tech-Blog/vm-advanced-iso-free-tools-for-advanced-tasks.html`.

The conversion can be verified by booting the new virtual machine while it is disconnected from the virtual switch and checking that the operating system and applications were converted correctly. Once verified, the physical server can be powered off or removed from the network, and the newly converted virtual machine can be connected to the network.

The migration of servers and applications can be time-consuming, and vCenter Converter Standalone provides a way to quickly convert physical servers into virtual machines.

Migrating servers into vSphere

It's not always possible to build new systems in a vSphere environment. Sometimes, it's necessary to migrate existing servers into the environment. The reasons for a migration might include a lack of time to build new systems or a lack of expertise to build new systems and migrate the data. Either way, we'll present some of the ways that you can plan and execute the migration of existing servers into a vSphere environment.

How to do it...

Planning server migrations can be done using the following steps:

1. Identify the existing platform of the server
2. Identify the possible methods for migration
3. Assess the feasibility and risks associated with each migration method
4. Execute the migration

How it works...

Some common source platforms for servers include physical Windows and Linux hosts, that is, operating systems that are installed on bare-metal servers. Some source systems are on other hypervisors, like Microsoft Hyper-V, while some systems already reside in a vSphere environment, but they need to be moved to a separate vSphere environment, perhaps one that is not owned or inherently trusted by the source. The application is an important component as well. Well-known applications that are easy migration candidates include Microsoft **Active Directory** (**AD**), SQL Server, or Exchange. All of these existing platforms are common sources for servers when moving to a new vSphere environment.

The method of migration is dependent on the source platform. Some common migration methods are listed as follows, along with their source platforms and associated drawbacks:

- Physical servers, Windows, or Linux:
  - **vCenter Converter**: This method is called a physical-to-virtual conversion, and it was discussed in the previous section. Drawbacks include downtime for the application during cutover. If the system is resource-intensive, downtime for the entire conversion process may be needed, which could take hours. Only some Linux distributions are supported.
  - **Third-party converter tools like PlateSpin Migrate**: These are very similar to vCenter Converter, but are licensed at a cost. The drawbacks are the same as those of vCenter Converter.

- Microsoft applications:
  - Often, the best way to migrate a server into a vSphere environment is to use native tools that are built into the system. Active Directory, for example, has a well-understood and well-supported replication engine that makes standing up a new Domain Controller relatively easy. The drawback to migrating with Active Directory replication is the need to add complexity to the AD environment and possible **Domain Name System** (**DNS**) changes, which could impact the entire environment.
  - **SQL Server:** There are many ways to migrate an SQL database: backup and restore, mirroring, log shipping, **Microsoft Cluster Services** (**MSCS**), and **Always-On Availability Groups** (**AAGs**). The drawbacks of migrating with native SQL tools include varying degrees of downtime for the database.
  - **Exchange**: Backup and restore, **Database Availability Group** (**DAG**), mailbox move; drawbacks include downtime and the length of time to migrate.

- Microsoft Hyper-V:
    - vCenter Converter is a good candidate for migrating VMs on Hyper-V. This is known as a **Virtual-to-Virtual (V2V)** conversion, and it has the same drawbacks as any other vCenter Converter migration.
    - The Zerto virtual replication software is mainly used for disaster recovery, but it's also an excellent migration tool. Downtime is minimal, and the setup is not difficult. The drawbacks include the cost, as it's a licensed product.

vSphere Security Design 10

The security requirements of the virtual environment are a critical part of the vSphere design. If components of the virtual data center are compromised, a great deal of damage can be done, from powering off virtual machines, to accessing sensitive data, to impacting business processes by disrupting or deleting virtual resources. To identify the security requirements, there are a few questions that the data center architect should ask:

- Which users require access? What resources should be available to the users (administrators, users, auditors, and so on)?
- Do the resources require physical separation to ensure security?
- Which resources should be separated? For example, concerning separating DMZ resources from internal production resources, is it OK to share storage between the DMZ and internal production resources? What about computing resources?
- Are there compliance policies (for example, **Health Insurance Portability and Accountability Act (HIPAA)** or **Payment Card Industry (PCI)** policies) that the design must adhere to?

In this chapter, we will take a look at some of the security features of vSphere that can be incorporated into a data center design, in order to satisfy the security requirements for authentication and access.

Beyond the security features available in vSphere, there are a few simple security best practices that should be applied as part of any data center design. These security best practices include the following:

- Using multiple layers of security to protect systems and services
- A physical or logical separation of systems and services, based on security domains
- Removing or disabling unnecessary services
- Control of access to resources within the environment, based on user roles
- Configuring firewalls, software, and hardware to allow and deny access to services
- Keeping security updates and patches up to date

In this chapter, we will cover the following topics:

- Managing single sign-on password policies
- Managing single sign-on identity sources
- Security design with the VMware Certificate Authority
- Using Active Directory for ESXi host authentication
- ESXi firewall configuration
- ESXi Lockdown Mode
- Configuring role-based access control
- Virtual network security
- Using the VMware vSphere 6 Hardening Guide

Managing the single sign-on password policy

When installing the vCenter **Platform Services Controller (PSC)**, a default **Single Sign-On (SSO)** domain is created. By default, this domain is vsphere.local, but with vSphere 6.x, this domain can be defined by the user during the installation.

The `vsphere.local` domain becomes an identity source for SSO. Users within this identity source can be configured to administer SSO. These users can also be assigned permissions within vCenter. Each user authenticates using a password. The password lifetime, complexity, and how to handle failed login attempts are configured by policies in SSO. These policies should be configured to maintain compliance with the security requirements of the design.

How to do it...

To configure SSO password policies, we need to follow these steps:

1. Use the vSphere Web Client to access the SSO **Configuration** and **Policies**. The **Password Policy** is shown in the following screenshot:

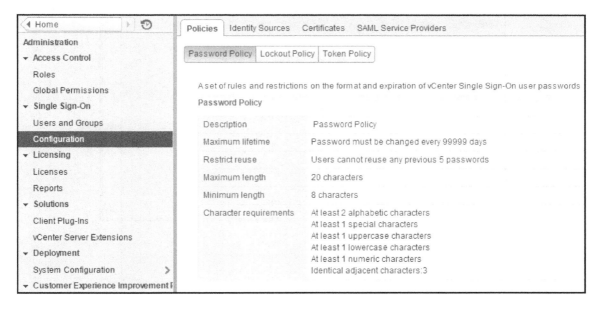

The SSO password policy section

2. Edit the **Password Policy** to set the password expiration and complexity requirements. The **Edit Password Policies** dialog is shown in the following screenshot:

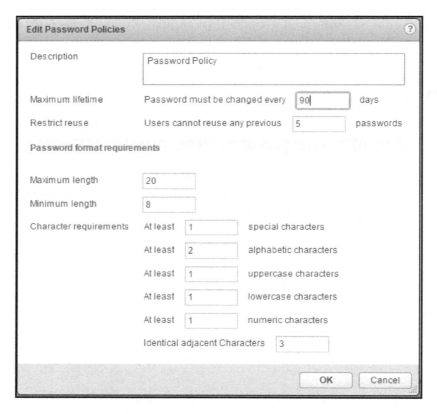

Editing the SSO password policy

3. Edit the **Lockout Policy** and configure the policies for how failed login attempts will be handled, as follows:

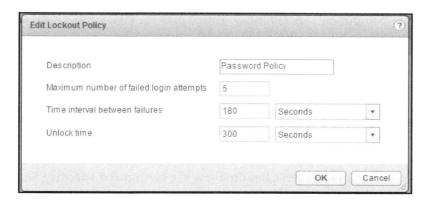

Editing the SSO password lockout policy

How it works...

Passwords are one of the first levels of security. Policies should be configured to meet the security requirements of the design.

The SSO password policy defines when a password will expire and when a password can be reused. The password format and complexity are also configured as a part of the password policy. When an SSO user's password has expired, the user will not be able to access the environment until the password has been changed. When the user creates or updates their password, it must meet the password format defined in the policy.

The SSO lockout policy is configured to protect the environment from a brute-force password attack. When a user attempts to log in with an incorrect password, the user's account is locked after the maximum number of attempts has been reached. The interval between failures defines the time period in which the attempts occur to set the lockout. When an account is locked, the user will not be granted access until after the unlock time has passed, even if the correct password is used.

Managing single sign-on identity sources

SSO identity sources integrate authentication databases that can be used by SSO to provide access to vSphere components. An identity source provides user and group authentication information. Users and groups within the identity source can be assigned permissions within the vSphere environment. The default identity source is the `vsphere.local` domain.

How to do it...

Use the following process to create, edit, or remove SSO **Identity Sources**:

1. Access the vSphere Web Client to view the configured **Identity Sources**, as shown in the following screenshot:

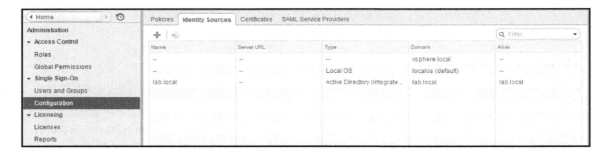

The SSO Identity Sources section

2. Identity sources are created using the **Add identity source**. The following screenshot is an example of creating an Active Directory identity source, using **Integrated Windows Authentication**:

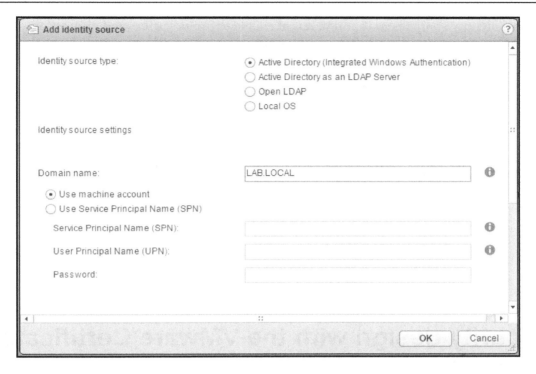

Adding an Active Directory domain as an identity source

How it works...

Identity sources can be configured from the following types:

- **Active Directory (Integrated Windows Authentication)**
- **Active Directory as an LDAP Server**
- **Open LDAP**
- **Local OS**

Once an identity source is configured, it is available to provide users and groups for creating permissions in the vSphere environment. The following screenshot shows the three domains associated with the configured identity sources that are available when creating permissions:

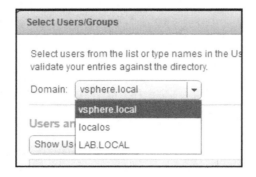

Choosing an identity source for new SSO users

Security design with the VMware Certificate Authority

Using digital certificates can give users confidence that the vSphere components with which they're communicating are trusted. With the introduction of the **Platform Services Controller** (**PSC**) in vSphere 6.0, VMware included an embedded certificate authority to manage certificates in a vSphere environment called the **VMware Certificate Authority** (**VMCA**).

This section will discuss how an architect can use the VMCA to design a secure and trusted vSphere environment. By default, the VMCA creates and issues self-signed certificates. Being self-signed, they're not trusted, because they're not issued by a trusted **Certificate Authority** (**CA**). A secure design should include trusted certificates.

How to do it...

Based on your security requirements, choose one of the following certificate management methods:

- **Default**: This method uses the VMCA as the root CA for the vSphere environment. Certificates issued by the VMCA in this mode are not trusted unless the VMCA root certificate is installed.
- **VMCA as a subordinate CA**: The VMCA can be incorporated into an enterprise **Public Key Infrastructure (PKI)** by becoming a subordinate CA to an enterprise root CA. The VMCA can then issue trusted certificate chains to vSphere components.
- **Custom certificate management**: Finally, the VMCA can be bypassed and certificates can be issued to vSphere components directly from an enterprise CA.

How it works...

For secure environments, you don't want to use the default, self-signed VMCA certificates. You'll either use the VMCA as a subordinate CA or install certificates directly from an enterprise CA. In either case, you'll use the built-in certificate manager to install certificates. If vCenter is installed on Windows, the certificate manager is at the following path (the drive letter depends on where vCenter is installed):

```
C:\Program Files\VMware\vCenter Server\vmcad\certificate-manager
```

If you're using the VCSA, the certificate manager is at the following path:

```
/usr/lib/vmware-vmca/bin/certificate-manager
```

The certificate manager application offers the options shown in the following screenshot to manage certificates:

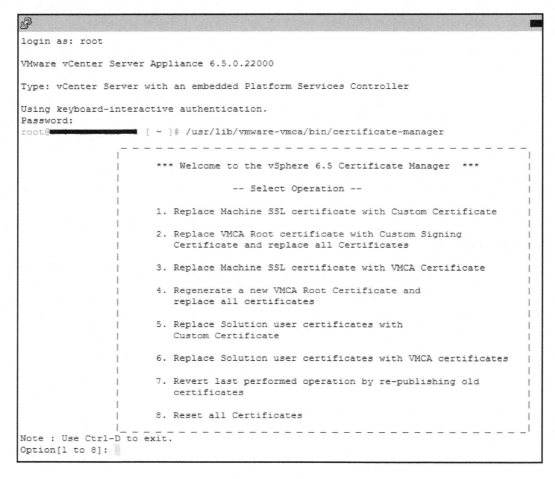

The Certificate Manager menu

If you are using the VMCA as a subordinate CA, choose option **2**. Choose option **5** to bypass the VMCA completely and install custom certificates from an enterprise CA.

Using Active Directory for host authentication

The default administrator user for ESXi is the root user. The root user can be used to manage the ESXi host directory, using either the vSphere Client or the CLI. As a security best practice, access to the vSphere hosts using the root account should be limited. For authentication on the ESXi host, local users can be created, or the host can be joined to Active Directory.

How to do it...

To use Active Directory for host authentication, follow these steps:

1. Use the vSphere Client or the vSphere Web Client to access the **Authentication Services** configuration for the ESXi host. The following screenshot shows the **Authentication Services** configuration in the vSphere Web Client:

The ESXi host Authentication Services section

2. Select **Join Domain** and provide the domain and credentials to join the ESXi host to a domain, as shown in the following screenshot:

Joining an ESXi host to an Active Directory domain

3. Select **OK** to join the ESXi host to the domain.

How it works...

The ESXi host is joined to the Active Directory domain and becomes a member server within the domain. Once the ESXi host is joined to the domain, domain users and groups can be used to create permissions for managing the ESXi hosts. The following screenshot of the **Select Users and Groups** dialog shows access to an Active Directory domain to configure permissions after the host has been joined:

Adding a vCenter user from an Active Directory domain

Once permissions are applied for Active Directory users on the host, the users can access the host using the vSphere Client or the CLI. The users' actions are logged and auditable when logging directly in to a host.

ESXi firewall configuration

The ESXi firewall can be configured to control access to and from services within the vSphere environment. The ESXi firewall can be configured to block incoming or outgoing network traffic or to limit traffic to or from specific hosts or networks.

How to do it...

Use the following process to configure and manage the ESXi firewall:

1. The ESXi firewall configuration is accessed through the **Security Profile** section of the host configuration, as shown in the following screenshot:

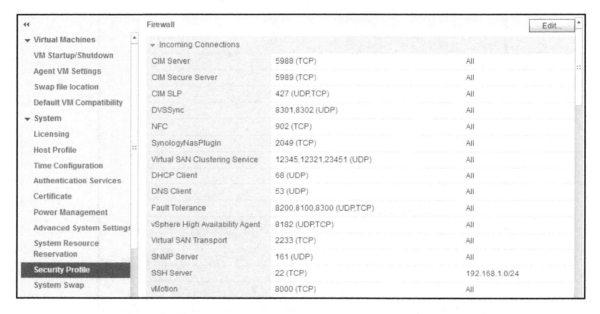

Firewall			Edit...
▼ Incoming Connections			
CIM Server	5988 (TCP)		All
CIM Secure Server	5989 (TCP)		All
CIM SLP	427 (UDP,TCP)		All
DVSSync	8301,8302 (UDP)		All
NFC	902 (TCP)		All
SynologyNasPlugin	2049 (TCP)		All
Virtual SAN Clustering Service	12345,12321,23451 (UDP)		All
DHCP Client	68 (UDP)		All
DNS Client	53 (UDP)		All
Fault Tolerance	8200,8100,8300 (UDP,TCP)		All
vSphere High Availability Agent	8182 (UDP,TCP)		All
Virtual SAN Transport	2233 (TCP)		All
SNMP Server	161 (UDP)		All
SSH Server	22 (TCP)		192.168.1.0/24
vMotion	8000 (TCP)		All

Left sidebar items: Virtual Machines — VM Startup/Shutdown, Agent VM Settings, Swap file location, Default VM Compatibility; System — Licensing, Host Profile, Time Configuration, Authentication Services, Certificate, Power Management, Advanced System Settings, System Resource Reservation, **Security Profile**, System Swap

The ESXi firewall configuration

2. Select **Edit** to configure the ESXi firewall.
3. Inbound access to a service or outbound access from a service can be enabled. Access can be configured to/from any IP address or can be limited to specific hosts or networks, as shown in the following screenshot:

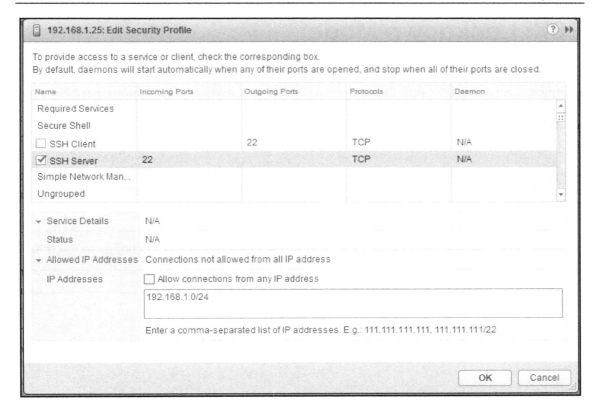

Allowing incoming connections from certain subnets

4. Click on **OK** to apply changes to the ESXi firewall.

How it works...

By default, the ESXi firewall opens the firewall port required for a service when the service is started. The ESXi firewall can be configured to only allow connections from specific IP addresses, to increase security.

ESXi Lockdown Mode

Environment security is greatly increased by limiting the ability to directly access ESXi hosts. Lockdown Mode can be enabled when first adding a host to the vCenter inventory, or can be configured by using the vSphere Web Client. Lockdown Mode can easily be disabled and enabled at any time, in order to directly access a host for support or troubleshooting.

How to do it...

Use the following process to enable Lockdown Mode on an ESXi host:

1. Access the **Security Profile** of the ESXi host by using the vSphere Web Client. The following screenshot displays the **Lockdown Mode** host configuration in the vSphere Web Client:

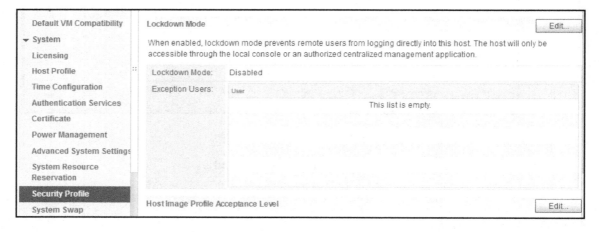

The Lockdown Mode host configuration

2. Select **Lockdown Mode** for the ESXi host, as shown in the following screenshot:

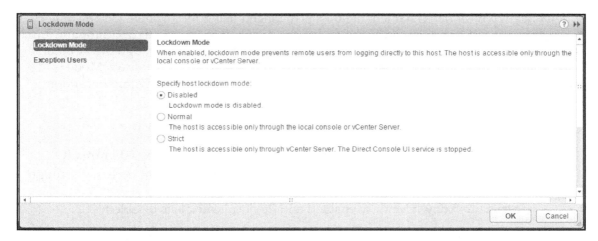

Selecting the Lockdown mode of an ESXi host

3. Configure the **Exception Users**, as shown in the following screenshot:

Configuring Lockdown Mode exception users

4. Click **OK** to complete the **Lockdown Mode** configuration.

How it works...

When Lockdown Mode is enabled, the host is managed using the vSphere Client connected to the managing vCenter Server, VMware PowerCLI, or VMware **vSphere Command-Line Interface (vCLI)**. The only difference is that access is authenticated through the vCenter Server, instead of by using a local account on the ESXi host. While Lockdown Mode is enabled, access to the host through SSH is unavailable, except for configured exception users.

There are three Lockdown Mode that can be configured for an ESXi host:

- **Disabled**: Lockdown Mode is disabled. The host can be accessed normally.
- **Normal**: Lockdown Mode is enabled and the host can only be accessed through vCenter or the local console.
- **Strict**: Lockdown Mode is enabled and the local console is disabled.

When Lockdown Mode is enabled on a host, attempts to access the host directly will result in an error, unless the user is an exception user. The following screenshot shows an attempt to access a host in Lockdown Mode using the vSphere Client:

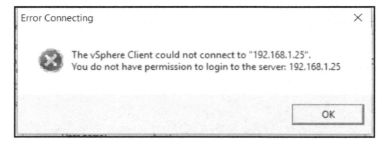

A typical access error when Lockdown Mode is enabled

Exception users can continue to access a host in Lockdown Mode. Exception users can be used for emergency troubleshooting or for third-party applications that require direct access to a host.

Configuring role-based access control

vSphere environments use **Role-Based Access Control** (**RBAC**) to provide access and permissions to vCenter inventory objects. Not everyone who accesses the vCenter Server should be set up as an administrator. Use roles and permissions to only assign the necessary permissions that a user or a group of users needs, in order to perform actions in the vSphere environment.

How to do it...

To configure RBAC in a vSphere environment, use the following steps:

1. Create a role with the necessary privileges. Preconfigured roles include **Administrator**, **Read-only**, and **No access**. Several sample roles are included and can be cloned or edited.

2. Create or edit roles to only provide the necessary privileges required to perform the role's function (for example, a role that only provides console access to a virtual machine).

3. Add permissions to vSphere inventory objects by assigning a user and a role to the object (for example, allow a specific user to access the console of a single virtual machine or a group of virtual machines).

How it works...

Privileges define access and actions that can be performed. A role is simply a collection of privileges. **Roles** can be created, edited, or deleted. The following screenshot displays the **Roles** administration with the **Privileges** listed for the **Administrator** role:

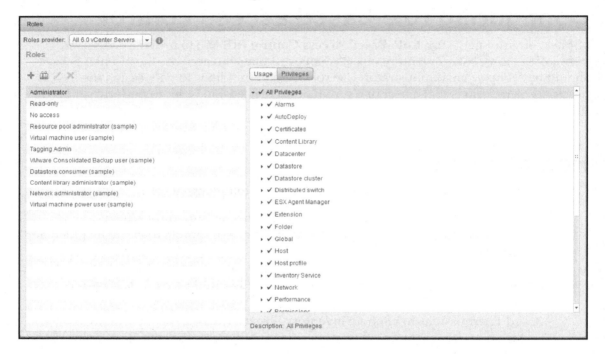

Default roles in vSphere

New roles can be created and existing roles can be edited. The available sample roles can be cloned and edited to meet the requirements.

A permission is created by assigning a user or a group of users to a **Role** and applying it to an object, such as a vCenter, data center, cluster, folder, or virtual machine, in the inventory. Permissions are managed from the vSphere Web Client and accessed from **Manage** | **Permissions** for the object.

When adding permission, a user or group is selected, as shown in the following screenshot:

Adding a user or group for certain roles

A **Role** is assigned to the **User/Group**, as shown in the following screenshot:

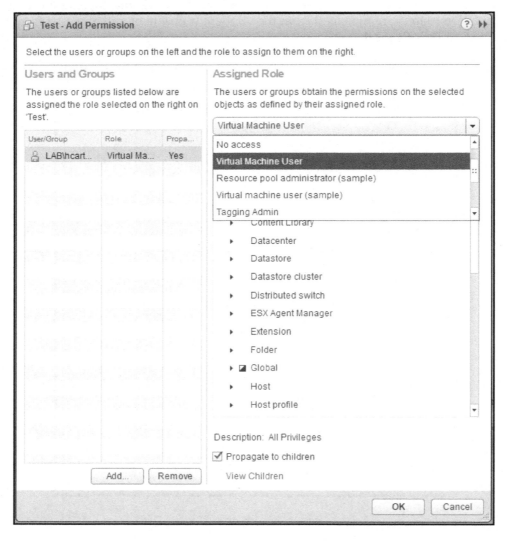

Assigning a role to an Active Directory security group

The permission can be propagated to children. This will apply the permissions to child objects in the inventory, for example, all of the virtual machines in a specific folder, or all of the objects in a data center. The **View Children** link will display all of the subordinate objects that the permission will be applied to.

When creating roles and assigning permissions, it is important to ensure that users are limited to the privileges needed to access the objects that they require. Limit the use of full administrator privileges, and discourage the use of shared logins.

Virtual network security

Security is an important factor that must be considered when designing virtual networks. Many of the same network practices that are used in the physical network can be applied to the virtual network. The virtual network provides several advantages for security, but it also introduces some challenges.

The security of virtual machine network traffic is critical, along with the security of the VMkernel traffic, to prevent attacks that may compromise the management, vMotion, fault tolerance, and IP storage networks.

How to do it...

1. Identify the available virtual switch security options
2. Select a virtual switch security configuration, based on design requirements
3. Apply security best practices to create a virtual network design, separating virtual machine services and network traffic into security zones based on design requirements

How it works...

Separate the virtual machine network traffic, based on services and security zones. Use separate vSwitches or VLAN tagging on port groups, in order to separate non-production, DMZ, test and development, management, vMotion, IP storage, and production virtual machine network traffic. The following are some things to take care of:

- The vSphere management network should be separated from other network traffic by using a management VLAN or a physically separate network.
- vMotion network traffic is transmitted unencrypted. It could be possible for an attacker to obtain the memory contents of a virtual machine during vMotion migration. The recommended practice is for the vMotion network to be on a separate VLAN or a physically separated, non-routable, or closed network from other production traffic.

- iSCSI and NFS IP storage traffic is also typically unencrypted. IP-based storage should be logically separated on its own VLAN or on a separate physical non-routable or closed network segment.

The following screenshot shows the **Security** settings that can be applied to both **Virtual Standard Switches** (**VSS**) and **Virtual Distributed Switches** (**VDS**):

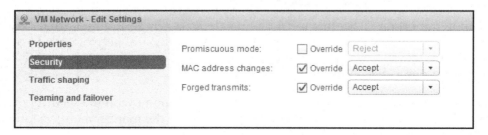

Virtual switch security settings

Virtual switch security settings are as follows:

- **Promiscuous mode**: This policy is set to **Reject**, by default. Setting it to **Accept** allows for guest network adapters connected to the virtual switch to detect all network frames passed on the virtual switch.
- **MAC address changes**: If this policy is set to **Reject** and the guest operating system changes the MAC address to a MAC address other than what is defined in the virtual machine configuration file, inbound network frames are dropped.
- **Forged transmits**: Setting this policy to **Reject** will drop any outbound network frame with a source MAC address different from the one currently set on the adapter.

There's more...

In addition to the standard security settings shared above, the vDS offers security features not available in the VSS. This includes NetFlow, port mirroring, and private VLANs. NetFlow allows you to send information about traffic flows to a NetFlow collector like SolarWinds' Real-Time NetFlow Analyzer. Port mirroring replicates all network packets to a network analyzer like WireShark. Finally, private VLANs allow you to further segment network traffic within a VLAN to individual or groups of devices.

Using the VMware vSphere 6 Hardening Guide

The VMware vSphere 6 Hardening Guide provides configuration guidance for securing a vSphere environment. The guide includes recommended security settings for ESXi hosts, virtual machines, and virtual networks.

How to do it...

1. Download the VMware vSphere 6 Hardening Guide from `https://www.vmware.com/security/hardening-guides.html`
2. Use the guide to apply security settings, based on design security requirements

How it works...

The vSphere Hardening Guide is an Excel spreadsheet that was created by Mike Foley of the VMware Technical Marketing team, a member of the vCommunity. The Hardening Guide contains security settings for ESXi hosts, virtual machine configurations, and virtual networks. Each guideline includes information such as a **Guideline ID**, **Description**, **Risk Profile**, **Vulnerability Discussion** (the reason for the guideline), **Configuration Parameter**, **Default Setting**, and the **Desired Setting** for the **Risk Profile**.

The following screenshot provides an example of the information available in the vSphere Hardening Guide:

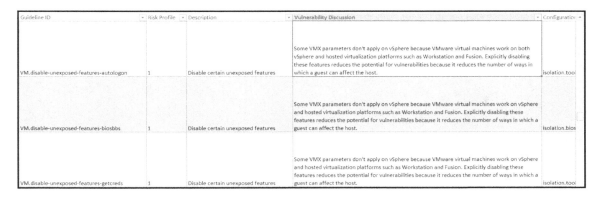

Example information found in the vSphere Hardening Guide

Guidelines are categorized into three **Risk Profiles**:

- **Risk Profile 3** should be implemented in all environments
- **Risk Profile 2** should be implemented in more security sensitive environments
- **Risk Profile 1** should be implemented in environments requiring the highest levels of security

A section for each guideline documents any potential negative effects that may be produced as a result of a specific setting. The guide also includes examples of how to check and fix settings by using the vSphere Web Client, the vSphere API, esxcli, vCLI, and PowerCLI.

11
Disaster Recovery and Business Continuity

The factors that influence the design of the backup and recovery of a virtual data center are the **Recovery Point Objective (RPO)** and **Recovery Time Objective (RTO)**. The RPO defines the amount of data loss that is acceptable. The RTO is the amount of time it should take to restore an application or service a workload after an outage.

The acceptable RPO and RTO should be defined for each workload. It is important to consider the application's dependencies when determining the RPO and RTO. Specifically, the RTO of an application will depend on the RTO of all of the application's dependencies. For example, if an application depends on a database server and the RTO of the database server is determined to be two hours, the RTO of the application itself cannot be less than two hours if the outage affects both the server running the application and the database server that supports the application.

vSphere provides many options that provide the continued operation of the virtual machines and the workloads they run in the event of an outage. These solutions do not replace the need for virtual machine backups.

The following are two different methods for backing up virtual machine workloads:

- Traditional backup using in-guest backup agents
- Agentless backup using the vSphere Storage APIs-Data Protection

The backup and recovery design should not only include virtual machines but also the backups of the virtual infrastructure configuration containing the management, network, and other configurations. This ensures that the virtual infrastructure can be restored after a failure within the infrastructure, such as a host failure or a vCenter failure.

This chapter will cover backing up vSphere infrastructure components. This includes backing up the ESXi host and the virtual distributed switch configurations to ensure that the infrastructure can be restored in the event of an outage.

VMware provides several products to protect virtual machines and recover them in the event of a virtual machine or infrastructure failure. This chapter demonstrates many of these options, including the deployment and basic configurations for the protection and recovery of virtual machines. The backup and recovery solution that will be selected will depend on the design factors.

In this chapter, we will cover the following topics:

- Backing up ESXi host configurations
- Configuring ESXi host logging
- Backing up virtual distributed switch configurations
- Deploying Veeam Backup and Replication
- Using Veeam backup and replication to back up virtual machines
- Replicating virtual machines with vSphere replication
- Protecting the virtual data center with Site Recovery Manager

Backing up ESXi host configurations

A full backup of an ESXi host is not necessary because the installation of ESXi is a quick and simple process. Host configurations should be backed up in order to quickly restore the configuration of a host in case ESXi needs to be reinstalled.

If hosts are deployed using Auto Deploy or the host configurations are stored in a host profile, the individual backups of host configurations may not be necessary, but are a good way to ensure that a backup of the host configuration is available in case there is an issue with vCenter or a configured host profile.

How to do it...

The simplest way to back up ESXi host configurations is to use the `vicfg-cfgbackup` vCLI command, as shown in the following steps:

1. Use the `vicfg-cfgbackup` vCLI command to create a backup of an ESXi host configuration:

   ```
   vicfg-cfgbackup -server <esxihostname> -s <pathtobackupfile>
   ```

2. Use the `vicfg-cfgbackup` vCLI command to restore an ESXi host configuration from a backup:

```
vicfg-cfgbackup —server <esxihostname> —l <pathtobackupfile>
```

How it works...

The **vSphere Command-line Interface (vCLI)** can be downloaded from VMware at `http://www.vmware.com/support/developer/vcli/` and installed on a Windows PC or Linux workstation. vCLI is also included as part of the **vSphere Management Assistant (vMA)**, which can be deployed in the vSphere environment.

> vMA is deprecated and version 6.5 was the final release in favor of vCLI and PowerCLI.

The ESXi backup is saved to the specified file. This file is not human-readable but contains the configuration information of the ESXi host and can be used to restore the configuration in the event that the host is lost and has to be reinstalled. The backup can also be used to return the host to a known good configuration if a configuration change is made that negatively impacts the host.

A configuration backup should be made before upgrading hosts or before making configuration changes to a host.

Restoring a host configuration using `vicfg-cfgbackup` will require the host to be rebooted once the restoration has completed. This will cause any virtual machines on the host to be shut down. The host should be placed in the maintenance mode, and all running virtual machines should be vMotioned to other hosts if possible.

> Full documentation on the `vicfg-cfgbackup` vCLI command can be found in the vSphere documentation at `http://pubs.vmware.com/vsphere-60/topic/com.vmware.vcli.ref.doc/vicfg-cfgbackup.html`.

There's more...

An ESXi host configuration backup can also be performed using PowerCLI, with the Get-VMHostFirmware PowerCLI cmdlet, as shown in the following command line:

```
Get-VMHostFirmware -vmhost <hostname or IP Address> -
BackupConfiguration -DestinationPath<PathtoBackupLocation>
```

The following screenshot demonstrates a host configuration backup using PowerCLI and the Get-VMHostFirmware cmdlet:

```
PowerCLI C:\>
PowerCLI C:\>
PowerCLI C:\> Get-VMHostFirmware -vmhost 192.168.1.25 -BackupConfiguration -Dest
inationPath C:\Temp\

Host              Data
----              ----
192.168.1.25      C:\Temp\configBundle-192.168.1.25.tgz


PowerCLI C:\> _
```

Host configuration backup using PowerCLI

To restore the ESXi host configuration, the Set-VMHostFirmware PowerCLI cmdlet is used:

```
Set-VMHostFirmware -vmhost <hostname or IP Address> -Restore -
SourcePath <PathtoBackupLocation>
```

As with restoring the ESXi configuration using vicfg-cfgbackup, the host will be rebooted once the configuration is restored. The Set-VMHostFirmware cmdlet will not run against an ESXi host that has not been placed in the maintenance mode.

Configuring ESXi host logging

Having access to the ESXi host logs is required in order to troubleshoot or determine the root cause of an ESXi host failure. Redirecting host logs to persistent storage or to a Syslog server is especially important when a host has not been installed to persistent storage, for example, a stateless host deployed using vSphere Auto Deploy or a host that has been installed to a USB stick.

Logging may not seem to be a key component in disaster recovery. Having a proper backup of the host configuration allows a host to be quickly returned to a service, but if the root cause of the failure cannot be determined, preventing the failure from happening again cannot be guaranteed. Logs are the best source for performing analyses to determine the root cause of a failure and to determine the best course of action required to prevent future failures.

How to do it...

ESXi logs should be redirected to the persistent storage or sent to a central Syslog server in order to ensure that the logs are available for analysis after a host failure. The following process details how to configure ESXi logging:

1. To redirect host logs, select the host and edit **Advanced System Settings** on the **Manage** tab. Use the **Filter** box to display the Syslog settings, as shown in the following screenshot:

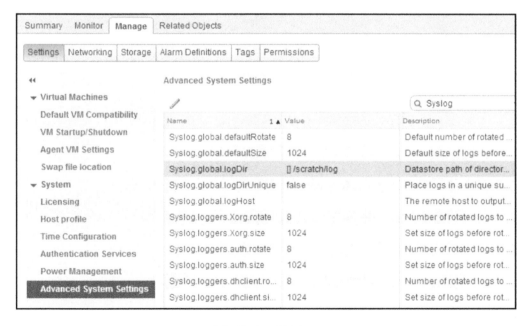

Redirect logs to persistent storage

2. Edit the **Syslog.global.logDir** setting in order to set the datastore path to output the logs to. This can be set to a VMFS or NFS datastore, which has been configured on the host, as shown in the following screenshot:

Editing the Syslog.global.logDir advanced setting

3. Edit the **Syslog.global.logDirUnique** setting to create a unique subdirectory for each host under **Syslog.global.logDir**. This setting is useful if logs from multiple hosts are being stored in the same directory. The following screenshot displays the enabling of the **Syslog.global.logDirUnique** setting by selecting the **Yes** option:

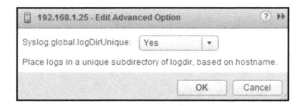

Option to automatically create unique log directories based on hostname

4. If the host logs are set to a central Syslog server, edit the **Syslog.global.logHost** setting and enter the FQDN or IP address of the Syslog server. The following screenshot shows the advanced configuration option for setting **Syslog.global.logHost**:

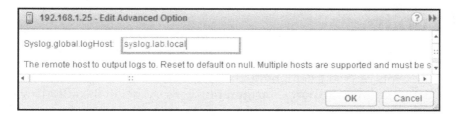

Redirecting logs to a syslog server

How it works...

When **Syslog.global.logDir** is configured, host log files will be stored in the configured path. With **Syslog.global.logDirUnique** set to **Yes**, a subdirectory with the FQDN of the host is created to store the logfiles. If **Syslog.global.logHost** has been configured, the host logs are sent to a centralized Syslog server. The host logs can be sent to multiple Syslog servers by separating the servers with a comma. The ESXi host logs can be configured to be stored on persistent storage and to be sent to a central Syslog server.

Backing up virtual distributed switch configurations

Virtual distributed switch configurations can be exported to a file. The file contains the switch configuration settings and can optionally contain information about the dvPortGroup configurations. This file can then be used to restore the virtual distributed switch configuration or to import the configuration into a different deployment.

> Virtual distributed switch import, export, and restore operations are available in the vSphere Web Client.

Virtual distributed switch configurations should be exported before making changes to the distributed virtual switches in a production environment in order to ensure that the switch can be restored to an operational state in the event of a configuration error.

How to do it...

Perform the following procedure to create a backup of the VDS configuration:

1. In the vSphere Web Client, right-click on the VDS to be exported. Navigate to **All vCenter Actions** | **Export Configuration...**, as shown in the following screenshot:

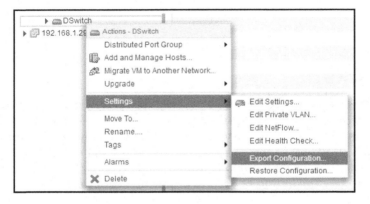

Context menu to backup a vDS

2. Select an option, depending on whether you want to export the distributed switch and all of the port groups or the distributed switch only. Selecting the **Distributed switch only** option exports only the virtual distributed switch configuration and does not include any configurations for the port groups associated with the dvSwitch. Give the exported configurations a short description, as illustrated in the following screenshot:

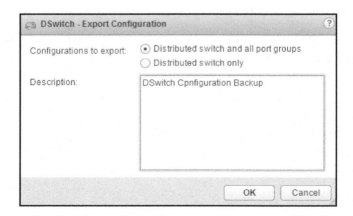

vDS export configuration options

3. Select **Yes** when the **Confirm Configuration Export** dialog is displayed. The **Confirm Configuration Export** dialog box is shown in the following screenshot:

Confirming the option to save the exported vDS configuration

4. Select the local path to which you want to save the configuration, and specify a filename for the exported configuration.

How it works...

Once exported, the configuration file will contain all of the settings for the VDS and the `dvPortgroup` configurations. This file can then be used to restore the VDS configurations of an existing distributed switch or to import the configurations if the VDS is accidentally deleted or lost.

Restoring the VDS configuration from the exported configuration file is a simple process. Right-click on the VDS to be restored and navigate to **All vCenter Actions** | **Restore Configuration...**, as shown in the following screenshot:

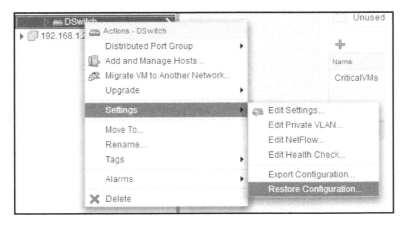

Context menu to restore a vDS backup

When restoring or importing a VDS from an exported configuration file, we can use one of the two options: **Restore distributed switch and all port groups** or **Restore distributed switch only**, as shown in the following screenshot:

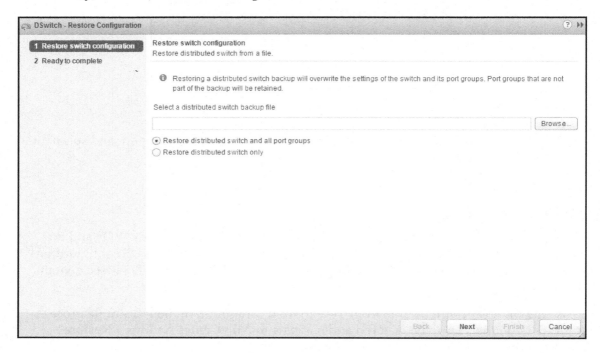

vDS restore wizard

When using the **Restore distributed switch only** option, only the distributed switch configuration is restored. dvPortGroups and their associated configurations are not restored. If the **Restore distributed switch and all port groups** option is selected, the virtual distributed switch configuration and the associated dvPortgroups are restored. Note that, during the restore process, the current settings of the distributed virtual switch and the associated dvPortgroups will be overwritten.

Deploying Veeam Backup and Replication

VMware has deprecated their **Advanced Data Protection (ADP)** application, which provided backup and restore capabilities in a virtual environment, in favor of letting the partner community develop their own solutions. One popular option for VM backups is **Veeam Backup and Replication (Veeam B&R)**. Veeam B&R is an easy-to-deploy Windows application that provides backup and recovery of virtual machines. Veeam B&R is installed on a Windows server and uses **VMware vSphere Storage APIs-Data Protection (VADP)** API calls to backup and restore virtual machines. Veeam B&R provides the following capabilities:

- Image-level and application-consistent backups
- Image-level replication for disaster recovery
- Automated backup verification
- Off-site and cloud-based backup copies
- File-level recovery
- Scale-out backup repositories
- Hardware-agnostic backup platform

How to do it...

In order to deploy Veeam B&R, perform the following steps:

1. Download Veeam B&R from `https://www.veeam.com/backup-replication-vcp-download.html`.
2. Since Veeam B&R is a Windows application, you'll need to mount the Veeam B&R ISO file on a supported Windows Server operating system.

3. On opening the mounted ISO file, click on **Veeam Backup and Replication Install**, as shown in the following screenshot. Install .NET if requested by the installer to do so and reboot. If you rebooted, the installation should automatically continue. Accept the license agreement and click **Next**:

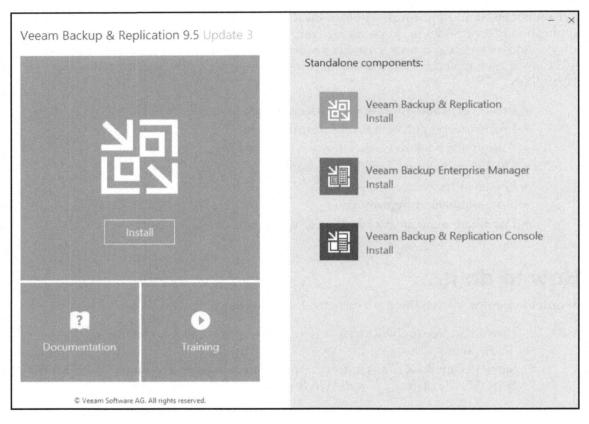

Veeam Backup and Replication installation splash screen

4. If you have a license file, upload it now. You can continue without a license to use the Community Edition, which is free for up to 10 instances.

5. When prompted regarding which components to install, choose the defaults to install an all-in-one Veeam B&R instance and click **Next**. This will install the Veeam B&R application, the Veeam Backup Catalog, and the management console.

6. Click **Install** to install any missing prerequisites. Otherwise, click **Next** to continue.

7. Review your chosen configuration settings and click **Install**. When the installation succeeds, click **Finish**.

8. Launch Veeam B&R from the desktop icon and choose **Connect**.

9. Add vCenter Servers or standalone ESXi hosts to the backup infrastructure by right-clicking on **VMware vSphere** and choosing **Add Server...** Enter the DNS name or IP address and credentials and select **Next**. The vCenter Server or ESXi host will be added to the backup inventory.

How it works...

The Windows Server machine used for the Veeam B&R installation should already have an IP address, subnet mask, gateway, and DNS configured. It should also have forward and reverse DNS records created for completeness.

Once the application is installed, the console is used to add backup sources, such as vCenter Servers and ESXi hosts, to the backup infrastructure inventory. Backup targets can be local or network NTFS repositories. UNC paths are used for network repositories.

Using Veeam Backup and Replication to back up virtual machines

Virtual machine backups using Veeam B&R are created and managed using the Veeam B&R Console, which has vCenter Server or ESXi hosts added to its backup inventory.

How to do it...

Perform the following steps to create a Veeam backup job, known as a VeeamZIP job in the free Community Edition of the software:

1. In the **Inventory** view of the Veeam B&R Console, select the ESXi host or vSphere container that hosts the VM you wish to back up. In the upper-left corner, select **VeeamZIP...** to open the **VeeamZIP** wizard, as shown in the following screenshot:

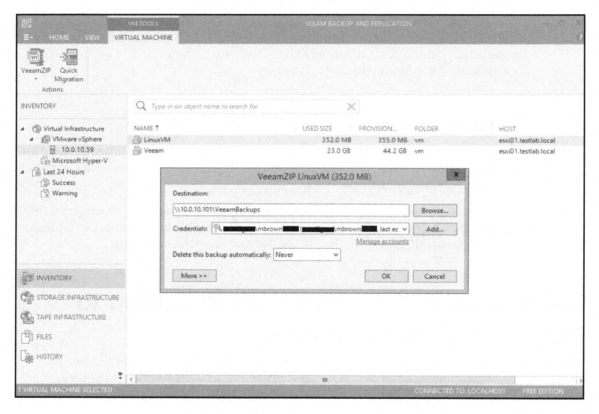

Veeam Backup and Replication VeeamZip wizard

2. Optionally, click the **More>>** button to set the retention level, encrypt the backup, set the compression level, or disable guest quiescence.

3. Allow the backup job to finish and review the status, as shown in the following screenshot. You should see the job successfully complete:

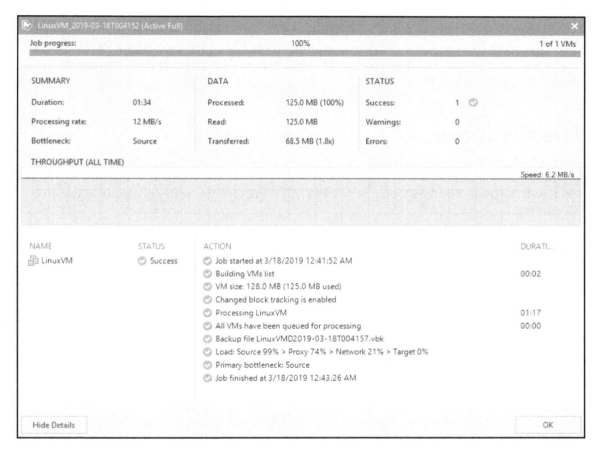

LinuxVM_2019-03-18T004152 (Active Full) ✕

Job progress: 100%   1 of 1 VMs

SUMMARY   DATA   STATUS

Duration: 01:34   Processed: 125.0 MB (100%)   Success: 1

Processing rate: 12 MB/s   Read: 125.0 MB   Warnings: 0

Bottleneck: Source   Transferred: 68.5 MB (1.8x)   Errors: 0

THROUGHPUT (ALL TIME)

Speed: 6.2 MB/s

NAME   STATUS   ACTION   DURATI...

LinuxVM   Success   Job started at 3/18/2019 12:41:52 AM

           Building VMs list   00:02

           VM size: 128.0 MB (125.0 MB used)

           Changed block tracking is enabled

           Processing LinuxVM   01:17

           All VMs have been queued for processing   00:00

           Backup file LinuxVMD2019-03-18T004157.vbk

           Load: Source 99% > Proxy 74% > Network 21% > Target 0%

           Primary bottleneck: Source

           Job finished at 3/18/2019 12:43:26 AM

Hide Details   OK

Veeam Backup and Replication job summary

How it works...

VeeamZIP jobs are created in order to back up virtual machines. VeeamZIP jobs include the backup targets and the backup retention policy, encryption, compression, and quiesce status. VeeamZIP jobs cannot be scheduled and can be considered as standalone or independent restore points.

Once the VeeamZIP job has run, the virtual machine can be restored to its original location or to a different location. Restoring to a different location provides a way to test the virtual machine backups without impacting the running virtual machine.

File-Level Restores (**FLR**) can also be performed by choosing the appropriate Windows or Linux file-level restore option. File-level restores require an FLR appliance to be deployed to an ESXi host. This appliance requires network connectivity, which it uses to access the files of the backed-up VM.

There's more...

Veeam B&R includes application-aware protection for Microsoft SQL, Microsoft Exchange, and Microsoft SharePoint. This requires VMware Tools to be installed. Veeam B&R acts as a **Microsoft Volume Shadow Copy Service** (**VSS**) requester and relies on applications to be VSS-aware.

Replicating virtual machines with vSphere Replication

vSphere Replication is included for free with vSphere Essentials Plus or higher. vSphere Replication allows virtual machines to be replicated between sites or between datastores on the same site. vSphere Replication leverages **Change Block Tracking** (**CBT**) to only replicate changes between the source virtual machines and the replication target.

vSphere Replication appliances are deployed at each site participating in replication. Multiple vSphere Replication appliances can be deployed to improve replication performance.

How to do it...

To deploy vSphere Replication and configure a virtual machine for replication, perform the following steps:

1. Download the vSphere Replication appliance ISO file from
   `http://www.vmware.com/go/download-vsphere`.
2. The vSphere Replication appliance is deployed from an OVF. During OVF deployment, the initial configuration of the administrator password, the database, and the management network IP address are configured, as shown in the following screenshot:

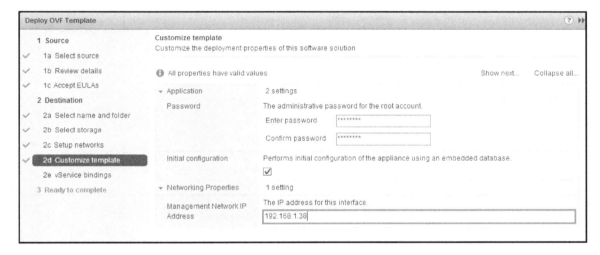

vSphere Replication OVF deployment wizard

3. Once the vSphere Replication appliance has been deployed, it can be managed from the vSphere Web Client, as shown in the following screenshot:

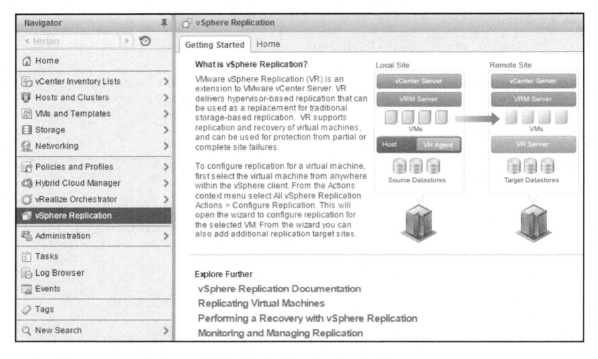

Managing vSphere Replication with the vSphere Web Client

4. Replication can now be configured for virtual machines. To enable replication, right-click on the virtual machine to be replicated. Then, navigate to **All vSphere Replication Actions | Configure Replication** from the menu, as shown in the following screenshot:

VM context menu to configure vSphere Replication

5. The replication wizard walks through the configuration of **Target site**, **Replication server**, **Target location**, and **Replication options**. The following screenshot displays the **Configure Replication** wizard for a virtual machine:

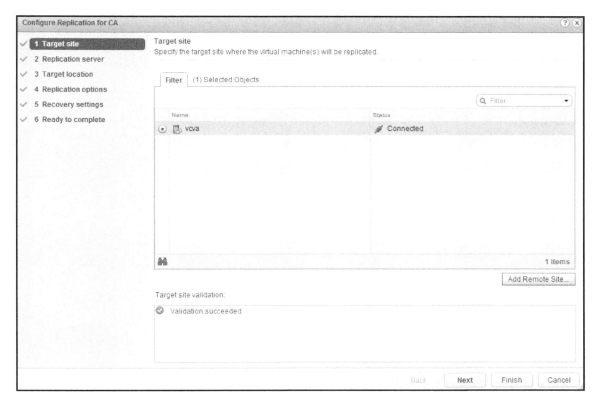

Configure vSphere Replication for a VM wizard

6. The **Recovery settings** menu allows you to configure the **Recovery Point Objective (RPO)**, time between replications, and the number of **Point in time instances** to keep of the replicated virtual machine. The best RPO that can be realized with vSphere Replication is 15 minutes. The following screenshot shows the configuration of an RPO of 15 minutes for the selected virtual machine:

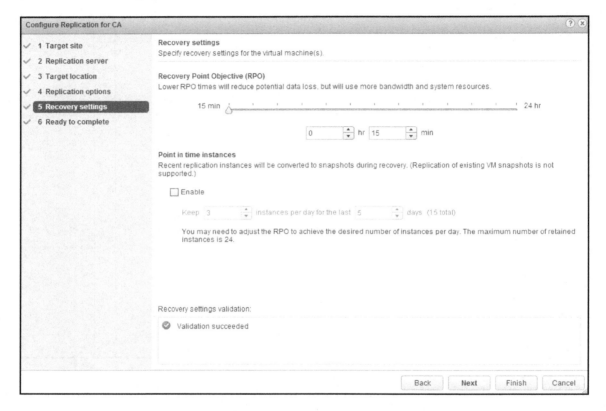

vSphere Replication recovery settings for a VM

7. Once the replication for a virtual machine has been configured, the replication can be monitored in the vSphere Web Client. The following screenshot shows the status of an **Initial Full Sync** on a virtual machine that has been configured for replication:

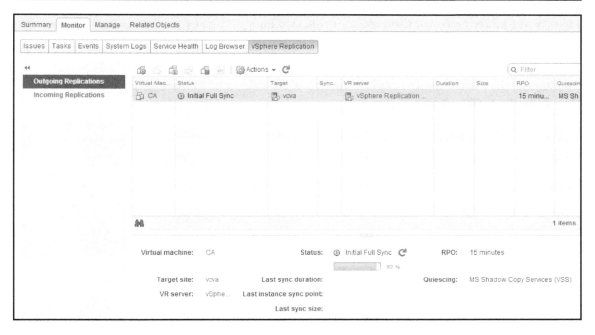

Monitoring vSphere Replication

How it works...

After the initial synchronization has been completed, the vSphere kernel tracks the writes to the protected virtual machine and transfers only the blocks that have changed. The following diagram illustrates the traffic flow for a virtual machine that's replicated with vSphere Replication:

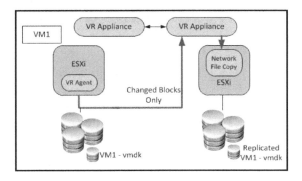

vSphere Replication architecture

Here, **VM1** has been configured for replication. Changed blocks are tracked and transferred to the target vSphere Replication appliance.

Once a replication has been set up, it can be recovered from the **vSphere Replication** management by selecting the replicated virtual machine and choosing **Recover**, as shown in the following screenshot:

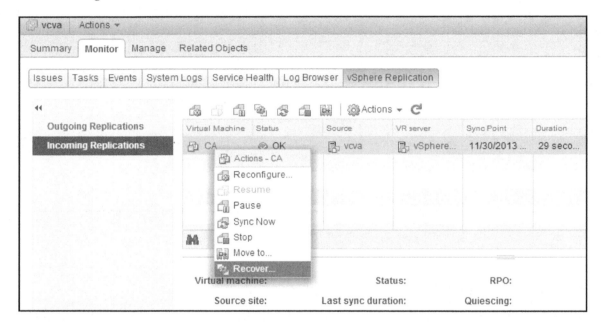

Context menu to recover a VM protected by vSphere Replication

Protecting the virtual data center with Site Recovery Manager

Site Recovery Manager (SRM) is a VMware product that provides a framework for automating the protection and failover between VMware virtualized data centers. SRM is licensed as a separate product. Licensing is per VM protected and there are two license editions: Standard and Enterprise. The **Standard Edition** provides for the protection of up to 75 virtual machines, and the **Enterprise Edition** can protect an unlimited number of virtual machines.

A complete book can be dedicated to the implementation and use of SRM. This book is just meant to be a quick overview of the configuration and capabilities of SRM. More information on the implementation and use of SRM can be found in the SRM documentation at `http://www.vmware.com/support/pubs/srm_pubs.html`.

How to do it...

Protecting the data center using SRM is accomplished through the following process:

1. Identify the requirements of Site Recovery Manager
2. Deploy Site Recovery Manager at the protected and recovery sites
3. Configure connections between the protected and recovery sites
4. Establish virtual machine replication between the protected and recovery sites
5. Create resource mapping between the protected and recovery sites
6. Create protection groups containing the virtual machines to be protected
7. Configure recovery plans to automate the recovery of virtual machines
8. Test the recovery plan to ensure that it will operate as expected

How it works...

SRM does not provide replication of virtual machines. It provides a framework to easily automate and manage the protection and failover of virtual machines. The SRM service runs on a Windows server and requires a supported database. Supported databases for the deployed SRM version can be found on the product and solution interoperability matrix at `http://partnerweb.vmware.com/comp_guide2/sim/interop_matrix.php`.

Virtual machines can be replicated between sites using either vSphere Replication or array-based replication. If array-based replication is used, a supported **Storage Replication Adapter (SRA)** is installed on the SRM servers at each site. SRA communicates with the array to control replication flow during normal, failover, and failback operations.

vSphere Replication can be deployed independently, or it can be deployed as part of the SRM installation. vSphere Replication connectivity between sites can be configured and managed from within SRM.

The following diagram illustrates a basic SRM architecture, using both vSphere Replication and array-based replication between the protected and recovery sites:

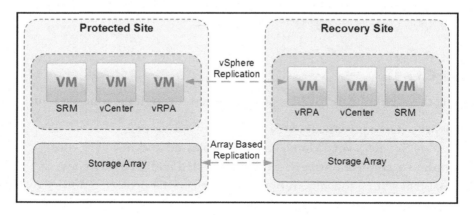

Basic SRM architecture

Compute resources (data centers, clusters, and resource pools) and network resources on the protected site are mapped to the resources at the recovery site. For example, the port group named `Production VM Network` at the protected site is mapped to a port group named `Failover VM Network` at the recovery site. The resource must exist at the recovery site before it can be mapped. A placeholder datastore is configured to hold the protected virtual machine configuration files at the recovery site.

Protection groups are created and contain virtual machines that are protected. When virtual machines are added to a protection group, a placeholder configuration file is created at the recovery site on the placeholder datastore. Protection groups can be used to group virtual machines that should be recovered together to ensure that workload dependencies are met. For example, an application that includes a virtual machine running a web frontend and another virtual machine running the support database can be placed in a protection group to ensure that all of the workload dependencies are recovered when a failover is initiated.

Recovery plans contain protection groups. Multiple recovery plans can be created, and a protection group can be included in more than one recovery plan. For example, a recovery plan can be created for a single protection group to facilitate recovery, or a single application and another recovery plan can be created to include all of the configured protection groups in order to facilitate the recovery of the entire site.

As part of the recovery plan, the virtual machine startup order can be configured with virtual machine network options. If the virtual machine network configuration (IP address or DNS servers) needs to be changed during recovery, the virtual machine network options are set on the individual virtual machines in the recovery plan. VMware Tools must be installed on the virtual machines if network changes are required.

A recovery plan can be tested without impacting the protected virtual machines by running a recovery test. During the test, an isolated vSwitch (a vSwitch with no uplinks) will be created at the recovery site. When virtual machines are recovered during the test, they are connected to this isolated switch. Once the test recovery has been completed, the virtual machine can be verified at the recovery site. Once the test has been completed and verified, the cleanup operation can be run to return the virtual machines to a protected state.

12
Design Documentation

Design documentation provides written documentation of the design factors and the choices that an architect has made in a design to satisfy given business and technical requirements.

Design documentation also aids in the implementation of a design. In many cases where the design architect is not responsible for the implementation, design documents ensure the successful implementation of designs by implementation engineers.

 Once you have created the documentation for a few designs, you will be able to develop standard processes and templates to aid in the creation of design documentation in the future.

Documentation can vary from project to project. Many consulting companies and resellers have standard documentation templates that they use when designing solutions. A properly documented design should include a minimum of the following information:

- Architecture design
- Implementation plan
- Installation guide
- Validation test plan
- Operational procedures

This information can be included in a single document or separated into different documents.

VMware provides Service Delivery Kits to VMware partners. These kits can be found on the VMware Partner University portal at `http://www.vmware.com/go/partneruniversity`, which provides documentation templates that can be used as a foundation for creating design documents. If you do not have access to these templates, example outlines are provided in this chapter to assist you in developing your own design documentation templates.

The final steps of the design process include gaining customer approval to begin implementation of the design and the implementation of the design itself.

In this chapter, we will cover the following topics:

- Creating the architecture design document
- Writing an implementation plan
- Developing an installation guide
- Creating a validation test plan
- Writing operational procedures
- Presenting the design
- Implementing the design

Creating the architecture design document

The architecture design document is a technical document describing the components and specifications required to support the solution and ensure that the specific business and technical requirements of the design are satisfied.

An excellent example of an architecture design document is the Cloud Infrastructure Architecture Case Study White Paper article that can be found at `http://www.vmware.com/files/pdf/techpaper/cloud-infrastructure-a chitecture-case-study.pdf`.

The architect creates the architecture design document to document the design factors and the specific choices that have been made to satisfy those factors. The document serves as a way for the architect to show their work when making design decisions. The architecture design document includes the conceptual, logical, and physical designs.

How to do it...

The architecture design document should generally follow the below format.

1. Write a purpose and overview
2. Write an executive summary
3. Describe the design methodology and include:
    1. Conceptual design—requirements, constraints, assumptions, and risks
    2. Logical management, storage, compute, network, and virtual machine design
    3. Physical management, storage, compute, network, and virtual machine design

How it works...

The *Purpose and overview* section of the architecture design includes the *Executive summary* section. The *Executive summary* section provides a high-level overview of the design and the goals the design will accomplish, and defines the purpose and scope of the architecture design document.

The following is an example executive summary in the *Cloud Infrastructure Architecture Case Study White Paper*:

Executive Summary
This architecture design was developed to support a virtualization project to consolidate 100 existing physical servers on to a VMware vSphere 6.x virtual infrastructure. The primary goals this design will accomplish are to increase operational efficiency and to provide high availability of customer-facing applications. This document details the recommended implementation of a VMware virtualization architecture based on specific business requirements and VMware recommended practices. The document provides both logical and physical design considerations for all related infrastructure components including servers, storage, networking, management, and virtual machines. The scope of this document is specific to the design of the virtual infrastructure and the supporting components.

The *Purpose and overview* section should also include details of the design methodology the architect has used to create the architecture design. This should include the processes followed to determine the business and technical requirements, along with definitions of the infrastructure qualities that influenced the design decisions.

Design factors, requirements, constraints, and assumptions are documented as part of the conceptual design. Chapter 3, *The Design Factors*, provides details on the key factors included as part of the conceptual design. To document the design factors, use a table to organize them and associate them with an ID that can be easily referenced.

The following table illustrates an example of how to document the design requirements:

ID	Requirement
R001	Consolidate the existing 100 physical application servers down to five servers.
R002	Provide capacity to support growth for 25 additional application servers over the next 5 years.
R003	Server hardware maintenance should not affect application uptime.
R004	Provide *N+2* redundancy to support a hardware failure during normal and maintenance operations.

The conceptual design should also include tables documenting any constraints and assumptions. A high-level diagram of the conceptual design can also be included.

Details of the logical design are documented in the architecture design document. The logical design of management, storage, network, and compute resources should be included. When documenting the logical design document, any recommended practices that were followed should be included. Also include references to the requirements, constraints, and assumptions that influenced the design decisions.

When documenting the logical design, show your work to support your design decisions. Include any formulas used for resource calculations and provide detailed explanations of why design decisions were made.

An example table outlining the logical design of compute resource requirements follows:

Parameter	Specification
Current CPU resources required	100 GHz
CPU and memory growth of 25 additional application servers (R002)	25 GHz
CPU required (75% utilization)	157 GHz
Current memory resources required	525 GB
Memory growth	131 GB
Memory required (75% utilization)	821 GB
Memory required (25% TPS savings)	616 GB

Similar tables will be created to document the logical design for storage, network, and management resources.

The physical design documents have the details of the physical hardware chosen along with the configurations of both the physical and virtual hardware. Details of vendors and hardware models chosen and the reasons for decisions made should be included as part of the physical design. The configuration of the physical hardware is documented along with details of why specific configuration options were chosen. The physical design should also include diagrams that document the configuration of physical resources, such as physical network connectivity and storage layout.

A sample outline of the architecture design document is as follows:

- **Cover page**: This includes the customer and project names.
- **Document version log**: This contains the log of authors and changes made to the document.
- **Document contacts**: This includes the subject matter experts involved in the creation of the design.
- **Table of contents**: This is the index of the document sections for quick reference.
- **List of tables**: This is the index of tables included in the document for quick reference.
- **List of figures**: This is the index of figures included in the document for quick reference.
- **Purpose and overview**: This section consists of an executive summary to provide an overview of the design and the design methodology followed in creating the design.
- **Conceptual design**: This is the documentation of the design factors: requirements, constraints, and assumptions.
- **Logical design**: This has the details of the logical management, storage, network, compute, and virtual machine design
- **Physical design**: This contains the details of the selected hardware and the configuration of the physical and virtual hardware.

Writing an implementation plan

The implementation plan documents the requirements necessary to complete the implementation of the design.

The implementation plan defines the project roles and defines what is expected of the customer and what they can expect during the implementation of the design.

This document is sometimes referred to as the **statement of work**. It defines the key points of contact, the requirements that must be satisfied to start the implementation, any project documentation deliverables, and how changes to the design and implementation will be handled.

How to do it...

The implementation plan should generally follow the below format.

1. Write a purpose statement
2. Include project contacts
3. State the implementation requirements
4. Include an overview of implementation steps
5. Define the project documentation deliverables
6. Describe the implementation of change management

How it works...

The purpose statement defines the purpose and scope of the document. The purpose statement of the implementation plan should define what is included in the document and provide a brief overview of the goals of the project. The purpose statement is simply an introduction so that someone reading the document can gain a quick understanding of what the document contains.

The following is an example purpose statement:

> *"This document serves as the implementation plan and defines the scope of the virtualization project. This document identifies points of contact for the project, lists implementation requirements, provides a brief description of each of the document deliverables, and provides an overview of the implementation process for the data center virtualization project. The scope of this document is specific to the implementation of the virtual data center implementation and the supporting components as defined in the architecture design."*

Key project contacts, their roles, and their contact information should be included as part of the implementation plan document. These contacts include customer stakeholders, project managers, project architects, and implementation engineers.

The following is a sample table that can be used to document project contacts for the implementation plan:

Role	Name	Contact information
Customer project sponsor		
Customer technical resource		
Project manager		
Design architect		
Implementation engineer		
QA engineer		

Support contacts for hardware and software used in the implementation plan may also be included in the table, for example, contact numbers for VMware support or other vendor support.

Implementation requirements contain the implementation dependencies, including the access and facility requirements. Any hardware, software, and licensing that must be available to implement the design is also documented here.

Access requirements include the following:

- Physical access to the site is required.
- Credentials necessary for access to resources are needed. These include active directory credentials and VPN credentials (if remote access is required).

Facility requirements include the following:

- Power and cooling to support the equipment that will be deployed as part of the design
- Rack space requirements

Hardware, software, and licensing requirements include the following:

- vSphere licensing
- Windows or other operating system licensing
- Other third-party application licensing

- Software (ISO, physical media, and so on)
- Physical hardware (hosts, arrays, network switches, cables, and so on)

A high-level overview of the steps required to complete the implementation is also documented. The details of each step are not a part of this document; only the steps that need to be performed will be included:

1. Procurement of hardware, software, and licensing
2. Scheduling of engineering resources
3. Verification of access and facility requirements
4. Performance of an inventory check for the required hardware, software, and licensing
5. Installation and configuration of storage array
6. Rack, cable, and burn-in of physical server hardware
7. Installation of ESXi on physical servers
8. Installation of vCenter Server
9. Configuration of ESXi and vCenter
10. Testing and verification of implementation plan
11. Migration of physical workloads to virtual machines
12. Operational verification of the implementation plan

The implementation overview may also include an implementation timeline documenting the time required to complete each of the steps.

Project documentation deliverables are defined as part of the implementation plan. Any documentation that will be delivered to the customer once the implementation has been completed should be detailed here. Details include the name of the document and a brief description of the purpose of the document.

The following table provides example descriptions of the project documentation deliverables:

Document	Description
Architecture design	This is a technical document describing the vSphere components and specifications required to achieve a solution that addresses the specific business and technical requirements of the design.
Implementation plan	This identifies implementation roles and requirements. It provides a high-level map of the implementation and deliverables detailed in the design. It documents change management procedures.

Document	Description
Installation guide	This document provides detailed, step-by-step instructions on how to install and configure the products specified in the architecture design document.
Validation test plan	This document provides an overview of the procedures to be executed post installation to verify whether or not the infrastructure is installed correctly. It can also be used at any point subsequent to the installation to verify whether or not the infrastructure continues to function correctly.
Operational procedures	This document provides detailed, step-by-step instructions on how to perform common operational tasks after the design is implemented.

How changes are made to the design, specifically changes made to the design factors, must be well-documented. Even a simple change to a requirement or an assumption that cannot be verified can have a tremendous effect on the design and implementation. The process for submitting a change, researching the impact of the change, and approving the change should be documented in detail.

The following is an example outline for an implementation plan:

- **Cover page**: This includes the customer and project names
- **Document version log**: This contains the log of authors and changes made to the document
- **Document contacts**: This includes the subject matter experts involved in the creation of the design
- **Table of contents**: This is the index of document sections for quick reference
- **List of tables**: This is the index of tables included in the document for quick reference
- **List of figures**: This is the index of figures included in the document for quick reference
- **Purpose statement**: This defines the purpose of the document
- **Project contacts**: This is the documentation of key project points of contact
- **Implementation requirements**: This provides the access, facilities, hardware, software, and licensing required to complete the implementation
- **Implementation overview**: This is the overview of the steps required to complete the implementation
- **Project deliverables**: This consists of the documents that will be provided as deliverables once implementation has been completed

Developing an installation guide

The installation guide provides step-by-step instructions for the implementation of the architecture design. This guide should include detailed information about how to implement and configure all of the resources associated with the virtual data center project.

In many projects, the person creating the design is not the person responsible for implementing the design. The installation guide outlines the steps necessary to implement the physical design outlined in the architecture design document.

The installation guide should provide details about the installation of all components, including the storage and network configurations required to support the design. In a complex design, multiple installation guides may be created to document the installation of the various components required to support the design. For example, separate installation guides may be created for the storage, network, and vSphere installation and configuration.

How to do it...

The installation guide should generally follow the below format.

1. Write a purpose statement
2. Create an assumption statement
3. Write step-by-step instructions to implement the design

How it works...

The purpose statement simply states the purpose of the document. The assumption statement describes any assumptions the document's author has made. Commonly, an assumption statement simply states that the document has been written, assuming that the reader is familiar with virtualization concepts and the architecture design.

The following is an example of a basic purpose and assumption statement that can be used for an installation guide:

Purpose
This document provides a guide for installing and configuring the virtual infrastructure design defined in the architecture design.

Assumptions
This guide is written for an implementation engineer or administrator who is familiar with vSphere concepts and terminologies. The guide is not intended for administrators who have no prior knowledge of vSphere concepts and terminology.

The installation guide should include details for implementing all areas of the design. It should include configuration of the storage array, physical servers, physical network components, and vSphere components. The following are just a few examples of installation tasks to include instructions for:

- Storage array configurations
- Physical network configurations
- Physical host configurations
- ESXi installation
- vCenter Server installation and configuration
- Virtual network configuration
- Datastore configuration
- High availability, distributed resource scheduler, storage DRS, and other vSphere components installation and configuration

The installation guide should provide as much detail as possible. Along with the step-by-step procedures, screenshots can be used to provide installation guidance.

The following screenshot is an example taken from an installation guide that details enabling and configuring the **Software iSCSI** adapter:

5.3 Configure Storage
1. Enable the Software iSCSI HBA.
    -   Select **Storage Adapters** in the **Hardware** menu.
    -   Select **Add** to create the Software iSCSI HBA

    -   Select the new Software iSCSI HBA and select **Properties**.
    -   In the iSCSI initiator properties select **Configure** to set the **iSCSI Name** and **iSCSI Alias**.

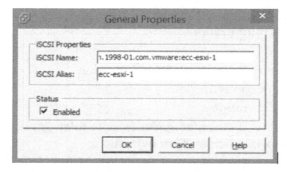

    -   Select the **Network Configuration** tab and **Add** the iSCSI-A VMkernel

Example of the detail included in an installation guide

The following is an example outline for an installation guide:

-   **Cover page**: This includes the customer and project names
-   **Document version log**: This contains the log of authors and changes made to the document
-   **Document contacts**: This includes the subject matter experts involved in the creation of the design

- **Table of contents**: This is the index of document sections for quick reference
- **List of tables**: This is the index of tables included in the document for quick reference
- **List of figures**: This is the index of figures included in the document for quick reference
- **Purpose statement**: This defines the purpose of the document
- **Assumption statement**: This defines any assumptions made in creating the document
- **Installation guide**: This provides the step-by-step installation instructions to be followed when implementing the design

Creating a validation test plan

The validation test plan documents how the implementation will be verified. It documents the criteria that must be met to determine the success of the implementation and the test procedures that should be followed when validating the environment. The criteria and procedures defined in the validation test plan determine whether or not the design requirements have been successfully met.

How to do it...

The validation test plan should generally follow the below format:

1. Write a purpose statement
2. Write an assumption statement
3. Define success criteria
4. Include the test procedures

How it works...

The purpose statement defines the purpose of the validation test plan and the assumption statement documents any assumptions the author of the plan has made in developing the test plan. Typically, the assumptions are that the testing and validation will be performed by someone who is familiar with the concepts and the design.

The following is an example of a purpose and assumption statement for a validation test plan:

Purpose
This document contains testing procedures to verify that the implemented configurations specified in the architecture design document successfully addresses the customer requirements.

Assumptions
This document assumes that the person performing these tests has a basic understanding of VMware vSphere and is familiar with the accompanying design documentation. This document is not intended for administrators or testers who have no prior knowledge of vSphere concepts and terminology.

The success criteria determines whether or not the implemented design is operating as expected. More importantly, these criteria determine whether or not the design requirements have been met. Success is measured based on whether or not the criteria satisfies the design requirements.

The following table shows some examples of success criteria defined in the validation test plan:

Description	Measurement
Members of the active directory group vSphere administrators are able to access vCenter as administrators	Yes/no
Access is denied to users outside the vSphere administrators active directory group	Yes/no
Access to a host using the vSphere Client is permitted when Lockdown Mode is disabled	Yes/no
Access to a host using the vSphere Client is denied when Lockdown Mode is enabled	Yes/no
Cluster resource utilization is less than 75%	Yes/no

If the success criteria are not met, the design does not satisfy the design factors. This can be due to a misconfiguration or error in the design. Troubleshooting will need to be done to identify the issue or modifications to the design that may need to be made.

Test procedures are performed to determine whether or not the success criteria have been met. Test procedures should include testing of usability, performance, and recoverability. Test procedures should include the test description, the tasks to perform the test, and the expected results of the test.

The following table provides some examples of usability testing procedures:

Test description	Tasks to perform test	Expected result
vCenter administrator access	Use the vSphere Web Client to access the vCenter Server. Log in as a user who is a member of the vSphere administrators AD group.	Administrator is granted access to the inventory of the vCenter Server.
vCenter access: no permissions	Use the vSphere Web Client to access the vCenter Server. Log in as a user who is not a member of the vSphere administrators AD group.	Access is denied.
Host access: Lockdown Mode disabled	Disable Lockdown Mode through the DCUI. Use the vSphere Client to access the host and log in as root.	Direct access to the host using the vSphere Client is successful.
Host access: Lockdown Mode enabled	Re-enable Lockdown Mode through the DCUI. Use the vSphere Client to access the host and log in as root.	Direct access to the host using the vSphere Client is denied.

The following table provides some examples of reliability testing procedures:

Test description	Tasks to perform test	Expected result
Host storage path failure	Disconnect the `vmnic` providing IP storage connectivity from the host.	The disconnected path fails, but IO continues to be processed on the surviving paths. A network connectivity alarm should be triggered and an email should be sent to the configured email address.
Host storage path restore	Reconnect the `vmnic` providing IP storage connectivity.	The failed path should become active and begin processing the IO. Network connectivity alarms should clear.
Array storage path failure	Disconnect one network connection from the active SP.	The disconnected paths fail on all hosts, but the IO continues to be processed on the surviving paths.
Management network redundancy	Disconnect the active management network `vmnic`.	The standby adapter becomes active. Management access to the host is not interrupted. A loss-of-network redundancy alarm should be triggered and an email should be sent to the configured email address.

These are just a few examples of test procedures. The actual test procedures will depend on the requirements defined in the conceptual design.

The following is an example outline of a validation test plan:

- **Cover page**: This includes the customer and project names
- **Document version log**: This contains the log of authors and changes made to the document
- **Document contacts**: This includes the subject matter experts involved in the creation of the design
- **Table of contents**: This is the index of document sections for quick reference
- **List of tables**: This is the index of tables included in the document for quick reference
- **List of figures**: This is the index of figures included in the document for quick reference
- **Purpose statement**: This defines the purpose of the document
- **Assumption statement**: This defines any assumptions made in creating the document
- **Success criteria**: This is a list of criteria that must be met to validate the successful implementation of the design
- **Test procedures**: This is a list of test procedures to follow, including the steps to follow and the expected results

Writing operational procedures

The operational procedure document provides the detailed, step-by-step procedures required for the successful operation of the implemented virtual data center design. These procedures should include monitoring and troubleshooting, virtual machine deployment, environment startup and shutdown, patching and updating, and any other details that may be required for the successful operation of the implemented design.

How to do it...

The operational procedures should generally follow the below format:

1. Write a purpose statement
2. Write an assumption statement

3. Create step-by-step procedures for daily operations
4. Include troubleshooting and recovery procedures

How it works...

As with other design documents, the purpose statement defines the purpose of the operational procedures document. The assumption statement details any assumptions the author of the plan made in developing the procedures.

Purpose
This document contains detailed step-by-step instructions on how to perform common operational tasks. This document provides a guide to performing common tasks associated with management, monitoring, troubleshooting, virtual machine deployment, updating, and recovery.

Assumptions
This document assumes that an administrator who uses these procedures is familiar with VMware vSphere concepts and terminology.

The operational procedure document provides step-by-step procedures for common tasks that will need to be performed by the administrator of the environment. Examples of procedures to include are as follows:

- Accessing the environment
- Monitoring resource usage and performance
- Deploying new virtual machines
- Patching ESXi hosts
- Updating VMware tools and virtual machine hardware

The operational procedure document should also describe troubleshooting and recovery. Examples of these procedures include the following:

- Monitoring alarms
- Exporting log bundles
- Restoring a virtual machine from a backup
- Environment shutdown and startup

The following screenshot is an example taken from an operational procedures document, which details the process for exporting a log bundle:

5. Exporting a vCenter Log Bundle

When a service request is submitted to VMware for support, VMware Support may require the system logs to troubleshoot the reported issue.

1. To export system logs right-click the vCenter Server inventory object and select **All vCenter Actions -> Export System Logs**.
2. Select the hosts and vCenter logs to include in the log bundle.

3. Select the logs to export. In most cases the default selections will be used unless otherwise stated by VMware Support. Click **Generate Log Bundle** to begin the log export.

4. After the log bundle has been generated click **Download Log Bundle** to download the logs.
5. Choose a location to save the log export. A zipped archive containing the exported logs will be downloaded to location selected.

Example of a typical task included in the operational procedures

The following is an example outline of an operational procedures document:

- **Cover page**: This includes the customer and project names
- **Document version log**: This contains the log of authors and changes made to the document
- **Document contacts**: This includes the subject matter experts involved in the creation of the design
- **Table of contents**: This is the index of document sections for quick reference
- **List of tables**: This is the index of tables included in the document for quick reference
- **List of figures**: This is the index of figures included in the document for quick reference
- **Purpose statement**: This defines the purpose of the document
- **Assumption statement**: This defines any assumptions made when creating the document
- **Operational procedures**: These are the step-by-step procedures for the day-to-day access, monitoring, and operation of the environment
- **Troubleshooting and recovery procedures**: These are the step-by-step procedures for troubleshooting issues and recovering from a failure

Presenting the design

Typically, once the design has been completed, it is presented to the customer for **Approval** before **Implementation**:

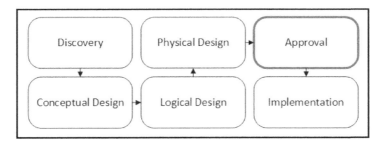

Approval phase in the vSphere design workflow

In order to obtain customer approval, typically, a high-level presentation is given to the project stakeholders to provide details on how the design satisfies the requirements and the benefits associated with the design.

 If you are not comfortable giving presentations, check out http://www.toastmasters.org/. Toastmasters can help you develop presentation skills and build confidence when speaking in front of people.

How to do it...

Presenting the design to stakeholders is a simple, but important, part of the design process:

1. Develop a presentation
2. Present the design to the customer

How it works...

The presentation should include the following information:

- An overview of the design methodology
- An overview of the discovery process
- The design factors: requirements, constraints, and assumptions
- A high-level overview of the logical and physical design

Remember to tailor your presentation to your audience. Keep the presentation at a high level, but be ready to provide details about the technical and business decisions made to support the design.

When presenting the design, explain the key design decisions and how they satisfy the requirements. Cover the entire design, but keep the presentation brief. Be ready to answer questions about the design and the reasons behind the design decisions.

Implementing the design

The final step of the design process is the **Implementation** of the design:

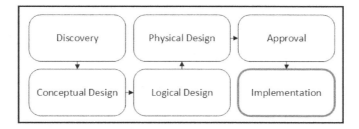

Implementation phase of the vSphere design workflow

Implementation takes the design from paper and puts it into practice. If time has been taken to create and correctly document a solid design, its implementation will be the easiest part of the process.

How to do it...

The following steps are part of the design implementation:

1. Implementation of the documented design
2. Validation and testing
3. Review and delivery

How it works...

Implement the design as documented in the architecture design. The implementation plan provides a guide to the implementation process, while the installation guide provides the details about performing the installation. The validation test plan is then used to test and validate the implementation against the design requirements.

Once the design has been successfully implemented, the design should be reviewed with the customer to identify any lessons learned for next steps. The documented deliverables are then provided to the customer.

Good luck!

Other Books You May Enjoy

If you enjoyed this book, you may be interested in these other books by Packt:

VMware vSphere 6.5 Cookbook - Third Edition
Abhilash G B, Cedric Rajendran

ISBN: 978-1-78712-741-8

- Upgrade your existing vSphere environment or perform a fresh deployment
- Automate the deployment and management of large sets of ESXi hosts in your vSphere Environment
- Configure and manage FC, iSCSI, and NAS storage, and get more control over how storage resources are allocated and managed
- Configure vSphere networking by deploying host-wide and data center-wide switches in your vSphere environment
- Configure high availability on a host cluster and learn how to enable the fair distribution and utilization of compute resources
- Patch and upgrade the vSphere environment
- Handle certificate request generation and renew component certificates
- Monitor performance of a vSphere environment

VMware NSX Cookbook
Bayu Wibowo, Tony Sangha

ISBN: 978-1-78217-425-7

- Understand, install, and configure VMware NSX for vSphere solutions
- Configure logical switching, routing, and Edge Services Gateway in VMware NSX for vSphere
- Learn how to plan and upgrade VMware NSX for vSphere
- Learn how to use built-in monitoring tools such as Flow Monitoring, Traceflow, Application Rule Manager, and Endpoint Monitoring
- Learn how to leverage the NSX REST API for management and automation using various tools from Python to VMware vRealize Orchestrator

Leave a review - let other readers know what you think

Please share your thoughts on this book with others by leaving a review on the site that you bought it from. If you purchased the book from Amazon, please leave us an honest review on this book's Amazon page. This is vital so that other potential readers can see and use your unbiased opinion to make purchasing decisions, we can understand what our customers think about our products, and our authors can see your feedback on the title that they have worked with Packt to create. It will only take a few minutes of your time, but is valuable to other potential customers, our authors, and Packt. Thank you!

Index

Made in the USA
Middletown, DE
08 May 2019